The Complete AZ-900 Handbook

Straightforward strategies to pass the exam

Tom Taulli

bpb

www.bpbonline.com

First Edition 2026

Copyright © BPB Publications, India

ISBN: 978-93-65895-551

To View Complete
BPB Publications Catalogue
Scan the QR Code:

Dedicated to

*My late father, Thomas Taulli, who bought me my first computer
when I was 12 years old and always encouraged me to learn*

About the Author

Tom Taulli is an author, developer, and entrepreneur. He is the founder of startups like ExamWeb, BizEquity, and Hypermart.net, which was sold to InfoSpace.

Over the years, Tom has written about AI and software development. His work has also been published in publications like BusinessWeek.com, Barrons.com, Bloomberg.com, and Inc.com.

Besides his writings, Tom teaches courses for various institutions. He is also an advisor to companies like TadHealth, MeasureSquare, and Aisera.

About the Reviewers

❖ **Gaurav Deshmukh** is a senior software engineer tech lead with over a decade of experience in software engineering and technical management. He specializes in full-stack development, cybersecurity, cloud technologies, and no-code, low-code automation platforms engineering. Currently, his focus is on building secure, cloud-native systems and streamlining enterprise processes through automation and self-service platforms. He has co-authored a book on building generative AI agents, where he explores practical applications of AI and distributed systems in business transformation. In addition, he contributes as a technical reviewer for books on systems engineering, DevOps, Kubernetes, generative AI, and cybersecurity. Gaurav is passionate about mentorship and knowledge sharing, engaging actively with global communities through IEEE, ACM, and platforms like ADPList and Topmate.io. His unique blend of technical depth, industry insight, and commitment to education continues to shape innovation in the technology landscape.

❖ **Peng Lu** is a seasoned IT application manager and senior member of the IEEE, bringing over 20 years of experience across consulting and in-house roles. As both a consultant and developer, Peng has built a strong track record in the evolving landscape of artificial intelligence.

A certified IT consultant, Peng possesses deep expertise across a broad spectrum of IT domains, including machine learning, artificial intelligence, ERP, cloud computing, and digital transformation. This cross-functional skill set enables Peng to deliver holistic, tailored solutions that meet the unique needs of diverse clients.

Peng is highly proficient in IT management and excels at leading complex projects to successful outcomes. Committed to staying at the forefront of innovation, Peng actively follows advancements in cloud technologies and AI to ensure forward-thinking, impactful results.

Acknowledgement

I want to thank the team at BPB Publications for believing in this project and for making the writing process much smoother. I also want to thank the technical reviewers, Gaurav Deshmukh and Peng Lu, whose insights and expertise greatly enhanced the quality of this book.

Preface

Cloud computing is critical for many businesses. The AZ-900 exam provides an effective way to become a part of this thriving field, and this book shows what you need to know to pass it. There are 11 chapters that cover all the key topics covered on the exam.

Besides chapters, the book includes a full-length practice exam to reflect the real testing experience, and a glossary to help readers quickly review essential terms. Whether new to IT or looking to advance in project management or business analysis, readers will find this guide an accessible path to mastering Azure fundamentals and passing the AZ-900 certification.

Chapter 1: Introduction to the AZ-900 Certification - shows why this exam is valuable for your career in cloud computing. It then covers details about the AZ-900 exam. They include the number and types of questions, scoring, and how to register. The chapter also covers other related Microsoft Certifications. The end of the chapter provides a demo for how to set up an Azure account and navigate the Azure portal.

Chapter 2: The Foundations of Cloud Computing - explains the different cloud deployment models, including public, private, and hybrid clouds, and looks into cloud service types such as IaaS, PaaS, and SaaS. You will learn about concepts like serverless computing, pricing models, and the differences between capital and operating expenses. The chapter also covers the shared responsibility model and explains the core benefits of cloud computing. They include scalability, high availability, and security.

Chapter 3: Architectural Components and Services of Azure - describes how Azure's data centers operate. There is an explanation of geographies, regions, and sovereign regions. There is also a discussion of availability zones for high resilience. The chapter then discusses how resources are organized within Azure with subscriptions, resource groups, management groups, licenses, and tenants.

Chapter 4: Compute Services - explains virtual machines. Topics include the setup, pricing, and connectivity. The chapter then goes on to cover supporting features like Virtual Machine Scale Sets, availability sets, and proximity placement groups. You will also learn about Azure Virtual Desktop for delivering virtual desktops, Azure App Services for running web applications, and serverless options like Azure Functions. Finally, container services are covered. They are Azure Container Instances, Azure Kubernetes Service, and Azure Container Apps.

Chapter 5: Networking - begins by looking at core networking concepts like IP addresses, protocols, and routing. The chapter then covers Azure's networking services, such as virtual networks, network security groups, peering, Azure DNS for domain management, Azure VPN Gateway for secure connectivity, and ExpressRoute for private connections to Microsoft's network.

Chapter 6: Storage - looks at the basics of Azure storage accounts, redundancy options to ensure data availability, and different storage tiers for performance and cost optimization. Next, there is coverage of specific storage solutions such as blob storage for unstructured data, using AzCopy for data transfer, Azure Files for file shares, and Azure Migrate to help transition workloads to the cloud. You will see how to select and implement the right storage options for their solutions.

Chapter 7: Identity, Access, and Security - describes Microsoft Entra ID, such as authentication and authorization. You will learn about Conditional Access policies, multifactor authentication, and passwordless solutions to enhance security. The chapter also details role-based access control for managing permissions, and explains security frameworks like Zero Trust and defense-in-depth, alongside tools like Microsoft Defender for Cloud.

Chapter 8: Cost Management for Azure - provides an overview of cloud cost management. You will learn about key Azure tools such as the total cost of ownership calculator to assess migration costs, Azure Cost Management tools for ongoing tracking and optimization, and the use of resource tags to improve cost analysis and accountability across services.

Chapter 9: Governance and Compliance in Azure - introduces the Azure Policy for enforcing organizational standards, resource locks for preventing accidental changes, and Microsoft Purview for data governance and compliance management. You will learn about how to maintain control, meet regulatory requirements, and implement best practices for governance across their cloud resources.

Chapter 10: Deployment and Monitoring of Azure Resources - starts with Azure Advisor, which provides for best practice recommendations. This is followed up with Azure Service Health for tracking service issues and maintenance, and Azure Monitor for collecting, analyzing, and acting on telemetry data.

Chapter 11: Strategies for the Exam - provides practical advice and tips for passing the AZ-900 exam. It offers strategies for managing time, understanding and focusing on exam objectives, and narrowing down multiple-choice options effectively. The chapter concludes with a high-level review of the main topics covered in the book.

Coloured Images

Please follow the link to download the
Coloured Images of the book:

https://rebrand.ly/275efc

We have code bundles from our rich catalogue of books and videos available at https://github.com/bpbpublications. Check them out!

Errata

We take immense pride in our work at BPB Publications and follow best practices to ensure the accuracy of our content to provide an indulging reading experience to our subscribers. Our readers are our mirrors, and we use their inputs to reflect and improve upon human errors, if any, that may have occurred during the publishing processes involved. To let us maintain the quality and help us reach out to any readers who might be having difficulties due to any unforeseen errors, please write to us at:

errata@bpbonline.com

Your support, suggestions and feedback are highly appreciated by the BPB Publications' Family.

At www.bpbonline.com, you can also read a collection of free technical articles, sign up for a range of free newsletters, and receive exclusive discounts and offers on BPB books and eBooks. You can check our social media handles below:

Instagram

Facebook

Linkedin

YouTube

Get in touch with us at: business@bpbonline.com for more details.

Piracy

If you come across any illegal copies of our works in any form on the internet, we would be grateful if you would provide us with the location address or website name. Please contact us at business@bpbonline.com with a link to the material.

If you are interested in becoming an author

If there is a topic that you have expertise in, and you are interested in either writing or contributing to a book, please visit www.bpbonline.com. We have worked with thousands of developers and tech professionals, just like you, to help them share their insights with the global tech community. You can make a general application, apply for a specific hot topic that we are recruiting an author for, or submit your own idea.

Reviews

Please leave a review. Once you have read and used this book, why not leave a review on the site that you purchased it from? Potential readers can then see and use your unbiased opinion to make purchase decisions. We at BPB can understand what you think about our products, and our authors can see your feedback on their book. Thank you!

For more information about BPB, please visit www.bpbonline.com.

Join our Discord space

Join our Discord workspace for latest updates, offers, tech happenings around the world, new releases, and sessions with the authors:

https://discord.bpbonline.com

Table of Contents

CHAPTER 1

Introduction to the AZ-900 Certification

Introduction

In this chapter, we will get an overview of the Azure Fundamentals exam. We will look at the details, such as the topics, number of questions, types of questions, scoring, and registration. We will also highlight the benefits of the certification. The cloud is a fast-growing industry, and those who have the skills in this important category can command lucrative salaries.

This chapter looks at other Microsoft certifications. Besides those for the cloud, there are also offerings for AI and data engineering. Finally, this chapter will give an overview of the Azure platform. This will include how to setup an account and use the portal.

Among the many IT certifications, the Azure Fundamentals exam is one of the most popular. It is a great way to get a good understanding of the fundamentals of cloud computing and Azure.

Structure

This chapter covers the following topics:

- Azure Fundamentals exam
- Taking the AZ-900 exam
- Benefits of the certification

- Exam topics
- Exam details
- Types of questions
- Other Microsoft Certifications
- The story of Azure
- Setting up an account
- The Azure portal

Objectives

By the end of this chapter, you will have a good understanding of what is covered in the exam and the benefits of getting the certification. You will also get hands-on experience with Azure.

Taking the AZ-900 exam

The Microsoft website says[1] that the Azure Fundamentals exam tests your *foundational knowledge of cloud concepts, core Azure services, plus Azure management and governance features and tools.*

This may sound complicated and even daunting, but the exam is at the beginner level, and you do not need to understand how to use Azure services for the same. The material is mostly at a high level. For the most part, it is about understanding general principles of cloud computing, as well as the capabilities and use cases for various Azure services.

The code for the Azure Fundamentals exam is AZ-900. The *AZ* is for Azure, and 900 indicates that the exam is the starting point for the certification path for Microsoft. There are several other 900-level exams, like Azure AI Fundamentals (AI-900), Azure Data Fundamentals (DP-900), and Microsoft 365 Certified: Fundamentals (MS-900).

The AZ-900 exam is for a wide audience. It is a good choice for those in IT roles or for someone who wants to transition to a role that involves cloud computing. However, the exam can also be taken by those with non-technical backgrounds. After all, cloud computing is a critical technology that impacts all departments. This means the AZ-900 exam could be a good fit for someone in sales, especially someone who sells technology products. The exam could be helpful for someone who is a project manager. For example, this could be for someone who is leading a cloud migration. Some of these people may ultimately want to make a career change and take on a role as a cloud expert.

Even executives and senior managers can benefit from the exam. The knowledge gained from it can go a long way in helping to evaluate cloud technologies and successfully implement them.

---

1 https://learn.microsoft.com/en-us/credentials/certifications/azure-fundamentals/?practice-assessment-type=certification

Benefits of the certification

Getting the AZ-900 certification can boost your career. It can be a way to set yourself apart and get the attention of employers. They will see the certification as a sign of your knowledge as well as your commitment to improving your skills. Let us take a look at other reasons for getting the certification.

Credibility

There are many certifications available, but the AZ-900 stands out as one of the most popular in the IT world. Of course, the backing of Microsoft is a big help. This brings much credibility. However, the certification has also been around since 2018. During this time, Microsoft has made changes to make the exam better and more relevant.

Growth of the cloud

Even though cloud computing has been around since the late 1990s, technology continues to grow rapidly. Then again, it has been shown to be beneficial for businesses. Cloud computing costs are generally lower than those of on-premises environments. The technology also allows for centralizing data, which provides better analytics and AI applications. Then there is the convenience of being accessible from a browser. This also means that there is no need to install updates.

The cloud computing market is massive. For 2024, the market was about $805 billion and is expected to double by 2028.[2] This represents a **compound annual growth rate** (**CAGR**) of 19.4%.

There are many factors that have powered the growth of the market:

- **Innovative technologies**: Mobile, AI, big data, and edge computing are just some of them. They all generally rely on cloud computing platforms.

- **Hybrid cloud services**: Hybrid cloud is a mix of cloud computing and on-premises systems. This is important for highly regulated industries that have strict security requirements. However, by leveraging the cloud for less critical workloads, this allows for lower costs. You will know more details in *Chapter 2, The Foundations of Cloud Computing*.

- **Digital transformation**: To remain critical, businesses need to modernize their IT systems. Often, this is about migrating to cloud-based approaches.

- **Remote work**: When the COVID-19 pandemic hit, companies had to scramble. They needed to invest in cloud-based technologies to allow for remote working.

- **Security:** Over the years, there have been innovations in cybersecurity solutions. These have provided much more protection for cloud computing platforms.

---

2 https://www.idc.com/getdoc.jsp?containerId=prUS52460024

Growth of Azure

Behind AWS, Azure is ranked second in the cloud computing market. The market share is estimated at about 25%.[3] By comparison, AWS is about 31% and Google is at 10% to 11%.

Going forward, Microsoft has major ambitions to invest in its platform, trying to become number one. To this end, the company announced in fiscal year 2025 that it would spend $80 billion on AI and data centers.[4] This is compared to $55.7 billion the previous year.

According to a 2024 report, Gartner concluded:[5]

- Microsoft is a Leader in this Magic Quadrant. Microsoft Azure maintains a comprehensive array of **infrastructure as a service (IaaS)** and **platform as a service (PaaS)** that meet all enterprise IT use cases. Azure provides robust hybrid cloud capabilities, allowing enterprises to integrate their on-premises, Windows-based environments with the cloud. Microsoft's vast network of partners worldwide makes Azure a logical choice for many customers in regional markets.

- Microsoft competes aggressively in every area of cloud computing and integrates Azure with its other leading cloud platforms to promote a *better together* story in the market. Microsoft is also a strategic partner with other market leaders, such as SAP, VMware, Oracle, NVIDIA, and OpenAI, to offer joint solutions.

The report also notes that AI has been critical for the success of Azure. A major part of this has been due to its strategic partnership with OpenAI, which is the developer of cutting-edge generative AI systems and applications like ChatGPT.

Compensation

Expertise in cloud computing and Azure can make a big difference for your salary, depending on your role, background, and location.

First, these are the average salaries in the U.S., based on a person's role:

- **Cloud engineer**: They design and manage cloud-based systems. For those with mid-level skills, the average salary is $136,794, and $156,482 for those with senior-level skills.[6]

- **Cloud architect**: This role is focused on designing cloud systems. They can expect a salary that ranges from $123,000 to $184,000.[7]

---

3 https://www.statista.com/statistics/967365/worldwide-cloud-infrastructure-services-market-share-vendor/
4 https://www.wsj.com/livecoverage/stock-market-today-dow-sp500-nasdaq-live-01-03-2025/card/microsoft-to-spend-80-billion-on-ai-data-centers-this-fiscal-year-2Iismn1QUr3mj7cp3G78
5 https://azure.microsoft.com/en-us/blog/microsoft-named-a-leader-in-2024-gartner-magic-quadrant-for-strategic-cloud-platform-services/
6 https://motionrecruitment.com/it-salary/cloud-computing
7 https://www.cloudinstitute.io/cloud-computing/cloud-computing-salary-guide-2024

- **Cloud security engineer**: They will set up and manage the security, compliance, and privacy for cloud systems. They can earn a salary of about $136,485.[8]

- **Cloud database administrator**: They will implement, secure, and manage cloud-based databases. They can earn about $180,000.[9]

Next, these are the salaries based on the level of experience:

- **Entry-level (0 to two years)**: The salaries typically range between $65,000 and $90,000.[10]

- **Mid-level (three to five years)**: The salaries are around $90,000 and $120,000.[11]

- **Senior-level (more than 5 years)**: The salaries can range from $115,000 to $160,000, or more.[12]

The long-term trends for cloud professionals look bright. Research from the U.S Bureau of Labor Statistics shows that IT jobs, which include cloud professionals, are forecast to grow by 11% from 2019 to 2029.[13]

Exam topics

Microsoft has a helpful study guide located at **https://learn.microsoft.com/en-us/credentials/certifications/resources/study-guides/az-900**. In it, there is a breakdown of the topics, and each one has a range of percentages for the number of questions.

Cloud concepts

This section covers the general concepts of cloud computing. In fact, there is little about Azure services. Anywhere from 25% to 30% of the questions on the exam are for this section. There are also three main topics covered:

- **Cloud computing**: This looks at the definition of cloud computing, along with the different types of models. These include public, private, and hybrid clouds. You will need to understand how each of these works, but also the use cases. Then there will be coverage of the consumption and pricing models, as well as understanding serverless.

- **Benefits of cloud computing**: The exam focuses on high availability, scalability, reliability, predictability, security, governance, and manageability.

- **Cloud service types**: There are three of them. They include IaaS, PaaS, and **software as a service (SaaS)**. These are how cloud computing services are delivered. This is also based on the shared responsibility model, which shows the division of responsibility between the cloud provider and the customer.

8 https://www.datacamp.com/blog/cloud-engineer-salary
9 https://www.simplilearn.com/cloud-computing-salary-article
10 https://veriipro.com/blog/the-rise-of-cloud-engineering-salary-trends-to-watch-in-2024/
11 https://veriipro.com/blog/the-rise-of-cloud-engineering-salary-trends-to-watch-in-2024/
12 https://veriipro.com/blog/the-rise-of-cloud-engineering-salary-trends-to-watch-in-2024
13 https://veriipro.com/blog/the-rise-of-cloud-engineering-salary-trends-to-watch-in-2024/

Azure architecture and services

Now, in this section, we will look at Azure services, which account for 35% to 40% of the questions on the exam. There are four main topic areas:

- **Core architectural components of Azure**: The exam will cover how Azure resources are set up geographically, such as regions, region pairs, and sovereign regions. This will include understanding availability zones, which allow for more resilience. You will also need to know how Azure resources are organized with resource groups, subscriptions, and management groups.

- **Azure computing and networking services**: This will look at how you can manage computing resources with containers, **virtual machines** (**VMs**), and functions. In fact, a big part of this will be about VMs. You will also need to understand networking tools like Azure Virtual Networks, Azure subnets, Azure DNS, and Azure VPN Gateway.

- **Azure storage services**: You will need to know about the different storage options, tiers, redundancy options, and account types. You will also need to understand tools to help manage files: AzCopy, Azure Storage Explorer, and Azure File Sync. Then there are the migration systems, which include Azure Migrate and Azure Data Box.

- **Azure identity, access, and security**: For this, you will need to know about Microsoft Entra ID, which is the identity service for Azure. This will mean understanding things like **single sign-on** (**SSO**), **multifactor authentication** (**MFA**), passwordless, **role-based access control** (**RBAC**), and conditional access. You will also need to know about zero-trust security, which is where you assume that a system will be breached.

Azure management and governance

The final section, which represents 30% to 35% of the questions on the exam, will also cover four topics:

- **Cost management:** While cloud computing is often cost-effective, there still needs to be monitoring. If not, there can easily be cost overruns and unexpected expenses. For the exam, you will need to know about what factors impact the costs for Azure. You will also need to know about the tools that can help manage costs, such as the **total cost of ownership** (**TCO**) calculator and tags.

- **Azure tools for governance and compliance**: These include Microsoft Purview in Azure and Azure Policy. You will also need to know about resource locks.

- **Managing and deploying Azure resources:** There are different ways to use Azure, including the Azure portal and Cloud Shell. The exam will also cover the tools, like Azure Arc and **Azure Resource Manager** (**ARM**), that provide for provisioning infrastructure, managing multi-cloud and on-premises environments.

- **Monitoring tools in Azure**: For the exam, you will need to know about Azure Advisor, Azure Service Health, and Azure Monitor.

Of course, some of the topics will change or be updated. However, this does not happen frequently. As much as possible, Microsoft wants stability with the exam.

Exam details

The instructions and details of the exam are as follows:

- You have 45 minutes to answer the questions on the AZ-900 exam. However, the total time allocated is 65 minutes. The only difference is that there is extra time for reading the instructions.

- Agreeing with the Microsoft Certification Exam Candidate Agreement, completing the test, and providing any feedback. There are anywhere between 35 and 50 questions.

- Microsoft allows you to take unscheduled breaks during the exam. In fact, there is one that is automatic, which is for five minutes. For any others, you will need to get permission.

- The score of the exam is based on points, not percentages. This is from 1 to 1000, and you need a minimum of 700 to pass the exam. For example, some questions are worth more than one point, depending on the difficulty.

- A handful of questions on the exam will not be factored into your score. The reason is that they are for experimental purposes. That is, they will be evaluated as potential candidates for future exams.

- You will receive your score within minutes of finishing the exam. This will include some feedback.

- In the U.S., the exam costs $99. You can schedule your test with Pearson VUE, located at **https://learn.microsoft.com/en-us/credentials/certifications/azure-fundamentals/?practice-assessment-type=certification**, and you get to choose between taking it online with a proctor or using a local test center.

- If you do not pass on your first try, you can retake it after 24 hours. For any after this, you will need to abide by the retake policy at **https://learn.microsoft.com/en-us/credentials/support/retake-policy**.

- Microsoft provides accommodations for those with disabilities, such as for visual impairments, mobility problems, or neurodiversity. For this, you will usually need to provide documentation, such as a letter from a doctor. The approval of accommodation can take up to ten days.

After you pass your exam, the certification will last, i.e., unless there is a major change to the exam, but it is highly unlikely to lose its credibility.

Types of questions

You will most likely come across multiple-choice and multiple-select questions on the AZ-900 exam. They are not long but can be tricky. For the last chapter of this book, we will look at strategies for this. Refer to the following samples:

1. Which Azure service do you use for managing resources in Azure?

    a. Azure Resource Manager

    b. Azure portal

    c. Azure Advisor

    d. Azure Monitor

   Answer: a

As for multi-selection questions, they require selecting two or more correct answers. This is an example:

1. **Which of the following are advantages of using cloud services?**

    a. High availability

    b. Scalability

    c. Increased capital expenditure

    d. Elasticity

   Answers: a, b, d

Besides these questions, the AZ-900 exam sometimes has drag-and-drop questions. This is where you use your mouse to move items that belong to the same category or have similar relationships. Refer to the following example:

1. **Match each Azure service to its correct description by dragging the service to the corresponding description**:

Azure Service	Description
Azure virtual machines	a. Fully managed relational database service
Azure App Service	b. Scalable cloud storage solution
Azure SQL Database	c. Hosting environment for web applications
Azure Blob Storage	d. On-demand, scalable computing resources

These are the correct matches:

- Azure virtual machines: d. On-demand, scalable computing resources
- Azure App Service: c. Hosting environment for web applications
- Azure SQL Database: a. Fully managed relational database service
- Azure Blob Storage: b. Scalable cloud storage solution

Other Microsoft Certifications

Microsoft offers over 70 certifications. They cover many of its applications, like Office, Fabric, Power Platform, Dynamics, and Windows Server. These certifications are for numerous roles. Some include business analysts, AI engineers, data analysts, database administrators, developers, and security engineers.

In terms of Azure, there are 22 certifications, and they fall into the following categories:

- **Fundamentals**: These are the entry-level certifications, such as the AZ-900 exam.

- **Associate**: This type of certification is for those who have some experience with a Microsoft application.

- **Expert**: This is a person who is highly skilled with a Microsoft application.

- **Specialty**: This is a niche area for Microsoft applications. Some examples include Microsoft Dynamics 365: Finance and Operations Apps Developer (MB-500) and Microsoft Information Protection Administrator (SC-400).

After you pass the AZ-900 exam, there are several paths to consider. A common one is found in *Table 1.1:*

Certification	Topics
AZ-104: Microsoft Azure Administrator Associate[14]	Manage Azure identities and governance (20 to 25%) Implement and manage storage (15 to 20%) Deploy and manage Azure compute resources (20 to 25%) Implement and manage virtual networking (15 to 20%) Monitor and maintain Azure resources (10 to 15%)
AZ-204: Microsoft Azure Developer Associate[15]	Develop Azure compute solutions (25 to 30%) Develop for Azure storage (15 to 20%) Implement Azure security (15 to 20%) Monitor, troubleshoot, and optimize Azure solutions (10 to 15%) Connect to and consume Azure services and third-party services (20 to 25%)
AZ-305: Microsoft Azure Solutions Architect Expert[16]	Design identity, governance, and monitoring solutions (25 to 30%) Design data storage solutions (20 to 25%) Design business continuity solutions (15 to 20%) Design infrastructure solutions (30 to 35%)

Table 1.1: Common path for taking certifications after obtaining the AZ-900

---

14 https://learn.microsoft.com/en-us/credentials/certifications/azure-administrator/?practice-assessment-type=certification

15 https://learn.microsoft.com/en-us/credentials/certifications/azure-developer/?practice-assessment-type=certification

16 https://learn.microsoft.com/en-us/credentials/certifications/exams/az-305/

You may want to specialize in a certain category, such as **artificial intelligence** (**AI**) or data. *Table 1.2* shows the AI path:

Certification	Topics
AI-900: Microsoft Azure AI Fundamentals[17]	Describe AI workloads and considerations (15 to 20%) Describe fundamental principles of machine learning on Azure (20 to 25%) Describe features of computer vision workloads on Azure (15 to 20%) Describe features of **natural language processing** (**NLP**) workloads on Azure (15 to 20%) Describe features of generative AI workloads on Azure (15 to 20%)
AI-102: Microsoft Azure AI Engineer Associate[18]	Plan and manage an Azure AI solution (15 to 20%) Implement content moderation solutions (10 to 15%) Implement computer vision solutions (15 to 20%) Implement natural language processing solutions (30 to 35%) Implement knowledge mining and document intelligence solutions (10 to 15%) Implement generative AI solutions (10 to 15%)

Table 1.2: Path for Azure certifications

Table 1.3 outlines the data path:

Certification	Topics
DP-900: Microsoft Azure Data Fundamentals[19]	• Describe core data concepts (25 to 30%) • Identify considerations for relational data on Azure (20 to 25%) • Describe considerations for working with non-relational data on Azure (15 to 20%) • Describe an analytics workload on Azure (25 to 30%)
DP-203: Microsoft Azure Data Engineer Associate[20]	• Design and implement data storage (15 to 20%) • Develop data processing (40 to 45%) • Secure, monitor, and optimize data storage and data processing (30 to 35%)
DP-100: Microsoft Azure Data Scientist Associate[21]	• Design and prepare a machine learning solution (20 to 25%) • Explore data and run experiments (20 to 25%) • Train and deploy models (25 to 30%) • Optimize language models for AI applications (25 to 30%)

Table 1.3: Data path for Azure certifications

---

17 https://learn.microsoft.com/en-us/credentials/certifications/azure-ai-fundamentals/?practice-assessment-type=certification

18 https://learn.microsoft.com/en-us/credentials/certifications/azure-ai-engineer/?practice-assessment-type=certification

19 https://learn.microsoft.com/en-us/credentials/certifications/azure-data-fundamentals/?practice-assessment-type=certification

20 https://learn.microsoft.com/en-us/credentials/certifications/ azure-data-engineer/ ?practice-assessment-type=certification

21 https://learn.microsoft.com/en-us/credentials/certifications/azure-data-scientist/?practice-assessment-type=certification

As for the specialty certifications for Azure, there are several to choose from, as you can see in *Table 1.4*:

Certification	Topics
Azure Cosmos DB Developer Specialty[22]	• Design and implement data models (35 to 40%) • Design and implement data distribution (5 to 10%) • Integrate an Azure Cosmos DB solution (5 to 10%) • Optimize an Azure Cosmos DB solution (15 to 20%) • Maintain an Azure Cosmos DB solution (25 to 30%)
Azure Virtual Desktop Specialty[23]	• Plan and implement an Azure Virtual Desktop infrastructure (40 to 45%) • Plan and implement identity and security (15 to 20%) • Plan and implement user environments and apps (20 to 25%) • Monitor and maintain an Azure Virtual Desktop infrastructure (10 to 15%)
Azure for SAP Workloads Specialty[24]	• Migrate SAP workloads to Azure (25 to 30%) • Design and implement an infrastructure to support SAP workloads on Azure (25 to 30%) • Design and implement **high availability and disaster recovery (HADR)** (20 to 25%) • Maintain SAP workloads on Azure (20 to 25%)

Table 1.4: *Specialty path for Azure certifications*

As for the rest of the chapter, we will get a high-level look at Azure. This will include its background, how to set up an account, and the Azure portal.

Story of Azure

In 2005, *Ray Ozzie* sold his company, Groove Networks, to Microsoft for $171 million[25]. *Bill Gates* said that the main reason for making the acquisition was to hire Ozzie. He considered him one of the world's top software developers.

Ozzie took the role of Chief Technical Officer, along with two others. He did not waste any time putting together a compelling vision for Microsoft. He set this forth in a 5000-word memo, which he titled, *The Internet Services Disruption*. In it, he declared that the future of software was the cloud and that there needed to be a rethinking of the Windows and Office franchises.

---

22 https://learn.microsoft.com/en-us/credentials/certifications/azure-cosmos-db-developer-specialty/?practice-as-sessment-type=certification
23 https://learn.microsoft.com/en-us/credentials/certifications/azure-virtual-desktop-specialty/?practice-assess-ment-type=certification
24 https://learn.microsoft.com/en-us/credentials/certifications/azure-for-sap-workloads-specialty/?practice-assess-ment-type=certification
25 https://www.businessinsider.com/the-man-who-bill-gates-once-hired-to-replace-him-has-a-new-startup-2012-1

He wrote[26]: *As much as ever, it is clear that if we fail to do so, our business as we know it is at risk. We must respond quickly and decisively.*

As should be no surprise, there was pushback on this message. After all, the cloud was still in the early stages, and there were concerns about security and scalability. However, **Amazon Web Services** (**AWS**) was already showing that the cloud was a viable and fast-growing business. So, Microsoft realized it needed to act quickly.

The company launched a major project, which was named *Red Dog* (the developers often wore red shoes). The priority was to completely rebuild Windows. Eventually, the platform would be renamed to Windows Azure and was launched in 2010.[27]

It was bare bones. Windows Azure had services for compute, APIs, storage, and basic SQL database capabilities, but Microsoft would continue to invest aggressively in the platform.

All this would pay off in a big way. In fact, without this ambitious investment in Azure, it seems likely that Microsoft would be a much smaller company today. Currently, the company has a market value of $3.2 trillion. During the fiscal second quarter in 2025, Microsoft reported revenues of $69.6 billion. As for Azure, it reported a 31% increase in sales.[28]

Amy Hood, the Executive Vice President and Chief Financial Officer of Microsoft, said this on the earnings conference call.[29] Azure and other cloud services revenue grew by 31%. Azure growth included 13 points from AI services, which grew 157% year-over-year and was ahead of expectations even as demand continued to be higher than the available capacity.

Setting up an account

Setting up an account with Azure is a straightforward process and involves:

- Creating an Azure account is a simple process. Go to the Azure website at **https://azure.com**[30] and click on **Get started with Azure**. Then choose **Try Azure for free**. When doing this, you will get a $200 credit.

- Unless you have a Microsoft account, you will need to set one up. This account will give you access not only to Azure but also to other Microsoft services and applications like *Outlook* and *OneDrive*.

- You will need to enter your phone number to verify your identity, as well as your credit or debit card. The free account will last for 30 days. It will then revert to the pay-as-you-go method. You can still use any remaining amount of your free credit. You can also cancel at any time.

26 https://www.seattlepi.com/business/article/microsoft-signals-big-shift-toward-online-services-1187024.php
27 https://www.forbes.com/sites/janakirammsv/2020/02/03/a-look-back-at-ten-years-of-microsoft-azure/
28 https://www.barrons.com/articles/microsoft-earnings-stock-price-today-025172dd?_gl=1*139db2i*_gcl_au*MTkx-Nzg0MDYyNi4xNzMyOTA2MzQ1*_ga*NjYxODk2Mjc1LjE3MjEyNTYwNzc.
29 https://seekingalpha.com/article/4753157-microsoft-corporation-msft-q2-2025-earnings-call-transcript?source=generic_rss
30 http://azure.microsoft.com/en-us/

- There are other perks as well. For example, there are more than 20 Azure services that are free for 12 months and 65 services that are always free.

The Azure portal

After you set up your account, you will be directed to the Azure portal, which you can see in *Figure 1.1*:

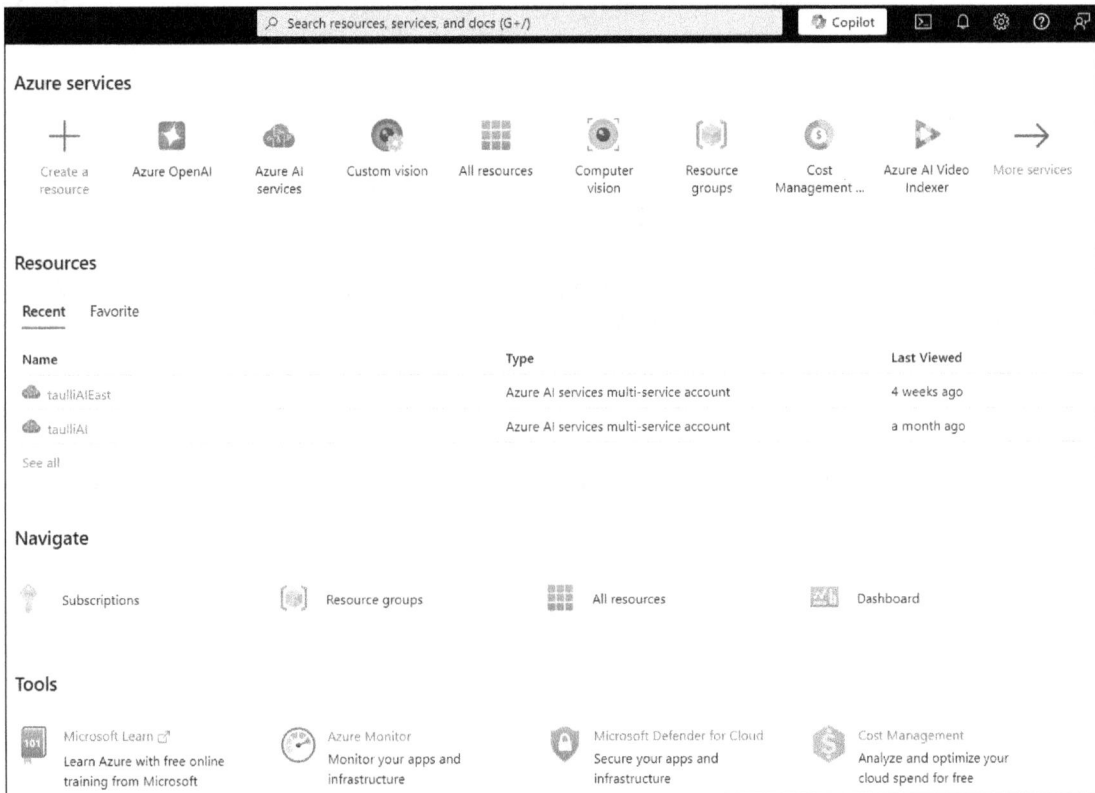

Figure 1.1: *The Azure portal*

The Azure portal is where you will select services and manage your account. Its graphical user interface is intuitive, making it easy to navigate and configure resources visually. However, Azure also offers a **command-line interface** (**CLI**), which is useful for automation, scripting, and performing advanced management tasks more efficiently. While the portal is ideal for interactive exploration, the CLI provides powerful capabilities for deploying and managing resources at scale through commands and scripts.

At the top of the screen for the Azure portal, there is the search box. This is certainly helpful, since there are so many services on Azure. You can also access Copilot, which is an AI-powered chatbot. This can answer many Azure-related questions.

The Azure portal is designed to make it easy to access services. There are icons for creating resources, Custom Vision, Computer Vision, Resource Groups, Cost Management, and Azure AI Video Indexer. Azure certainly wants to encourage people to use its AI services.

Below this section, you will find a list of recently accessed items. This is a convenient feature. You will often find that you use certain resources and tools regularly.

Azure's interface and the names of its services will change from time to time. So, in this book, the figures may not necessarily be the same. This is to be expected, but the good news is that there usually are not many changes.

Conclusion

In this chapter, we got an overview of the AZ-900 exam. We looked at the benefits of getting this certification, such as the credibility among employers, the growth of the cloud and Azure, and the potential career boost. After this, we covered the topics of the exam, which include three main categories. We also looked at other certifications like the Microsoft Azure Administrator Associate, the Microsoft Azure Developer Associate, and the Microsoft Azure Solutions Architect Expert. Finally, we got a quick demo of Azure.

In the next chapter, we will get started with the first topic area for the exam, i.e., cloud computing concepts. This will cover the types of cloud platforms, like the public cloud, private cloud, and hybrid cloud, along with the benefits and drawbacks. The chapter will also discuss the pricing models and the shared responsibility model.

Join our Discord space

Join our Discord workspace for latest updates, offers, tech happenings around the world, new releases, and sessions with the authors:

https://discord.bpbonline.com

CHAPTER 2
The Foundations of Cloud Computing

Introduction

In this chapter, we will get an overview of the fundamentals of cloud computing. While we will look at some Azure services, the primary focus will be on general concepts. These will include learning about cloud models, public cloud, private cloud, and hybrid cloud, and cloud service types, such as **infrastructure as a service (IaaS)**, **platform as a service (PaaS)**, and **software as a service (SaaS)**. The cloud is quite diverse, with many options.

The chapter will also look at the financial aspects of cloud computing. These include understanding capital versus operating expenses, as well as pricing models. We will also cover the shared responsibility model. This is a framework for understanding the levels of control between the cloud provider and customer. Finally, we will look at the primary benefits of cloud computing. Some of the main ones include high availability, scalability, and security.

Structure

This chapter covers the following topics:

- Cloud computing
- Cloud models
- Cloud service types

- Serverless
- Capital versus operating expenses
- Pricing for the cloud
- Shared responsibility model
- Benefits of the cloud

Objectives

By the end of this chapter, you will have a good understanding of the fundamentals of cloud computing. This will cover cloud models and cloud types. You will also know about the monetary characteristics, such as the pricing models, the shared responsibility model, and the core benefits of the cloud, which will allow for evaluating this technology.

Cloud computing

The term *cloud computing* seems to be everywhere. It has become a must-have way to describe most software. Unfortunately, cloud computing is also a source of marketing hype, and because of this, the definition of this term can be tough to pin down. However, for the purpose of the AZ-900 exam, you need to have a clear understanding of this concept.

The following is the definition of cloud computing on Microsoft's website:

Cloud computing is the delivery of computing services, including servers, storage, databases, networking, software, analytics, and intelligence, over the internet (*the cloud*) to offer faster innovation, flexible resources, and economies of scale. You typically pay only for cloud services you use, helping you lower your operating costs, run your infrastructure more efficiently, and scale as your business needs change.[1]

This is certainly a good way of explaining cloud computing. It covers the main aspects, such as the delivery of the technologies, the key benefits, and the business model. There is much more involved, and we will learn about these details in this book. However, it is a good idea to commit Microsoft's definition to memory. It will provide you with the necessary context to better understand what will be covered in the exam.

Cloud models

There are three main types of cloud computing, which are called cloud models. They include:

- Public cloud
- Private cloud
- Hybrid cloud

---

1 https://azure.microsoft.com/en-us/resources/cloud-computing-dictionary/what-is-cloud-computing

Each has its pros and cons. As with any complex technology, the use of a cloud model depends on requirements, goals, and budgets.

Public cloud

When we talk about Azure, or other cloud providers like *AWS* or *Google Cloud*, the public cloud is what we are referring to. It is the most common cloud model. The cloud provider will buy real estate for data centers, acquire the hardware and software, set up the physical security, and hire the IT personnel.

The core computing resources for the public cloud will be shared among customers. This is known as the multi-tenant model, which provides for lower costs and higher efficiency.

Private cloud

The private cloud, which is also called on-premises, uses the single-tenant model. This is where an organization will build, manage, and maintain its own data centers. The real estate, though, may be leased. Yet the organization will have total control over the IT systems.

A key advantage is that this allows for customization. This can be particularly important for highly specialized businesses. An example is an automated manufacturing facility. Managing robots would require **Internet of Things (IoT)** capabilities, such as real-time communications with devices and robots.

Another advantage of the private cloud is that it is suitable when there are high levels of regulation and compliance. This is the case for industries like healthcare, financial services, and energy. With a private cloud, they can focus resources on security and privacy systems.

Azure offers a variety of tools to help operate and manage private clouds. Some include Azure Arc and Azure ExpressRoute, which we will learn more about in this book.

Hybrid cloud

As the name implies, the hybrid cloud is a mix of the public cloud and the private cloud. This has sophisticated systems that allow the sharing of data across applications. For Azure, there are tools to help with this. The two main ones include Azure Arc and Azure Stack. Regardless, the hybrid cloud is complex to manage. You will need skilled IT personnel.

A major benefit of the hybrid cloud is that it can help to lower overall costs. For example, the mission-critical workloads can be managed with the private cloud, and the rest can be handled with the public cloud. In fact, the hybrid cloud is a popular strategy for organizations to embark on cloud transformation.

The hybrid cloud is also sometimes confused with multicloud. Multicloud is when an organization uses more than one public cloud. The purpose is to increase the redundancy, but a multicloud environment will also have an on-premises setup.

Over the years, the hybrid cloud has shown much interest. Consider research from SkyQuest Technology, which predicts that spending on this category will jump from $97.8 billion in 2023 to $348.14 billion by 2031.[2]

For the AZ-900 exam, you will need to understand the differences between the cloud models. You can find these in *Table 2.1*:

Feature	Public cloud	Private cloud	Hybrid cloud
Definition	• Most common cloud model • Computing resources shared among customers (multi-tenant model)	• Also known as on-premises cloud • Single-tenant model	• Combination of public and private cloud • Enables data and application sharing across both environments
Costs	Lower cost due to shared resources	• Higher costs due to dedicated resources • Requires investment in hardware, software, and personnel	• Costs vary based on workload distribution • Can optimize spending by using the public cloud for less mission-critical workloads
Customization	Limited customization of the underlying infrastructure	Highly customizable to meet specific business needs	Partial customization

Table 2.1: Comparison between cloud models

Cloud service types

There are three main cloud service types:

- IaaS
- PaaS
- SaaS

As you can see, all of these have the phrase *as a service*. Simply put, this is another way of describing how computing services are delivered via the internet or on demand. This phrase has become a shorthand for many types of technologies. In fact, it has become a common part of branding, such as **database as a service (DBaaS)**, **security as a service (SECaaS)**, **artificial intelligence as a service (AIaaS)**, and **backup as a service (BaaS)**.

As for IaaS, PaaS, and Saas, these are the core offerings of Azure. They provide different levels of computing services depending on the needs. We will look at each of them in the following sub-sections.

---

2 https://www.globenewswire.com/news-release/2024/10/22/2967003/0/en/Hybrid-Cloud-Market-is-Poised-to-Reach-USD-348-14-Billion-by-2031-SkyQuest-Technology.html

Infrastructure as a service

With IaaS, Azure provides the main infrastructure services for a customer. This is virtualized, which means that you access the hardware via the internet. The resources available for IaaS include **virtual machines** (**VMs**), storage, and networking. A VM can be thought of as a software-based simulation of a server. It has everything that a physical system has, including its own **operating system** (**OS**), applications, and hardware, like **central processing units** (**CPU**), memory, storage, and network interfaces.

However, the underlying physical server, which is hosted in an Azure data center, will usually have more than one VM. Yet they each run separately and appear to be their own machines. As a result, virtualization allows for more efficiency and scale, but this requires highly sophisticated technology, known as a hypervisor. This handles the allocation of the resources for each of the VMs and how they connect to the physical server.

Two of the most common hypervisors are Microsoft's Hyper-V and VMware's ESXi. Hyper-V is integrated with Microsoft's Windows Server and is also a standalone product. VMware's ESXi, on the other hand, is a bare-metal hypervisor, which runs without an OS.

A key advantage of IaaS is that you have much control over your IT infrastructure. You can set it up in the way you want, such as with the software you install and configure. It is as if you have access to the physical servers, storage, and networking, but you do not have to take on the heavy investments of setting up a private cloud.

However, there you will need a skilled team to manage the environment. This includes not only setting up the IT infrastructure but also the ongoing requirements for updates, patches, and security monitoring.

Platform as a service

PaaS is an abstraction of IaaS. This means that it is a more simplified platform. You still get access to the underlying computing resources of IaaS, but also numerous managed services, such as an OS, middleware, databases, and development tools. This also includes auto-scaling and built-in security and compliance. There is no need to manage the underlying IT infrastructure for this. Instead, you can focus on using and creating applications.

To illustrate this, we will look at an example. Suppose you are developing an inventory management app. You first use Visual Studio to write it using ASP.NET and a SQL Server backend. Once you are finished, you will use Azure App Service, which is a PaaS tool. This will manage the process for hosting the application and the database.

However, if you did this using IaaS, you would have spent hours setting up the IT infrastructure. You would need to configure the VM, install the OS, web server, and SQL server. For this, you would have to make the correct configurations for the network and security protocols. Then you would need to manage the traffic for the app, such as by using load balancers. The bottom line is that the PaaS approach can save considerable time.

Software as a service

SaaS is the highest level of abstraction for cloud computing. The cloud service provider manages the IaaS and PaaS services. The user only focuses on using the application. Common examples of SaaS apps include OneDrive, Office 365, and Teams.

Generally, you will access a SaaS app from a web browser. However, there is a trend for having versions available on the desktop. As for the pricing, it is usually based on subscriptions per user, and they are typically on a monthly or annual basis, at which you may get a discount.

Table 2.2 shows comparisons among the cloud types:

Features	IaaS	PaaS	SaaS
Service scope	Provides virtualized computing resources over the internet for servers, storage, and networking. Users manage operating systems, applications, and data.	Provides IaaS infrastructure and the OS, middleware, databases, and development tools. Developers can focus on creating applications, not the details of the infrastructure.	Users have access to fully functional applications.
Advantages	High level of control over computing resources, and no need to own or manage physical hardware.	Simplifies app development, provides development frameworks and tools, and manages underlying infrastructure.	No need for maintenance
Disadvantages	Requires management of operating systems and applications. Need skilled IT personnel.	Limited control over the underlying infrastructure.	Minimal customization options

Table 2.2: Comparison between cloud service types

Serverless

The term *serverless* can be confusing. It does not mean there are no servers. No, this technology is critical for this service. Serverless means that a cloud provider will manage the provisioning of the servers.

Serverless is a way to describe a cloud service where a developer does not have to worry about the underlying infrastructure. It is like a PaaS application, but it has even less need for configuration and management.

Another difference is that serverless is event-driven, which means that the code is executed only based on certain conditions. In terms of the pricing, Azure only charges according to the events. This can lead to lower costs if the workloads are irregular and not at high volumes.

Azure has a few serverless offerings. One is Azure Functions, which uses a myriad of event triggers. Just some include scheduled timers, HTTP requests, and activities with message queues. Azure Functions also support various programming languages to write the functions. Some include C#, Python, Java, and JavaScript.

The other type of serverless application is Azure Logic Apps, which allows for creating automated workflows for applications and data. This can be done with little or no code. Instead, you will create the workflows using a visual designer. There is also a large catalog of components. For example, there are more than 1,400 integrations with platforms like Salesforce, Office 365, and SQL Server. There is even one for Azure Functions.

These are examples of some of the workflows you can create:

- **E-commerce**: You can automate the workflow for when a customer submits an order. Azure Logic Apps can then automate the process to update the inventory, process the payment, and send the shipping details to the customer.

- **Enterprise application**: Suppose an employee submits a request for leave. Azure Logic Apps will automatically send this to HR, fill out the application, and update the employee's status in the payroll department. There will also be notifications to the manager and HR representative.

- **Social media**: Let us say you want to monitor the mention of your company's brand. You can create a workflow in Azure Logic Apps that analyzes the sentiment on X using an AI service.

Capital versus operating expenses

Evaluating the financial costs of IT infrastructure and applications is often complex. However, there is a high-level way for this. It is to look at two financial models:

- **Capital expenditures (CapEx)**: CapEx describes expenditures for long-term assets. These include real estate, facilities, hardware systems, servers, and other software. For CapEx, the expenditures need to be made up front. Although there may be a need to use debt financing, such as with real estate and certain types of equipment, there is a tax benefit for CapEx. You can deduct the depreciation on the assets. In some cases, this can be accelerated, which can allow for higher deductions in the early years. With CapEx, there needs to be a forecast, such as estimating IT needs for the next two to five years. However, this can be challenging since there could be a recession, new innovations, or an adverse impact from competition. On the other hand, you can easily underestimate the expenditures. Perhaps your industry will get a lift from positive trends, but as we have seen earlier, there may be little choice. Some businesses must use CapEx investments because of regulatory requirements or the need for highly customized IT systems.

- **Operating expenditures (OpEx)**: OpEx, in contrast, is about the day-to-day expenses of cloud computing. Since the model is generally based on consumption, the expenses are made as you use the services. Depending on the arrangement with the cloud provider, this can be made monthly or annually.

Another advantage is that there is no need to make long-term forecasts. However, this can be an issue with some companies. The reason is that the expenditures can be unexpected, such as when there is a spike in traffic. This is why it is a good idea to use cost optimization strategies, which we will cover in this book.

Pricing for the cloud

On its face, the pricing model for Azure is straightforward. It is pay-as-you-go, but the reality is that this approach can be quite complicated. There are a variety of factors for the pricing of Azure services that span compute resources, storage, and data transfers. There are also differences based on the regions. The result is that it can be difficult to come up with an estimate, even for the month. This is especially the case when you get started with Azure. It can take some time to gauge the needs of your organization. It is also important to monitor the costs as they can sometimes change significantly based on changes to your Azure account.

To help out, Azure has a useful tool called the Azure pricing calculator, which is available at **https://azure.microsoft.com/en-us/pricing/calculator/**. You can also see the UI in *Figure 2.1*:

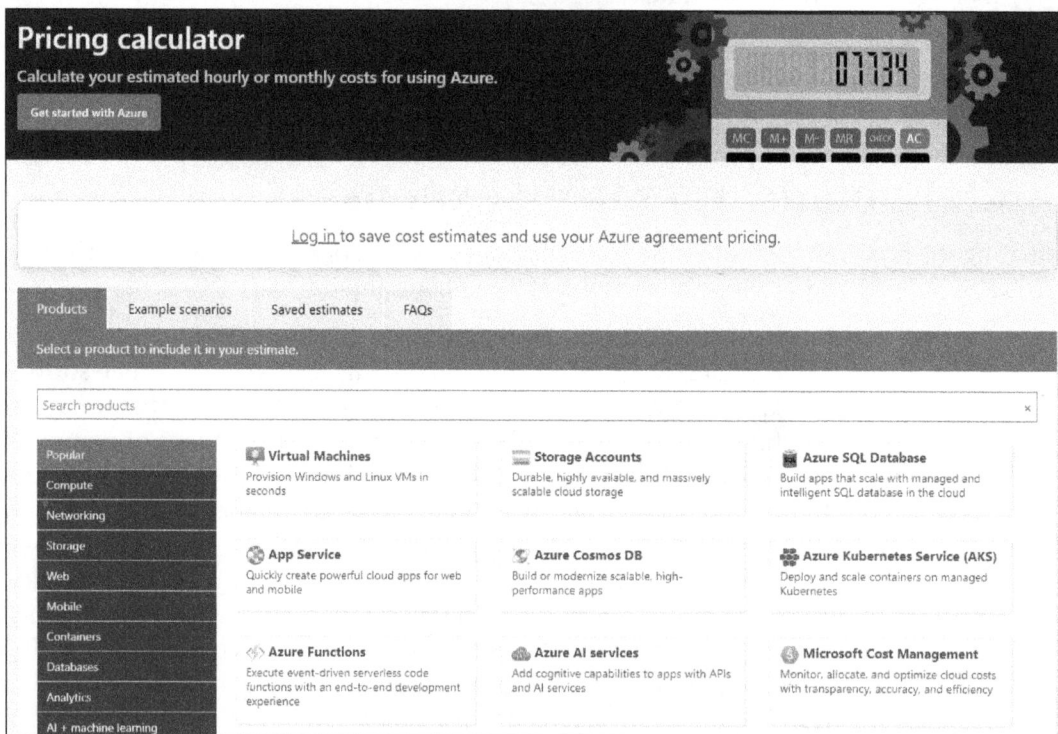

Figure 2.1: Azure pricing calculator

First, you will browse a list of Azure services. They are for VMs, storage, and databases. For each of these, you will click **Add to Estimate** for those you want to include in the estimate. You will then configure each for a variety of factors.

Here is a look at this for VMs:

- **VM size and series**: These are according to CPUs.

- **Operating system**: If you use Windows, there will likely be a license, but this will probably not be the case for Linux, which is open source.

- **Region**: This is the geographical location of the VM. This could be a country or parts of one, but the costs can vary. For example, you may pay higher fees for having VMs in Europe versus Asia.

- **Billing options:** Besides pay-as-you-go, there are reserved instances. This is when you prepay for one or three years of the service, which usually means getting a significant discount. Next, there is spot pricing. This is buying unused Azure capacity at a discount, but there is a catch: Azure can reclaim this at any time.

- **Storage**: There are many types of options, which are generally **hard disk drives (HDDs)** and **solid-state drives (SDDs)**.

- **Networking**: Typically, inbound data is free, while there is a charge for outbound data. There will also be fees for static and dynamic IP addresses, as well as load balancers.

- **Licensing**: You will have to pay fees for certain types of software, like Windows Server or SQL Server.

- **Add-ons and features**: Examples include backups, monitoring, and accelerated networking.

- **Support plans**: Azure offers support plans with different tiers.

It is important to emphasize that the pricing calculator provides an estimate. It could very well be off the mark. However, the more information you can provide, the better the results should be. Besides the calculator, there are other tools to manage costs. We will look at these later in the book.

Shared responsibility model

With offerings like IaaS, PaaS, and SaaS, there are different levels of roles for the cloud provider and the customer. This is known as the shared responsibility model. It is a framework to understand who has obligations for critical areas like IT services, security, and compliance.

The shared responsibility model is critical for the success of a cloud deployment. Here are some reasons for this:

- **Efficiency:** In economics, the concept of *division of labor* allows for lower costs and specialization. This goes for the shared responsibility model as well. It is about making sure there is an effective allocation of resources and little duplication of efforts.

- **Data privacy:** The shared responsibility provides a way to control the levels of data privacy. Sometimes, this needs to be high. There may be little choice if there are regulations or laws.

- **Mitigating confusion**: The shared responsibility model allows for better organization and management. The roles are much clearer, which allows for faster and better decision-making.

To get a sense of how the shared responsibility model works, let us look at *Figure 2.2*:

Service/Layer	SaaS	PaaS	IaaS
Customer Data	C	C	C
User Access & Identity	C	C	C
Application Configuration	C	C	C
Platform Configuration	P	S	C
Network Security	P	S	C
Operating System	P	P	S
Runtime Environment	P	P	S
Middleware	P	P	S
Virtualization	P	P	P
Servers	P	P	P
Storage	P	P	P
Networking	P	P	P
Physical Security	P	P	P

Cloud Shared Responsibility Model

C Customer Responsible (C)
S Shared Responsibility (S)
P Provider Responsible (P)

Figure 2.2: Key elements of the shared responsibility model

Granted, there is a lot here, but we will break things down. At the top of the diagram, we have services that are in the control of the customer regardless of the service model. These are customer data, user access, identity, and application configuration. The customer has the responsibility for the protection of their own data and the users who can have access to it.

In the middle tier of the figure is a blend of responsibility for the customer and the cloud provider. For example, for platform configuration and network security, this is managed by the cloud provider for SaaS, shared with PaaS, and managed by the customer for IaaS. This is similar for the OS, runtime environment, and middleware. This highlights the increase in security and management responsibilities as an organization goes from SaaS to IaaS.

Finally, at the bottom layer, there are the core services like virtualization, servers, storage, networking, and physical security. These are strictly the responsibility of the cloud provider. They are about the critical infrastructure, which requires significant IT capabilities. As for an on-premises environment or private cloud, there is no shared responsibility model. The customer is responsible for the whole IT environment.

Benefits of the cloud

There are major benefits to using a cloud platform. This helps to explain the strong growth over the years. When it comes to IT environments, it is common that the priority is to focus on the cloud.

For the AZ-900 exam, you will need to know some of these benefits:

- High availability
- Scalability
- Reliability
- Predictability
- Security
- Governance
- Manageability

In the next few sections, we will take a deeper look at each of them.

High availability

On July 19, 2024, cybersecurity company CrowdStrike released an update for its platform. Unfortunately, it would quickly lead to a cascade of disruptions across its customer base that relied on Windows-based systems. Airlines like Delta, United, and American Airlines experienced outages, which resulted in thousands of delayed or cancelled flights. There were also serious issues with hospitals, financial institutions, and other industries.

It would take CrowdStrike more than a week to fix the problem and get all the systems running properly, but the company's stock price got hit. Of course, there was damage to the company's reputation and brand. It would take time and effort to rebuild trust with customers.

In a Congressional hearing, CrowdStrike's senior vice president of counter adversary operations, *Adam Meyers*, had this to say:

Trust takes years to make, and seconds to break. We understand that we broke that trust, and that we need to work to earn it back.[3]

This is not to single out CrowdStrike. The fact is that maintaining high availability of complex IT systems is challenging, and there are occasional mishaps. HA describes a system that operates without interruption for a defined period.

There are numerous ways availability can be negatively impacted:

- **Power outage**: A small one can have a major impact on a system. Even if a power outage is for a minute, this can mean having to restart and reboot the operations.

---

3 https://www.wsj.com/articles/crowdstrike-faces-lawmaker-questions-over-july-outage-55e7985a

This can lead to considerable downtime. To deal with this, cloud providers will have extensive backup systems and battery power.

- **Network outage**: This could be due to bugs in the software, human error, or outside factors, like bad weather. Regardless, a network outage can result in prolonged downtime.

- **Application failure**: This is usually a problem for the customer. An application may have bugs or errors. This is why it is important to have strong code reviews and testing. Azure has a tool called Application Insights that helps with this.

- **Cyberattacks**: Threats like malware and **distributed denial of service** (**DDoS**) attacks can be devastating for an IT platform.

There are different types of disruptions. One is planned downtime, which is a scheduled pause in services, allowing for maintenance, patches, hardware replacements, or upgrades. Then there is unplanned downtime, which is when a system is hit with an unexpected problem that we mentioned in the preceding example. Of course, unplanned downtime is what needs to be avoided, and this is where HA plays a critical role.

Azure is built with capabilities to enhance HA. Part of this is done by using an intricate set of data centers, where it is difficult for an outage in one to impact another data center nearby. This redundancy does add to the costs, but this can be well worth it. Many companies require HA.

This is not to say that a system can be 100% available. This is clearly impractical. Instead, the focus is on achieving benchmarks, such as the *nines*. For example, five nines means that availability is 99.999%. This amounts to about five minutes of downtime annually.

HA metrics and requirements are set forth in a **service level agreement** (**SLA**). This is a contract where the cloud provider commits to certain levels of uptime and reliability for a particular customer.

Scalability

Scalability describes an IT system that can manage increases and decreases in workloads, adding or lowering resources automatically or based on certain policies. A workload is defined as an application, service, or process that uses cloud resources. This can be for numerous tasks, like storage, application hosting, or analytics.

There is a balancing act with scalability. On the one hand, you want seamless performance, with no interruptions. At the same time, you want to help minimize the costs. As for Azure, it provides tools to help with these two factors.

Scalability is a key factor for many businesses, as they try to adapt to dynamic environments:

- **E-commerce platforms:** The changes in traffic and transaction volumes can be highly volatile. This is especially the case during certain holidays, like Christmas, or shopping events, such as Black Friday or Cyber Monday.

- **Streaming services**: They consume massive workloads, which could be due to a breakout hit. Or it could be for an upcoming event, such as sports. Unfortunately, managing the scalability can be extremely difficult, even with modern cloud platforms. An example was the streaming of a boxing match between *Jake Paul* and *Mike Tyson* in late 2024. Netflix's systems suffered from low-quality video, interruptions, and glitches.[4]

- **Healthcare**: When there are outbreaks, like the COVID-19 pandemic, there is a need for high levels of scalability.

There are two main approaches to scalability. One is vertical scaling, which is also referred to as scaling up or scaling down. It is a more straightforward method. Vertical scaling is where you increase or decrease the capacity of an existing VM or service. For example, suppose you have a Basic B2 VM with two vCPUs and 4GB of RAM. Generally, it works for your workload, but suppose there is a spike in volume. Through Azure, you can upgrade the VM to a D4. This has four vCPUs and 16GB of RAM.

There are some limitations to vertical scaling, listed as follows:

- It is usually used when an application is on one VM.

- You often need to restart the VM, which can mean a brief amount of downtime.

- The scalability is constrained based on a single VM. This could mean that there will not be enough capacity for the increased workload.

- Upgraded VMs can be much more costly. In this situation, it is often better to have multiple VMs.

- By having one VM, there is the risk of a single point of failure.

- There is no automatic scaling. An administrator needs to monitor the performance of a system and manually make the adjustments.

The next approach is horizontal scaling, which is also called scaling out or scaling in. This is about adding or reducing the number of VMs. Horizontal scaling addresses some of the limitations of vertical scaling. There is improved fault tolerance because workloads are distributed across different VMs. There is also automatic scaling. Generally, horizontal scaling is a good option when an application has unpredictable and widely fluctuating workloads.

The main drawback is complexity. Here are some of the considerations:

- **Load balancing**: This distributes traffic evenly across VMs, which helps to minimize bottlenecks and improve reliability, but load balancing requires configuration, such as using solutions like Azure Load Balancer, Azure Application Gateway, and Azure Front Door.

- **Configuration consistency**: It is important to maintain consistency across all the VMs. If not, there is likely to be degradation of performance. For this, you can use

---

4 https://www.sportsbusinessjournal.com/Articles/2024/11/20/netflix-streaming-live-sports-impacts

Azure **Virtual Machine Scale Sets** (**VMSS**), which allows for creating predefined configurations.

- **State management**: State refers to information about the status of a system. This is essential for making sure an application is stable and consistent. With horizontal scaling, you will need to manage state for a VM. It is usually recommended to have the information stored in different caches and databases.

Reliability

Reliability describes a system that consistently performs as intended, based on predefined conditions. We have already mentioned some of the strategies for this, such as avoiding single points of failure and leveraging distributed resources across different VMs and services. However, it is also important to have deployments in various locations, which can increase the number of redundancies. Then there should be data backup and replication. Finally, an organization should perform ongoing monitoring and testing of the IT systems. This would include failure mode analysis and disaster recovery drills.

HA and reliability share features, but the main difference is that HA is about the amount of time a system is operational, while reliability is about assessing a system's ability to function without failure for a period. What this means is that a system can have HA but not be reliable if issues are not resolved quickly. Ultimately, the focus should be on having strong HA and reliability.

Predictability

Predictability is where you can consistently anticipate the performance and costs of an IT system. This helps create a better user experience. In terms of the capabilities for predictability, they include having strong scaling, often horizontal scaling, and HA.

We have already seen how to help estimate costs using the Pricing Calculator, but there are other tools built into Azure that allows for real-time tracking of resource consumption. There are also APIs that provide access to this data. With them, you can build your own applications to manage costs that are tailored to your organization's requirements.

Security

Azure invests heavily in security for its platform. There are many layers of protection and systems. Azure also has thousands of security professionals who monitor threats, research vulnerabilities, and maintain systems.

Here are some of the safeguards:

- **Physical security**: The data centers are surrounded by tall concrete and steel fences. Access is guarded by strict authentication systems, including biometrics. Then there is surveillance, with 24/7 video feeds.

- **Network security**: This is software and hardware that filters inbound traffic in the Azure platform. The tools include advanced firewalls and DDoS protection.

- **Data security**: Azure uses encryption to protect data that is at rest and in transit. The private keys are stored in vaults.

- **Compliance certifications**: Azure has undergone numerous audits of its systems, such as with FedRAMP and SOC 3.

Azure also provides customers with access to a variety of security tools, like Microsoft Defender and Microsoft Entra ID. We will learn more about these later in this book.

Governance

Governance is a set of policies, procedures, and controls for cloud resources. The focus is on effective management, security, and compliance.

Setting up a governance structure should not be rushed. It takes research, planning, and collaboration across the organization. There also needs to be a legal review to determine what regulations and compliance requirements are applicable. Some of the main ones are:

- **Health Insurance Portability and Accountability Act (HIPAA)**: This is a U.S. statute that governs the privacy of patient health data.

- **Payment Card Industry Data Security Standard (PCI DSS)**: This refers to several security standards for organizations that accept, process, store, and transmit credit card data.

- **General Data Protection Regulation (GDPR)**: This is a set of regulations for privacy. GDPR is applicable to the **European Union (EU)**.

- **Federal Information Security Management Act (FISMA)**: This is a U.S. statute that mandates that federal agencies adopt security systems and methods for protecting federal data.

- **ISO/IEC 27001**: This is an international standard for **information security management systems (ISMS)**.

- **ISO/IEC 27017**: These are security guidelines for cloud services. It is focused on the shared responsibilities between cloud providers and customers.

- **ISO/IEC 27018**: This is for the security of **personally identifiable information (PII)** for cloud systems.

- **Federal Risk and Authorization Management Program (FedRAMP)**: These are standards for cloud security used by federal agencies.

To help with these requirements and crafting guidelines, there are various templates available. One is Azure Blueprints, which is a package of policies, role assignments, and resource templates.

You can also bolster governance by using auditing and reporting tools, which monitor systems to identify anomalies and issues. Then there are systems for automated patching, such as for security and compliance standards.

Azure has several useful tools, such as Azure Policy. This allows you to create, assign, and manage governance policies. It is comprehensive, covering cloud resources and enforcing corporate standards, along with SLAs. You can also use management groups to organize resources and users. We will look more at this in this book.

Manageability

Manageability describes the ease and efficiency for a cloud system to be managed, controlled, and optimized. There are two flavors. First, there is management of the cloud, which is about the tools and practices to streamline the management of resources. Examples include scaling, monitoring, and alerts.

Then there is self-healing. This is where the cloud platform identifies and fixes the issues, such as by restarting systems or reallocating services.

The management of the cloud can be automated with **infrastructure as code** (**IaC**) tools like **Azure Resource Manager** (**ARM**) templates, Bicep, and Terraform. They allow for defining and deploying infrastructure using a language, which helps to provide for consistent and repeatable processes.

Next, there is management in the cloud. This is about effectively interacting with cloud resources. We already saw a way to do this, that is, by using the Azure portal, but you can also use a **command-line interface** (**CLI**) and PowerShell Scripts, such as for automation, scripting complex tasks, or managing resources programmatically. Finally, you can leverage **application programming interfaces** (**APIs**). These integrate Azure services into applications. In *Table 2.3*, there is a summary of the main benefits of using a cloud platform:

Benefits	Description
High availability (HA)	Ensures the system operates without interruption for defined periods Provides redundancy and backup systems Helps achieve specific uptime benchmarks (e.g., *five nines* 99.999% availability)
Scalability	Adapts to increases and decreases in workloads automatically Supports dynamic business needs (e.g., seasonal spikes, unexpected traffic)
Reliability	Maintain consistent system performance under predefined conditions Provides redundancy through multi-location deployments Includes data backup and replication for system stability
Predictability	Consistent anticipation of performance and costs Real-time tracking of resource consumption

Benefits	Description
Security	Multiple layers of protection (physical, network, data)
	Advanced tools like firewalls and DDoS protection
	Compliance with various security certifications
Governance	Clear policies and procedures for cloud resource management
	Compliance with regulatory requirements (HIPAA, GDPR, etc.)
	Templates and tools for policy implementation
Manageability	Multiple management interfaces (Portal, CLI, PowerShell)
	Automation through IaC
	Self-healing capabilities for system issues

Table 2.3: Benefits of cloud computing

Conclusion

In this chapter, we got an overview of cloud computing. We reviewed the three main cloud types and cloud models. These are ways to understand how cloud computing is deployed and managed. This chapter also looked at the approaches to pricing, the shared responsibility model, and the benefits of this powerful technology.

Remember, the AZ-900 exam primarily tests your conceptual understanding and knowledge of definitions rather than hands-on implementation details. Keeping this in mind will help you focus your study effectively.

As for the next chapter, we will move beyond general cloud fundamentals and start to look deeper at the Azure platform. This will include a review of the structures of data centers. There will also be coverage of how Azure is organized, such as with regions and availability zones.

Sample questions

1. **Which of the following best describes cloud computing?**

    a. The use of physical servers located on-premises

    b. The delivery of computing services over the internet to offer faster innovation and flexible resources

    c. Hosting software on personal devices for local access

    d. The deployment of hardware components for networking within an organization

    Correct answer: b

    Explanation: Cloud computing is defined as the delivery of computing services, including servers, storage, databases, networking, software, analytics, and intelligence, over the internet. This model allows for faster innovation, flexible resources, and economies of scale. The key benefit is that organizations pay only for the cloud services they use.

2. **Which cloud model uses a multi-tenant architecture where resources are shared among customers?**

    a. Public cloud

    b. Private cloud

    c. Hybrid cloud

    d. Multicloud

Correct answer: a

Explanation: The public cloud uses a multi-tenant model. This is where computing resources are shared among multiple customers, which provides for lower costs and increased efficiency. This model is typically provided by companies like Azure, AWS, and Google Cloud. They manage the data center operations, hardware, software, security, and IT personnel.

3. **Which cloud service type provides the highest level of abstraction, where the user only focuses on using the application?**

    a. IaaS

    b. PaaS

    c. SaaS

    d. Serverless

Correct answer: c

Explanation: SaaS offers the highest level of abstraction among cloud service types. The cloud provider manages the infrastructure, platform, and application. This means that users will focus solely on using the application without worrying about underlying hardware, operating systems, or middleware. Common examples of SaaS applications include Microsoft Office 365, Google Workspace, and Salesforce.

4. **Which financial model involves long-term investments for assets like real estate, servers, and hardware systems?**

    a. OpEx

    b. CapEx

    c. Pay-as-you-go

    d. Spot pricing

Correct answer: b

Explanation: CapEx refers to long-term investments in assets such as real estate, hardware systems, and servers. These expenditures are made upfront and are usually used for building private cloud infrastructures. A key advantage of CapEx is the tax benefit of asset depreciation.

5. **In the shared responsibility model, who is responsible for managing user access and identity?**

   a. Cloud provider

   b. Managed service provider

   c. Third-party security vendor

   d. Customer

Correct answer: d

Explanation: In the shared responsibility model, the customer is responsible for managing user access and identity. This also includes protecting their own data and configuring application settings.

6. **Which benefit of cloud computing allows an application to automatically adjust resources based on workload demands?**

   a. High availability

   b. Scalability

   c. Governance

   d. Manageability

Correct answer: b

Explanation: Scalability is the ability to adjust computing resources automatically or based on policies. This includes vertical scaling (increasing the capacity of a VM) and horizontal scaling (adding or reducing VMs). Scalability ensures that applications can maintain performance during traffic spikes and optimize costs during low usage periods.

7. **Which Azure service type is designed for creating automated workflows with minimal coding?**

   a. Azure Functions

   b. Azure SQL Database

   c. Azure Virtual Machines

   d. Azure Logic Apps

Correct answer: d

Explanation: Azure Logic Apps is a serverless cloud service that allows developers to design and automate workflows with minimal coding. This is done by using a visual designer. Azure Logic Apps offers extensive integration options with over 1,400 connectors, including Salesforce, Office 365, and SQL Server.

8. **Which of the following cloud models provides the highest level of customization and control?**

    a. Public cloud

    b. Private cloud

    c. Hybrid cloud

    d. Multicloud

Correct answer: b

Explanation: Private cloud, which is also known as on-premises, offers the highest level of customization and control. It is built, managed, and maintained by the organization itself. This model is best suited for organizations that require specialized configurations or high regulatory compliance.

9. **Which cloud service type allows developers to focus on building applications without managing underlying infrastructure?**

    a. IaaS

    b. PaaS

    c. SaaS

    d. Serverless computing

Correct answer: b

Explanation: PaaS abstracts the underlying infrastructure, such as the servers, storage, and networking. It then provides developers with tools, middleware, and frameworks. This allows developers to focus on building and deploying applications.

10. **Which type of cloud service is best suited for running custom virtual machines and managing networks?**

    a. IaaS

    b. PaaS

    c. SaaS

    d. Serverless computing

Correct answer: a

Explanation: IaaS provides virtualized computing resources, such as virtual machines, storage, and networking components. It allows for full control over operating systems, custom VMs, and network configurations.

11. **Which of the following describes a cloud environment that uses multiple public cloud providers?**

    a. Public cloud

b. Private cloud

c. Hybrid cloud

d. Multicloud

Correct answer: d

Explanation: Multicloud describes an architecture where an organization uses multiple public cloud providers, such as AWS, Azure, and Google Cloud, to avoid vendor lock-in and increase redundancy.

12. **Which of the following best explains vertical scaling in cloud computing?**

    a. Adding more virtual machines to handle increased traffic

    b. Increasing the capacity of an existing virtual machine

    c. Using multiple cloud providers to distribute workload

    d. Setting up failover systems for high availability

Correct answer: b

Explanation: Vertical scaling (scaling up or down) involves increasing or decreasing the capacity of an existing VM. This is done by upgrading its CPU or RAM. It is suitable for applications on a single VM but may require a restart.

13. **Which pricing model allows cloud customers to pay based on actual usage?**

    a. Reserved instances

    b. Spot pricing

    c. Pay-as-you-go

    d. Subscription-based

Correct answer: c

Explanation: Pay-as-you-go pricing allows customers to pay only for the resources they consume. This model is flexible and cost-efficient. This is especially the case for dynamic workloads with variable usage patterns.

14. **Which benefit of cloud computing ensures system redundancy and minimal downtime?**

    a. HA

    b. Scalability

    c. Cost efficiency

    d. Customization

Correct answer: a

Explanation: HA ensures that systems operate continuously without interruption. It involves redundancy and failover mechanisms to minimize downtime and meet SLAs.

15. **Which of the following is a characteristic of the shared responsibility model in cloud computing?**

    a. The cloud provider manages all aspects of security

    b. The customer manages data, user access, and application configuration

    c. The cloud provider is responsible for customer identity management

    d. The customer is responsible for physical data center security

Correct answer: b

Explanation: In the shared responsibility model, customers are responsible for managing their data, user identities, and application configurations. The cloud provider manages the underlying infrastructure, including physical security, networking, and virtualization.

16. **Which Azure tool is designed for estimating cloud costs?**

    a. Azure Monitor

    b. Azure Pricing Calculator

    c. Azure DevOps

    d. Azure Functions

Correct answer: b

Explanation: The Azure Pricing Calculator allows users to estimate cloud costs by configuring different Azure services, including virtual machines, storage, and databases. It provides a cost breakdown based on usage and location.

17. **Which of the following cloud service types is event-driven and charges based on code execution?**

    a. IaaS

    b. PaaS

    c. SaaS

    d. Serverless computing

Correct answer: d

Explanation: Serverless computing is event-driven and charges customers only for the actual execution time of code. It automatically scales with workload demand.

18. **Which cloud deployment model allows for seamless data sharing between on-premises infrastructure and cloud services?**

    a. Public cloud

    b. Private cloud

    c. Hybrid cloud

    d. Multicloud

Correct answer: c

Explanation: Hybrid cloud provides for seamless data sharing and application portability between on-premises infrastructure and public cloud services. It allows organizations to keep sensitive data on-premises while leveraging cloud scalability for other workloads.

19. **Which type of scaling adds or removes virtual machines to accommodate fluctuating workloads?**

    a. Vertical scaling

    b. Horizontal scaling

    c. Auto scaling

    d. Manual scaling

Correct answer: b

Explanation: Horizontal scaling, also known as scaling out or in, involves adding or removing VMs to distribute the workload across multiple instances. It enhances fault tolerance and allows for automatic scaling based on demand.

20. **Which pricing model allows cloud customers to purchase unused capacity at a discount but with the risk of interruptions?**

    a. Reserved instances

    b. Spot pricing

    c. Pay-as-you-go

    d. Subscription-based

Correct answer: b

Explanation: Spot pricing allows customers to buy unused cloud capacity at a discount. However, these resources can be reclaimed by the cloud provider with short notice. This is why spot pricing is more suitable for non-critical, interruptible workloads.

Join our Discord space

Join our Discord workspace for latest updates, offers, tech happenings around the world, new releases, and sessions with the authors:

https://discord.bpbonline.com

CHAPTER 3
Architectural Components and Services of Azure

Introduction

In this chapter, we will focus on the core architectural components and services of Azure. These include the underlying infrastructure that powers the cloud platform.

We will first look at the data center, such as its operations and capabilities. A data center is a true marvel of technology. It allows for the powerful applications we use every day, like Instagram, OpenAI, and Office 365.

For Azure, it is composed of many data centers, but this can lead to considerable complexity. To help further, Azure has provided a structure, which is generally based on geographic locations. These include regions, availability zones, and sovereign regions, which represent the main divisions across the Azure global footprint.

However, there are also resources that help organize these for your account. They include four categories: resources, resource groups, subscriptions, and management groups. These allow for configurations, access permissions, security precautions, and tracking for billing.

Finally, there are some other ways Azure specifies its resources and services. These include licenses and tenants. In this chapter, we will cover all these topics.

Structure

This chapter covers the following topics:

- Data centers
- Geographies and regions
- Sovereign regions
- Availability zones
- Data center website
- Organizing resources
- The resource hierarchy
- Licenses and tenants

Objectives

By the end of this chapter, you will have a good understanding of core architectural components and services of Azure. This will include two main parts. First, you will know how Azure services are allocated, such as with regions, availability zones, and sovereign regions. Furthermore, you will understand how to organize the services using a four-part hierarchy: resources, resource groups, subscriptions, and management groups.

Data centers

At the heart of a cloud computing platform is the data center. It is what powers the amazing capabilities. The data center is the location for a facility that holds the physical assets like servers, equipment, storage, and networking systems.

In the U.S., there are over 5,300 data centers, which is the largest for any country.[1] On a global basis, there are nearly 12,000.[2]

A typical data center will have the following characteristics:

- **Racks and cabinets**: Here, you can place the servers, networking system, storage, and other hardware. A rack is usually 19 inches wide and organized in rows. Racks can also be enclosed in cabinets. Arranging these is critical in terms of better management of cooling and maintenance.

- **Cabling**: There is a complex maze of cables, which can be in the ceilings or under the floors. They help to manage power and data flows.

---

1 https://www.statista.com/statistics/1228433/data-centers-worldwide-by-country/
2 https://datacentre.solutions/news/68654/the-united-states-counts-5388-data-centres

- **Power systems**: There is redundancy for energy supplies for a data center. These include backup generators and uninterruptible power systems. These typically run on diesel fuel.

- **Environmental control systems**: Because of the high levels of energy consumption, a data center can overheat. This is why there are systems to maintain temperature and humidity.

- **Fire protection**: An outage or mistake can result in a fire, which can spread quickly. To minimize this problem, a data center will have smoke detectors and sensors, along with fire suppression systems like sprinklers.

- **Physical security**: A data center will have multiple ways to prevent unauthorized access. Just some of the measures include surveillance cameras, perimeter fencing, biometric controls, and secure logins for racks and cabinets.

Given all these advanced systems and capabilities, the costs of building and managing a data center are significant.

For example, in the U.S., the construction costs average about $7 million to $12 million per **megawatt** (**MW**) of capacity.[3] In Europe, the range is $8 million to $14 million per MW. They are generally higher because of the stringent environmental regulations. Then again, as for emerging markets, the expenses are about $4 million to $7 million per MW.

Next, a data center will have operating expenses. The biggest line item is typically energy, which can range from 30% to 60% of the total costs.[4] The location of the data center can also be a major factor. After all, energy prices can vary widely based on access to cheap sources and the differences in climate. Because of this, cloud providers will try to locate a data center next to a major source of energy. An example is Apple's facility in Foulum, Denmark, which provides direct access to hydroelectric power from Norway.

Data centers come in different sizes. Some are fairly small and may serve specialized needs. Others may be for companies. However, a typical data center, at least for a cloud provider, will be roughly 100,000 square meters.

Yet some are massive. This is especially the case for those who handle complex workloads, such as for AI.

Consider the data center that Meta is building in Richland Parish, Louisiana. The plan is for it to be a staggering four million square feet. Meta estimates the costs for the construction at $10 billion.[5] Once finished, which is expected in 2030, there will be about 500 employees to manage the data center. There will also be $200 million in improvements for surrounding roads and water systems.

---

3 https://danacloud.com/blog/how-much-does-it-cost-to-build-a-data-center
4 https://www.datacenters.com/news/impact-of-geographic-location-on-data-center-energy-costs
5 https://www.opportunitylouisiana.gov/news/meta-selects-northeast-louisiana-as-site-of-10-billion-artificial-intelligence-optimized-data-center-governor-jeff-landry-calls-investment-a-new-chapter-for-state

As for energy, Meta has entered a partnership with Entergy Louisiana, which is a utility company. They will build power generation systems.

However, other mega tech companies like *Microsoft*, *Apple*, *Oracle*, and *Amazon* are also exploring their own mega projects. In other words, the growth of the data center market is expected to grow at a rapid clip.

But this will mean that an increasing amount of electricity will be devoted to these facilities. According to the *Electric Power Research Institute*, data centers may consume up to 9% of the total electricity in the U.S. by 2030, up more than 100%.[6]

However, it will be a major challenge to accommodate this spike in usage. Simply put, the traditional power grid was not built for these modern applications. Inevitably, the system will need to be modernized, which will be expensive and time-consuming.

There are other issues, such as with wind and solar, which are not consistent power supplies. Then there are the issues with regulatory approval.

Many of the mega tech companies are looking at nuclear energy as an alternative energy source. Here are some examples:

- **Amazon**: In March 2024, it purchased a 960-MW data center powered by the Susquehanna nuclear power plant in Pennsylvania.[7]

- **Google**: In October 2024, Google announced a partnership with Kairos Power to develop **small modular reactors** (**SMRs**) to supply up to 500 MW of carbon-free electricity by 2035.

- **Microsoft**: Microsoft has entered into an agreement with Constellation Energy to reopen the Unit 1 reactor at the Three Mile Island nuclear facility.[8]

There are clear advantages to nuclear energy. It can handle variable demands at a high scale and is carbon-free. On the other hand, it can be devastating if there is a malfunction or meltdown. Building nuclear facilities is also expensive and can take years to complete.

Geographies and regions

The Azure global infrastructure is enormous. To help simplify this for customers, it has organized it into geographic boundaries or country borders. Each has a specific market, with at least one region (but usually more).

Some of the geographies are the United States, Canada, Brazil, Europe, and the Asia Pacific. For example, the United States geography includes regions like East US, West US, and Central US, while Europe includes regions like North Europe and West Europe.

---

6 https://www.reuters.com/business/energy/data-centers-could-use-9-us-electricity-by-2030-research-institute-says-2024-05-29/

7 https://www.datacenterdynamics.com/en/analysis/nuclear-power-smr-us/

8 https://apnews.com/article/nuclear-tech-ai-data-11baf04fc4e7e7570313d5f7e4e64eb1

Each region has multiple data centers, which operate on their own. For the Azure global infrastructure, there are more than 60 regions and over 300 data centers.[9] This footprint is larger than any other cloud provider.

The regions and data centers are connected with a massive fiber optic network. It is also the largest in the world, with 165,000 miles of cabling.[10] This connects the services of many customers as well as Microsoft's own platforms like Xbox and Office 365.

Azure provides naming conventions for its regions. They include:

- **Geography**: There is a main area, such as *East US*. Then there is a secondary description, which adds more detail. An example is *South Central US*.

- **Sequence**: To identify the multiple data centers in a region, there is a version, such as *East US 2*. This is for the second data center in the East US region. Sometimes, these may be abbreviated like *eus2*.

When choosing a region, there is not necessarily a right answer. Rather, the decision involves weighing a variety of factors:

- **Proximity**: Generally, you want a region that is closer to your organization. This can mean less latency and lower costs. There are several third-party websites that can help measure the speed of the connections among regions and data centers, such as Azure Latency Test. You can find it at: **https://www.azurespeed.com/Azure/Latency**

- **Services**: A particular Azure service may not be available in a region. You may have to select one that is farther away.

- **Availability zones and disaster recovery**: If you have mission-critical applications, then you probably want these capabilities. They will help with high availability.

- **Data residency**: Because of regulatory requirements, you may have no choice but to use a data center in another region or country.

- **Pricing**: Services may have different cost structures in other regions. If you use a service frequently, you may want to select the region with the lower pricing. You can use the Pricing Calculator to help out with this.

- **Capacity**: Some regions may have capacity constraints. If you have a need for significant scaling, you might need to consider another region. For the decision, you will need to talk to an Azure representative.

- **Network**: If you are running a hybrid cloud, you should use a region that provides a service like Azure ExpressRoute. This will allow for more seamless networking connections.

There are also region pairs. This is where two Azure regions with the same geography – separated by at least 300 million—are linked to each other. The main purpose is to provide high availability and disaster recovery.

---

9 https://azure.microsoft.com/en-us/explore/global-infrastructure
10 https://learn.microsoft.com/en-us/azure/networking/microsoft-global-network

Here are some of the main features:

- **High-speed connection**: The regions are connected with low-latency, high-bandwidth networks. This provides for higher performance with data replication and synchronization.

- **Planned maintenance**: Azure sets schedules based on a sequential order for the different region pairs. By doing this, there is a mitigation of downtime.

- **Automatic replication**: Azure services like **geo-redundant storage (GRS)** automatically replicate data to the paired region. This provides another layer of redundancy and helps with data durability, even if the main region is unavailable.

Table 3.1 shows examples of region pairs:

Primary region	Secondary paired region
East US	West US
East US2	Central US
North Europe	West Europe
Southeast Asia	East Asia
Japan East	Japan West
Canada Central	Canada East
Germany West Central	Germany North
Brazil South	South Central US

Table 3.1: Examples of region pairs

While most region pairs are within the same country, there are exceptions. For instance, as seen above, the Brazil South region is paired with South Central US.

Sovereign regions

In July 2022, Microsoft announced Microsoft Cloud for Sovereignty (we will refer to it as the sovereign cloud). It is an Azure cloud platform that is built specifically for the unique needs of governments, the public sector, and regulated organizations. The sovereign cloud operates in an independent region.

These are some of the key benefits:

- **Data residency**: Governments and regulated organizations may be required to have their data physically located in the country of origin. This would be impossible with a public cloud platform. However, the sovereign cloud allows for data to stay in a certain country.

- **Security**: There are advanced options to protect data, such as encryption and confidential computing capabilities. There are also systems in place that allow for compliance with regulatory requirements and laws.

- **Transparency**: The sovereign cloud has deep visibility into cloud operations. This provides regulators with the ability to understand the inner workings of the platform and the level of security in place.

- **Local partners**: Azure has a rich ecosystem of consulting organization that helps customers implement and maintain their sovereign clouds. They will have the local expertise required.

An example of a sovereign cloud is Azure Government. It has a myriad compliance capabilities, such as for the **Department of Defense (DoD)**, the **Criminal Justice Information Services (CJIS)** Security Policy, and the **Health Insurance Portability and Accountability Act (HIPAA)**.

Many of the services for Azure Government are the ones found in the standard Azure cloud, like VMs, storage, networking, and databases, but there are usually different configurations.

The Azure Government platform is also only available for U.S. federal, state, local, and tribal governments. This includes access to vetted partners and contractors.

Another example of a sovereign cloud is Azure China, which is specifically built to comply with Chinese regulations and requirements. The cloud is operated by 21Vianet, a leading Chinese data center service provider. Access to Azure China is available to Chinese entities and foreign businesses operating within China, so long as they abide by the nation's regulatory standards.

Availability zones

An availability zone refers to different groups of data centers in a region. Each region generally has a minimum of three, but in some cases, there may not be availability zones. This is the case with the Canada East region. Regardless, the purpose of availability regions is to provide for high availability if there is an outage.

An availability zone is usually separated by several kilometers (Azure does not provide exact locations). This is to allow for low latency on the network, with a round-trip for data at less than two milliseconds.

Azure provides two methods of support for availability zones. Understanding them is important when formulating your own strategy for reliability.

These are the methods:

- **Zone-redundant deployments**: This is when resources are distributed and replicated across multiple availability zones—such as in the event of an outage. Azure will automatically perform this on your behalf. If there is an outage, it will handle the failover to another availability zone. This helps to increase high availability.

- **Zonal deployments**: A resource is deployed to the one availability zone that you select. You do not get the advantage of high availability. However, you do get lower latency and higher performance. If you want high availability, you will need to customize the architecture to handle multiple availability zones.

For some resources, you do not get the use of availability zones until you specify this in the configuration. An example is the Azure App Service. You must configure this for availability zones when you create the application. Moreover, existing applications cannot be converted. When a service is not configured for an availability zone, it is known as a nonzonal or regional deployment.

When Azure makes updates to its services, this will be done for one availability zone at a time. This helps to reduce the impact of a faulty update on the other availability zones.

Data center website

To get a better sense of Azure's global data center infrastructure, you can check out the Data Center Website at **https://datacenters.microsoft.com**. It is informative and even fun. In a visual way, you will see the myriad data centers, regions, and availability zones.

These are some of the key features:

- **Global infrastructure overview**: This is a 3D experience that shows the global footprint of data centers. *Figure 3.1* shows what this looks like.

- **Virtual data center tour**: This is an interactive view of Azure's data center operations. You can learn about the core technologies and security measures.

- **Cloud culture series**: These are interesting stories that highlight how Azure's cloud infrastructure supports innovation and cultural exchange in various regions. This includes Chile, South Africa, and Spain.

- **Latest news and updates**: You will see a list of recent announcements. Often, these are about new launches of data centers.

Refer to the following figure:

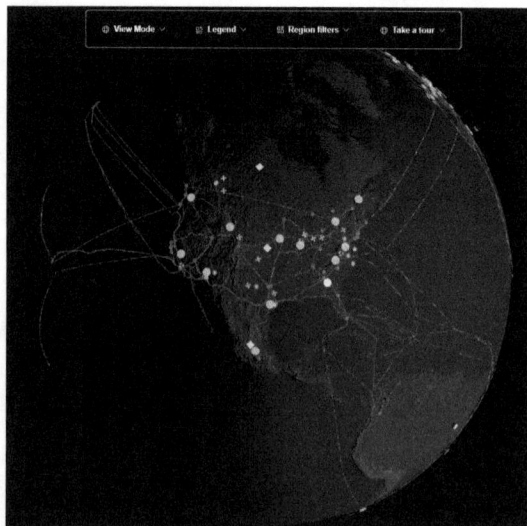

Figure 3.1: Map of Azure's regions across the globe

Let us look at the global infrastructure overview. This is located at **https://datacenters. microsoft.com/globe/explore/**.

At the top, there are different options:

- **View mode**: You can see the map as a globe, flat, or as a table.

- **Legend**: You can turn on or off different elements on the map, like geographies, regions, networking, and sustainability projects.

- **Region filters**: You can filter for what you want to see for a region. Some of the options are: compliance, disaster recovery, sustainability, and availability zone presence.

- **Tour**: You can tour a datacenter. This is even for a map of the assets in outer space, such as satellites.

On the map, you will see various circles and squares. They represent geographies and availability zones. Suppose you select a circle on the U.S. Map. For this, you will get a profile, which you can see in *Figure 3.2*:

West US
Region with Availability Zones

Location	**Data residency**
California	Stored at rest in the United States
	Learn more
Year opened	**Availability Zones**
2012	Coming soon
Products	**Disaster recovery**
See products in this region	Learn more about options for this region
Regional compliance	**Industry compliance**
EU-US Privacy Shield	SOX
	SEC Regulation SCI
	SEC 17a-4
	MPAA
	MARS-E
	+ 14 more

Global compliance
SOC 3
SOC 2
SOC 1
ISO 9001
ISO 27701

Figure 3.2: Profile of the West US region in Azure

This is useful information, especially when you are planning your Azure setup. The profile is for a region that has been in operation since 2012 and does not have any availability zones. However, it shows that Azure is in the process of implementing them.

Under the *Products* section, you can see the available products for the region. Next to this, you can click to get information about options for disaster recovery. Then there is information about regional, industry, and global compliance.

Organizing resources

A resource is defined as a manageable item that is provided by Azure. Common examples are VMs, storage, web applications, virtual networks, and databases. You organize resources according to a structured hierarchy, which you can find in *Figure 3.3*. This allows for better management, access control, policy enforcement, security, and cost monitoring.

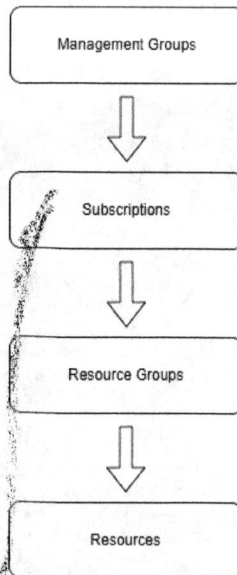

Figure 3.3: *This is the hierarchy of resources in Azure*

This is top-down. This means that policies and access controls from higher levels are applied to the lower levels. It provides for more consistency within an Azure environment.

For the next few sections, we will look in more detail at this hierarchy. We will do this by starting at the bottom of it, with resources.

Resources

Resources are the key building blocks for creating and managing cloud applications and services. Let us look at the steps for creating one:

1. Log in to Azure.

2. Where it says, *Azure services*, click **Create a resource**.

3. You will see a list of services, as shown in *Figure 3.4*. Each of these requires a resource.

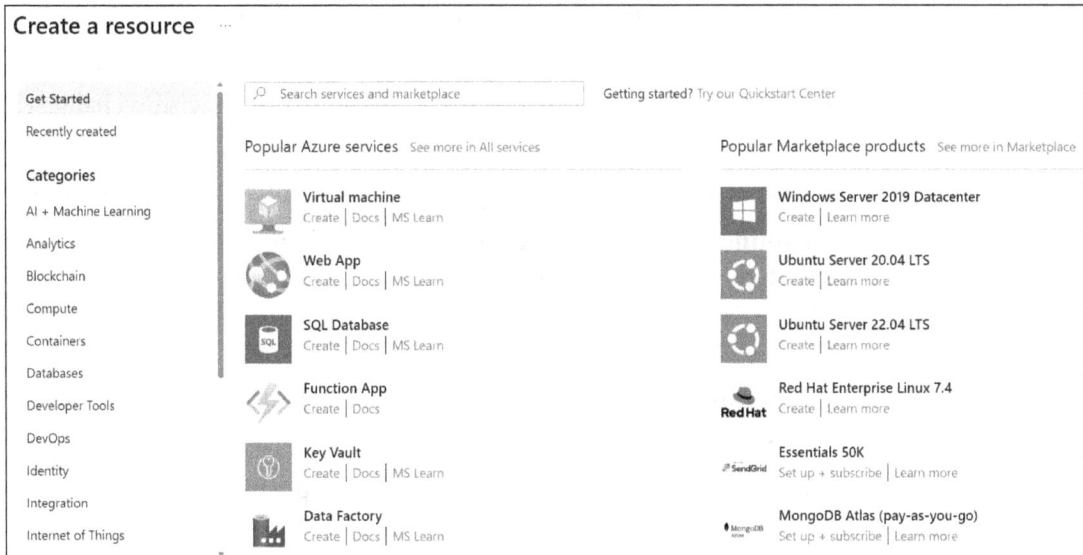

Create a resource

Get Started	Search services and marketplace	Getting started? Try our Quickstart Center
Recently created		
Categories	Popular Azure services See more in All services	Popular Marketplace products See more in Marketplace
AI + Machine Learning	Virtual machine Create | Docs | MS Learn	Windows Server 2019 Datacenter Create | Learn more
Analytics	Web App Create | Docs | MS Learn	Ubuntu Server 20.04 LTS Create | Learn more
Blockchain		
Compute	SQL Database Create | Docs | MS Learn	Ubuntu Server 22.04 LTS Create | Learn more
Containers		
Databases	Function App Create | Docs	Red Hat Enterprise Linux 7.4 **Red Hat** Create | Learn more
Developer Tools		
DevOps	Key Vault Create | Docs | MS Learn	Essentials 50K *SendGrid* Set up + subscribe | Learn more
Identity		
Integration	Data Factory Create | Docs | MS Learn	MongoDB Atlas (pay-as-you-go) *MongoDB* Set up + subscribe | Learn more
Internet of Things		

Figure 3.4: List of available resources in Azure

4. By default, the most popular services will be displayed on the screen, such as for a VM, Web App, and SQL Database. There is also a list of popular services from the Azure Marketplace, which is where third parties can promote their own. On the sidebar, you can filter the services based on the categories like AI + Machine Learning, Compute, and Identity.

5. For each service, there is a **Create** button. If you click this, you will go through the setup process for the resource.

This is not the only way to create a service. You can also use the Azure **Command-Line Interface** (**CLI**), PowerShell, and **Azure Resource Manager** (**ARM**) templates. These approaches allow for different levels of customization and automation.

When a resource is created, it is usually deployed in a specific region to optimize for performance and compliance requirements. However, there are some resources, like Microsoft Entra ID, that operate on a global basis.

When deployed, you can manage and monitor the resource with the Azure portal. There are various tools for this. Most resources will have a cost, typically based on usage. However, there are some that have free tiers or trial periods. Each resource is also connected to a single Azure subscription, which allows for centralized billing and access control.

Resource groups

A resource group is a container that includes the relevant resources for an Azure solution. This is done based on the needs of your organization. There are no strict guidelines or requirements for the resources that you include, yet there are best practices to consider.

It is recommended that the resources in a resource group have the same lifecycle. This means that deployment, updates, and deletions can be handled consistently. Otherwise, a change can cause major problems.

Here are other recommendations for streamlining operations and analytics:

- **Use consistent naming conventions**: A cryptic name can make it tough for other members to understand what a resource group is for. When coming up with a name, it is a good idea to include the resource type, application or business unit, region, and a unique identifier. Here is an example: rg-finance-app1-prod-eastus-001.

- **Manage access**: You can use **role-based access control** (**RBAC**) for this. You can set user permissions for the group, which can help bolster security.

- **Use resource locks**: For critical resources, you can implement locks to prevent accidental deletion or modification. This can also be used for subscriptions.

- **Tagging**: You can apply tags to resources and resource groups. This is another method of classification, say based on workload, environment, data type, or cost center.

These best practices highlight some of the advantages of resource groups, such as the use of RBAC and resource locks, but there are others as well. A resource group streamlines the process of making changes, which can be tedious, time-consuming, and prone to error. For example, if you make an update, this will impact all the resources in the group.

Another benefit is that it is easier to track costs. They are all centralized in the resource group.

There are also other factors to keep in mind:

- A resource can be in only one resource group.

- At any time, you can add or remove a resource from a resource group. You can also move a resource from one group to another.

- Resources in a resource group can be located in different regions, but this is not necessarily good practice. It is often better to centralize the resources.

- When you delete a resource group, all its resources are deleted. So, make sure you want to do this.

- Most resource groups are limited to 800 instances of a resource type.

To create a resource group, you can follow these steps:

1. Log in to Azure.

2. Where it says, *Navigate*, click **Create**.

3. You will see a configuration screen for the resource group, as shown in *Figure 3.5*:

Create a resource group ⋯

Basics	Tags	Review + create

Resource group - A container that holds related resources for an Azure solution. The resource group can include all the resources for the solution, or only those resources that you want to manage as a group. You decide how you want to allocate resources to resource groups based on what makes the most sense for your organization. Learn more

Subscription * ⓘ	Pay-As-You-Go ⌄
Resource group name * ⓘ	
Region * ⓘ	(US) East US ⌄

Figure 3.5: List of available resources in Azure

4. At the top, there are three tabs. It defaults to *Basics*, which has three required fields. You need to specify the subscription, resource group name, and the region.

5. The next tab is for Tags, which is optional. Each tag has a name and a value. For example, suppose you want to create one for the deployment environment of the resource. It could be something like: Environment: Production.

6. Select the **Review + create tab** and then click **Create**.

You may need to specify a region for a resource group because it contains metadata about the resources, and this may be sensitive information. For compliance reasons, you may be required to have this stored in a particular region.

Subscriptions

A subscription is an agreement between you and Azure to use and pay for one or more services. They can be for **software as a service (SaaS)** offerings like Office 365, or **platform as a service (PaaS)**, or **infrastructure as a service (IaaS)** cloud offerings.

A subscription is essentially a billing entity that has access control. It is linked to a payment method, like a credit card.

It is also typical that an organization will have multiple subscriptions. They can be for different roles, departments, geographies, or access policies. This can help to streamline the billing and governance.

Azure has different types of subscriptions:

- **Free trial**: You can use Azure services for free, but you still need to enter your payment information.

- **Pay-as-you-go**: This charges users according to resource consumption.

- **Enterprise agreement (EA)**: This is for larger organizations, which can benefit from volume discounts or flexible payment options.

- **Startup plans**: These are for smaller organizations. There are benefits like usage credits and discounted plans.

Management groups

Management groups are containers that provide comprehensive management of access, policies, and compliance for your subscriptions. These are not required, but they can be beneficial, especially for larger organizations. They can help to streamline Azure resources.

This is an example. Suppose you work for a multinational corporation. Because of the complex use of Azure resources, you set up management groups for the different departments, which you can see in *Figure 3.6*. These include those for finance, marketing, and IT. There is also a root management group, which Azure creates automatically, that is the container for these. The finance and marketing groups also have two subscriptions. For all role assignments of the management group, they will be inherited by any of the child resources.

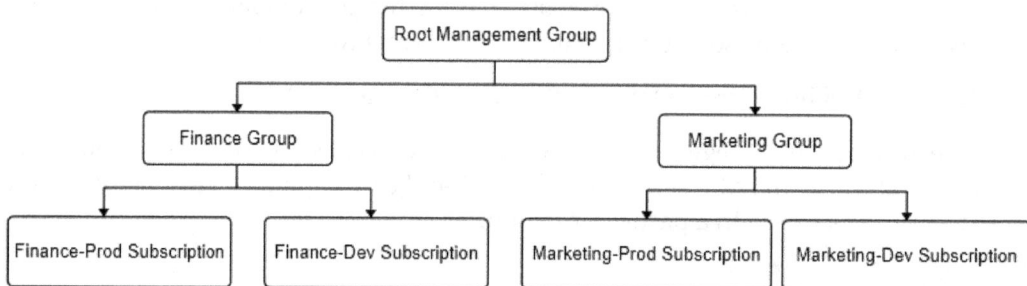

Figure 3.6: Management groups for finance and marketing

Generally, it is recommended to structure management groups for an organization's main structures, resource ownership, or billing. It is also a good idea not to nest too many of the levels. Otherwise, the management groups can get overly complicated.

The resource hierarchy

As mentioned earlier, when you have management groups or subscriptions, the policies and permissions are automatically applied to lower levels. Each child object has one parent, which helps to provide more clarity.

To see how this works, let us look at an example. *Figure 3.7* shows how an Azure region policy cascades through different levels of the resource hierarchy:

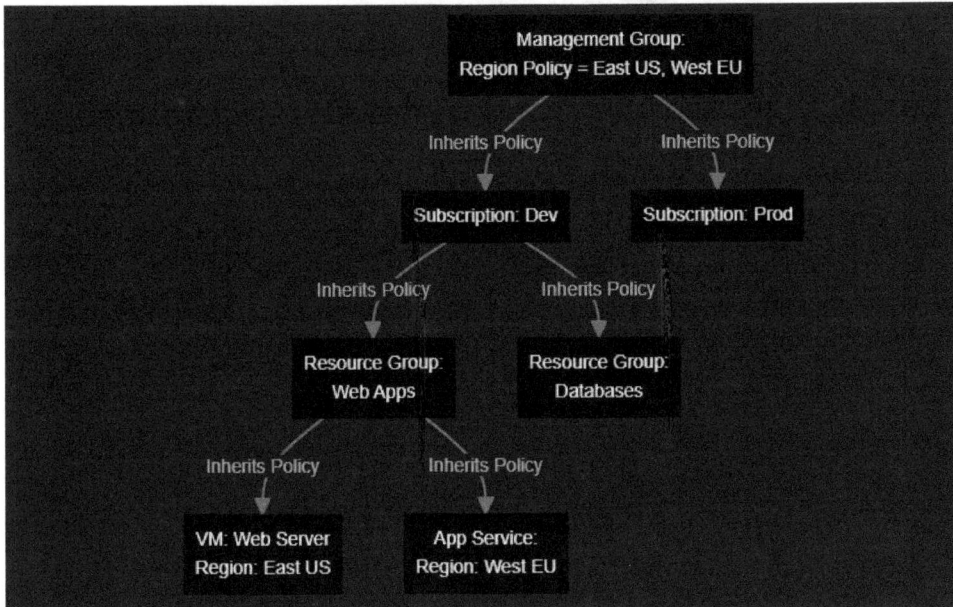

Figure 3.7: *Azure resource hierarchy for policy inheritance*

At the top, there is the management group that sets forth the policy that limits resource generation to two regions: East US and West Europe. Below this, there are two subscriptions, which are divided into **development (dev)** and **production (prod)**. These automatically inherit two subscriptions from the parent group. This means you cannot create resources outside of East US or West Europe.

For the dev subscription, there are two resource groups: *web apps* and *databases*. Since these are children of the dev subscription, they also must abide by the region policy.

At the bottom level, there are the resources for the web apps resource group:

- A VM Web Server, which has been deployed in East US
- An App Service, which has been deployed in West Europe

These will comply with the policy set at the management group level. So, if anything tries to deploy either of these resources, say, in South Asia or Northern Europe, they will fail.

Let us take another example, which you can see in *Figure 3.8*:

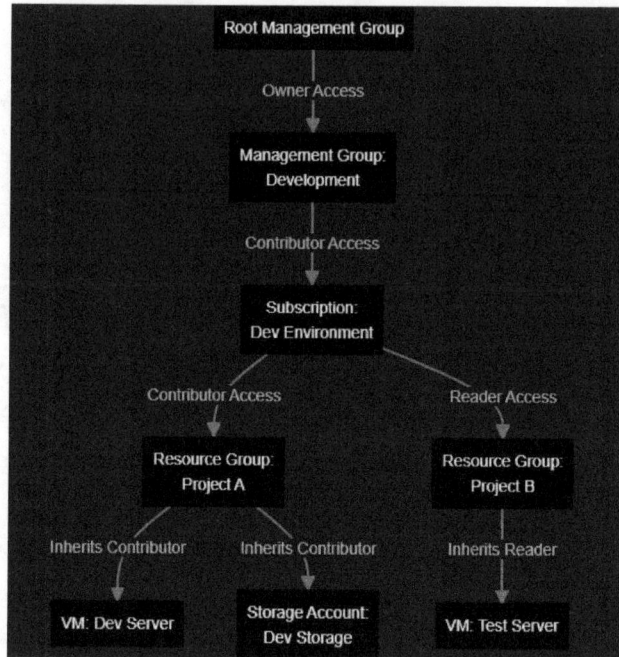

Figure 3.8: *Access permissions in the Azure hierarchy*

This shows how access permissions are inherited through the Azure hierarchy. We start with Root Management Group, which connects to a Development Management Group with Owner access. This Owner access represents the highest level of permission—that is, they have full control over all resources below it.

Next, the Development Management Group connects to a Dev environment subscription with Contributor access. The hierarchy is divided into two resource groups: Project A and Project B. Interestingly, these Resource Groups have different access levels:

- Project A inherits Contributor access. This allows the team members to create and manage resources

- Project B receives Reader access, which allows only view permissions

At the bottom level, we see individual resources. For Project A, they include:

- A Dev Server VM

- A Dev Storage account

Both inherit Contributor access, which means that the teams can modify these resources. Then there is Project B. It has a test server VM. There is Reader access, where teams can only view but not modify the resource. This hierarchy clearly shows the inheritance flows with permissions, while maintaining a single-parent relationship for each resource.

Licenses and tenants

When it comes to managing Azure resources, there are a couple of other concepts to understand. One is a license. This means you have the legal right to use the resource or service. It generally has a monthly fee per user. For an organization, an administrator will usually be the person who assigns or revokes access to the licenses. This certainly means having considerable power. Because of this, there should be guardrails. For example, an administrator should not be assigned a license for the service they administer.

Another important concept is that of a tenant. In this chapter, we use tenant to refer to the regional location that hosts the servers for a cloud service. For a SaaS service, this is generally determined by the application developer. As for other Azure services—such as PaaS—you will typically set the region, which we covered earlier in this chapter.

However, note that in Azure more broadly, *tenant* often refers to an organization's dedicated instance of Microsoft Entra ID used for identity and access management. Keep this in mind to avoid confusion when encountering the term in different Azure contexts.

Conclusion

In this chapter, we got an overview of the architectural components of the Azure platform. For this, we learned about how data centers work and the ways they are organized, such as with geographies, regions, sovereign regions, and availability zones. These help provide benefits like lower costs, higher efficiencies, improved security, and lower latency.

The next part of the chapter focused on how to manage the services of Azure. These include a four-part hierarchy: resources, resource groups, subscriptions, and management groups.

As for the next chapter, we will cover compute services in Azure. These are for deploying and managing applications, such as with VMs.

Sample questions

1. **Among these choices, what is the best description of an Azure data center?**

   a. A location for on-premises systems.

   b. A location that contains servers, storage, and networking systems for cloud applications.

   c. A serverless infrastructure for creating applications.

   d. A local system for edge devices.

   Correct answer: b

   Explanation: Azure data centers are physical locations, which are often massive, that include servers, storage, and networking systems. They help to house cloud applications.

2. **Of these options below, which is not included in Azure's global infrastructure?**

   a. Regions

   b. Availability zones

   c. Virtual machines

   d. Sovereign regions

   Correct answer: c

   Explanation: VMs are an Azure resource, not part of Azure's global infrastructure.

3. **What is the main purpose of availability zones in the Azure platform?**

   a. Security for the data centers.

   b. High availability and disaster recovery for applications.

   c. Lower costs for the Azure platform.

   d. Storage on edge devices.

   Correct answer: b

   Explanation: A key reason for availability zones is to allow for high availability and disaster recovery. This is done by allocating resources across various data centers in a region.

4. **Among these choices, which is the primary benefit of sovereign regions in Azure?**

   a. Improved speed for streaming services.

   b. Increased speed for local systems.

   c. Lower costs.

   d. Data residency for legal and regulatory compliance.

   Correct answer: d

   Explanation: A sovereign region is generally for governments. They help provide data residency, which is critical for compliance.

5. **What is the purpose of a resource group?**

   a. Organize and manage associated resources based on their lifecycle.

   b. Manage storage systems.

   c. Configure networking systems.

   d. Manage servers.

   Correct answer: a

   Explanation: A resource group is a container for resources. It allows for organizing and managing them, such as with updates.

6. **Which of the following applies to Azure region pairs?**

   a. They include two regions that are separated by at least 300 miles.

   b. They are available in AWS, not Azure.

   c. They are only for enterprise customers.

   d. They are only available in the EU because of regulatory reasons.

   Correct answer: a

   Explanation: As the name implies, a region pair has two regions that are in the same geography. They are separated by at least 300 miles. A region pair helps improve high availability and disaster recovery.

7. **What is the purpose of management groups?**

   a. To exclude the use of certain files.

   b. Manage access, policies, and compliance for selected subscriptions.

   c. To lower the latency with the Azure platform.

   d. To develop specialized applications.

   Correct answer: b

   Explanation: With a management group, you can configure access, policies, and compliance for subscriptions.

8. **In the Azure platform, which describes how resources are distributed across different availability zones?**

   a. Axis deployments.

   b. Nonzonal deployments.

   c. Zone-redundant deployments.

   d. Private cloud deployments.

   Correct answer: c

   Explanation: A zone-redundant deployment allows for distributing resources across different availability zones. This helps with high availability and automatic failover.

9. **Why would you use an Azure region?**

   a. To access resources in other countries.

   b. To comply with data residency regulations and requirements.

   c. To provide for user authentication.

   d. To connect to a private cloud.

   Correct answer: c

Explanation: Generally, you will select a closer region, but in some cases, this may not be an option. One of the main reasons is data residency.

10. **What is a tenant?**

    a. A storage system for edge devices.

    b. A virtual machine.

    c. The region where a cloud service is located.

    d. A software license.

    Correct answer: c

    Explanation: A tenant is the region where the servers host a cloud service. This is often important when it comes to data residency and regulatory compliance.

11. **Which one of these is a manageable item provided by the platform, like a virtual machine or database?**

    a. Management group

    b. Resource container

    c. Subscription

    d. Resource

    Correct answer: d

    Explanation: A resource is a manageable item in the Azure platform. It can be for a virtual machine, storage system, or database.

12. **What is a resource lock?**

    a. A security guardrail in Azure storage.

    b. A way to prevent accidental deletion of a resource.

    c. A control for a networking system.

    d. A way to prohibit certain users from accessing an application.

    Correct answer: b

    Explanation: When you work with management groups, you can delete multiple resources, but this can sometimes be done accidentally. This is why you would want to implement a resource lock.

13. **Why would you use tags?**

    a. To implement Zero Trust security.

    b. To provide access permissions for users.

    c. To help better manage resources.

    d. To manage structured data.

Correct answer: c

Explanation: You use tags to organize Azure resources. This can help lower costs and improve tracking.

14. **What type of method would a startup likely choose?**

    a. Pay-as-you-go
    b. Enterprise agreement
    c. Startup plan
    d. Consumption model

Correct answer: c

Explanation: Azure has startup plans. They are geared for smaller organizations that may not have many resources. Startup plans will have credits and discounted pricing for services.

15. **Which one describes automatic data replication for a secondary region?**

    a. Resource containers
    b. Geo-Redundant Storage
    c. Region pairs
    d. Nonzonal deployments

Correct answer: b

Explanation: With Geo-Redundant Storage, you can automatically replicate data to a secondary region. This helps to improve high availability.

16. **What is a hierarchical structure in Azure?**

    a. To increase security for the authentication process.
    b. To lower costs.
    c. To provide for analytics.
    d. To allow for consistent policy enforcement and access control.

Correct answer: d

Explanation: Azure has a hierarchical structure for managing resources. They include resources, resource groups, subscriptions, and management groups.

17. **What is the key benefit of a region pair?**

    a. It improves the bandwidth of the Azure platform.
    b. It provides for automatic failover and data replication when there is a regional outage.

    c.   It has lower costs.

    d.   It allows for security for governments.

Correct answer: b

Explanation: Azure region pairs allow for automatic failover and data replication. This ensures high availability and disaster recovery during regional outages.

18. **Why would a larger organization use management groups?**

    a.   To provide for centralized management of access, policies, and compliance.

    b.   To improve security and privacy.

    c.   To gain access to virtual machines.

    d.   To set up region pairs.

Correct answer: a

Explanation: A management group is particularly useful for a larger organization. After all, they tend to be complex. However, with a management group, it is much easier to handle access, policies, and compliance across multiple Azure subscriptions.

19. **Which one of these provides for lower latency and higher performance but does not necessarily allow for high availability?**

    a.   Zonal deployments.

    b.   Zone-redundant deployments.

    c.   Regional deployments.

    d.   Private cloud deployments.

Correct answer: a

Explanation: Zonal deployments have lower performance, but can achieve high performance; they are available only in one region. This means there is less high availability.

20. **What is the key benefit of using the CLI in Azure for creating resources?**

    a.   Automatic scaling

    b.   Customized automation and deployment of resources

    c.   Automatic data residency compliance

    d.   Advanced analytics

Correct answer: b

Explanation: With CLI, you can customize the automation and deployment of resources, such as with scripts.

CHAPTER 4
Compute Services

Introduction

In this chapter, we will look at compute services and understand virtual machines, including how to set them up and connect to them. Later, we will review the pricing.

After this, the chapter will cover other supporting systems for virtual machines. These include Azure **Virtual Machine Scale Sets** (**VMSS**), which are for load balancing, as well as Availability Sets. These help to evaluate redundancy and availability with applications on Azure. Finally, we will look at **proximity placement groups** (**PPGs**), which are about the placement of VMs and other resources in a data center.

After this, we will look at different tools to help with compute on Azure. One is the **Azure Virtual Desktop** (**AVD**), which is for remote access to services. Then we will evaluate some of the application tools, like Azure App Services and Azure Functions.

Finally, you will be guided on containers, which allow for deploying applications. We will review several of the key tools, like **Azure Container Instances** (**ACI**), **Azure Kubernetes Service** (**AKS**), and Azure Container Apps.

Structure

This chapter covers the following topics:

- Virtual machines
- Setting up a virtual machine
- Connecting a VM
- Pricing of a VM
- Understanding Azure Virtual Machine Scale Sets
- Availability sets
- Proximity placement group
- Azure Virtual Desktop
- Azure app services
- Azure Functions
- Container services

Objectives

By the end of this chapter, you will have a good understanding of the compute services in Azure. This will include three main parts. First, you will learn about virtual machines, in terms of how they work, their setup, and supporting tools. Next, you will understand some of the important tools for creating applications in Azure. Then you will learn about containerization, such as how it works and the use cases. This will also include reviewing key tools from Azure.

Virtual machines

In *Chapter 2, The Foundations of Cloud Computing*, we learned about virtual machines or VMs. This is a critical topic for the exam. As we saw, a VM is essentially a software-based server, and it is the heart of IaaS.

A key advantage of this technology is the **total cost of ownership** (**TCO**). This is a calculation for the expenses of purchasing and managing an IT asset. It is for the entire lifecycle.

To understand this, we will look at the TCO of a server system, which is in an on-premises environment. These are the main costs:

- **Hardware**: You will need to buy a physical machine. For a low-end server, this may be about $2,000 to $5,000. However, if you want one that is for enterprise purposes, they can easily be more than $10,000.
- **Storage**: For smaller systems, the expense may be a few thousand dollars, but storage can be quite costly for enterprise environments, especially for large applications. The expenses can easily be $50,000 or more.

- **Networking**: This is equipment for routers, switches, and firewalls. These systems can also cost over $50,000, especially when you need high performance and strong security.

- **Software licenses**: You will need to purchase software for the OS, virtualization, and middleware. You may be able to use open source, which usually has no fees, but if you want premium systems, the licenses can run $5,000. These fees are not one-time either. These are typically on an annual basis.

- **Data center**: You need to host your server. This can be done either by leasing a data center or building your own, which can cost more than $100,000. There are also the ongoing expenses for cooling, power, and physical security. These can be more than $1,000 per square foot.

- **Maintenance**: You will need trained personnel to manage the server. This can mean having to pay six-figure salaries.

As you can see, the costs can add up. In light of this, it should be no surprise that using VMs is often a more attractive option. While the pricing can be complicated, the overall cost is usually lower than what you would pay for a physical server. For example, a basic VM can cost about $140 to $150 per year. If you want something more advanced, it can be $500 or more. It depends on what features and capabilities you want.

Besides the lower costs, there are other advantages of VMs, which are as follows:

- **Rapid deployment**: You can quickly create a VM. In Azure, there is a form you will fill out (we will see a demonstration of this in the next section). It can take just a few minutes.

- **Flexibility**: You can easily adjust the compute resources of a VM. You can also leverage Azure's capabilities for scaling.

- **Maintenance**: Azure provides seamless updates and patching. What this means is that there is usually less need to hire IT personnel.

- **Easier migration**: With VMs, the transfer from on-premises to the cloud can be more streamlined. This is known as the lift-and-shift process.

Then again, VMs do have drawbacks, which are outlined as follows:

- **Complexity**: While Azure helps to streamline the process, it still requires some personnel who have experience with IT. There is certainly a learning curve. You probably want people who have certifications, such as with the AZ-900 and other exams.

- **Costs**: Even though they are usually much less than running an on-premises environment, they still need to be monitored. If not, there can easily be wasted expenditures, such as for underutilized resources.

- **Latency**: By running in the cloud, a VM has a delay in processing. However, this may not be acceptable for high-stakes applications that require real-time capabilities.

- **Security**: As we learned in *Chapter 2, The Foundations of Cloud Computing,* Azure provides substantial security systems. However, customers still may not want to rely on a third party for this. This is especially the case for regulated industries, where control of security is essential.

Setting up a virtual machine

We will take a look at the steps for creating a VM in Azure:

1. Log in to Azure.
2. Select **Create a resource**.
3. Where it says **Virtual machine**, click **Create**.
4. You will see the screen in *Figure 4.1*:

Create a virtual machine   ⋯   ✕

| Help me create a low cost VM | Help me create a VM optimized for high availability | Help me choose the right VM size for my workload |

Basics Disks Networking Management Monitoring Advanced Tags   ⋯

Create a virtual machine that runs Linux or Windows. Select an image from Azure marketplace or use your own customized image. Complete the Basics tab then Review + create to provision a virtual machine with default parameters or review each tab for full customization. Learn more ☐

Project details

Select the subscription to manage deployed resources and costs. Use resource groups like folders to organize and manage all your resources.

Subscription * ⓘ   Pay-As-You-Go   ⌄

    Resource group * ⓘ   (New) Resource group   ⌄
                           Create new

Instance details

| < Previous | Next : Disks > | Review + create |

Estimated monthly costs ⓘ   ↖

Costs indicated here are estimates only. Pricing may vary depending on your Microsoft agreement, date of purchase, subscription type, usage costs, licensing and currency exchange rates. Total costs may include other resource costs, licensing and subscription implications. This feature may have limited or restricted functionality, but is made available on a preview basis for evaluation and feedback.

⧉ Give feedback about your estimate experience

⌄ **Basics** $85.41

Estimated monthly cost $90.69

⅋ Give feedback

Figure 4.1: Virtual machine setup

5. You will then configure the VM.
6. Once finished with this, you will select **Review + create**.

At the top of the screen, there are seven tabs for the configuration: **Basics, Disks, Networking, Management, Monitoring, Advanced,** and **Tags**. Because of the large number of options, it is usually a good idea to do some planning before creating a VM.

Moreover, there are only a few options that are required:

- **Subscription**: Depending on your setup, there are several options, like pay-as-you-go.
- **Resource group**: You can use an existing one. There is also an option to create a new resource group.

- **Virtual machine name**: This needs to be unique. You cannot change it after it is created.

- **Region**: There is a drop-down of all the regions, but some types of VMs are not available in certain regions.

- **Availability zone**: Your managed disk and public IP will be created in this area, too. Azure also allows for selecting multiple availability zones.

- **Image**: This is the OS or application for the VM. Some examples include Windows Server 2022 Datacenter, Red Hat Enterprise Linux 8.10, and Ubuntu Server 24.04 LTS.

- **Size**: This is where you set how much of a workload you want to run, based on a VM's processing power, memory, and storage. Azure provides many options, like Standard_D2s_v3 (two vCPUs, 8 GB memory). In this naming convention, *D* indicates the VM series, *s* means it supports premium storage, and *v3* is the version.

- **Username**: This is for the administrator of the VM.

- **Key pair name**: This is the name of your SSH key, which is used to authenticate users.

Besides these options, there are others that are common for setting up VMs:

- **Disks**: You can select from a variety of disks, like **solid state drives** (**SSDs**).

- **Management**: You can allow for boot diagnostics and auto shutdowns.

- **Security**: You can set up Microsoft Defender for the Cloud, which provides unified security management and advanced threat protection. This is for hybrid cloud workloads.

- **Identity**: You can establish log access using Microsoft Entra ID.

When you create a VM, Azure will automatically create a virtual network, subnet, and public IP. This will allow for connections via the internet for resources like databases, storage, and other VMs.

However, depending on your requirements, you may want to configure the networking options for the **network interface card** (**NIC**):

- **Public IP**: This is a globally unique address that you assign to your VM. This allows for communication on the internet.

- **NIC network security group**: This contains security rules for permitting and denying inbound or outbound network traffic to the VM. It is usually a good idea to assign a network security group to subnets, not specific network interfaces within the subnet. Azure provides two levels of security: basic and advanced.

- **Public inbound ports**: The default option is that a VM cannot allow traffic from the public internet for a common port, but you can turn this off and select the ports that are open, such as for HTTP, HTTPS, SSH, and **Remote Desktop Protocol** (**RDP**). However, Azure recommends this only for testing purposes.

- **Load balancing**: This distributes inbound traffic for multiple servers and resources to improve reliability, availability, and performance. Azure has two main options for load balancing. One is primarily for TCP/UDP network traffic, while the other is for HTTP/HTTPS traffic.

In a VM, virtual networks are kept separate from each other. However, the VMs in the same network can access each other.

Note: **When creating a VM or many other services, you will be charged. In other words, when doing demos for this book, you probably should delete them after you create them.**

Connecting a VM

Azure provides a myriad of ways to connect to a VM. The approach depends on your OS, security requirements, and use cases. Here are the main approaches:

- **Remote Desktop Protocol (RDP)**: This is for Windows environments. RDP has an intuitive **graphical user interface** (**GUI**) and can perform many administrative tasks in Azure. However, port 3389 is open, which is a potential security vulnerability. If this is an issue for your organization, you might want to use Azure Bastion.

- **Azure Bastion**: This is a highly secure system, as there is no need to use public IP addresses. It is also available for Windows and Linux platforms. However, Azure is more expensive than options like RDP and SSH.

- **SSH**: This is a CLI remote access system for Linux platforms, such as Ubuntu and CentOS, and can handle complex operations like managing Kubernetes clusters. SSH uses private or public keys for security, so it is best to use SSH key authentication rather than passwords for stronger protection and easier management. You should also use **network security groups** (**NSGs**), which are virtual firewalls that control inbound and outbound traffic based on rules for IP addresses, ports, and protocols. This provides simpler management, consistent security policies across VMs, and fewer potential conflicts.

- **PowerShell**: This is for Windows environments. PowerShell is particularly good for automating Windows Server, such as with updates, configurations, and deployments. For better security, it is recommended to use PowerShell within a private network.

- **Azure Cloud Shell**: This is built into Azure. This means you can run CLI commands without setting up a local environment.

Let us see how to use Azure Cloud Shell:

1. Log in to Azure.
2. In the navigation bar at the top of the screen, click the icon that looks like an input prompt.

3. You can then select either Bash or PowerShell, which will be the default. You can change this any time.

4. You will have some other options. You can select a storage account. You will also need to choose a subscription type.

5. Select **Apply**.

6. You will see the shell, as shown in *Figure 4.2*:

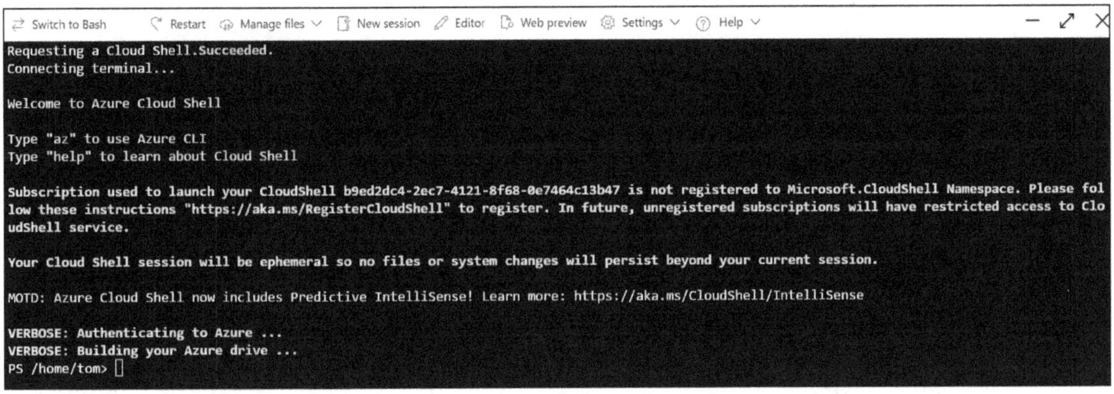

Figure 4.2: Azure Cloud Shell

7. At the top of the screen, there are different options, such as to switch to Bash, restart the shell, establish a new session, and change settings.

8. At the bottom of the screen, you can enter a script. For example, this is the structure to use when starting a VM: `az vm start --resource-group <ResourceGroupName> --name <VMName>`.

Pricing of a VM

As mentioned earlier, the pricing of a VM can be complex. The calculation is based on a wide array of factors, which include the following:

*   **Compute resources**: You are charged based on the CPU and the amount of **random access memory (RAM)** that you use, which is calculated per second. The minimum is one minute. So long as the VM is running, you will be charged.

*   **Storage**: You pay for hard drives, SSDs, and data disks on a continuous basis. It does not matter if you stop your VM.

*   **Licenses**: You will pay an hourly fee for the Windows Server. You are charged when the VM is running.

You will also be charged for the public IP address, and there are two types:

- **Dynamic IP addresses**: This is automatically assigned by the network's **Dynamic Host Configuration Protocol** (**DHCP**), which can change periodically. Azure charges for a dynamic IP address when the VM is being used.

- **Static IP address**: This is fixed and is manually assigned to your VM. Azure charges for this even if the VM is not being used.

Understanding Azure Virtual Machine Scale Sets

With Azure VMSS, you can deploy and manage identical VMs that are load-balanced, such as with the Azure Load Balancer (for TCP/UDP) and Azure Application Gateway (for HTTP/HTTPS). There is no extra cost for this feature. Rather, the VMSS is a way to better manage your existing VMs.

Here are some other features:

- **Autoscaling**: This is automatic, with Azure increasing or decreasing the number of VMs according to CPU usage and memory. You can set the criteria for this, such as with performance metrics and schedules.

- **Maintenance**: There are automatic updates and upgrades.

- **Monitoring**: You get access to a dashboard to track the performance of the VMSS.

- **High availability**: The VMs are distributed across availability zones to mitigate downtime.

- **OS**: There is support for Windows and Linux.

- **Capacity**: You can use a VMSS to manage up to 1,000 VMSS instances.

- **Simplified process**: You can easily manage VMs by using one configuration or a baseline image.

There are a variety of use cases for a VMSS. Some include big data analytics, AI workloads, batch processing, high-performance clusters, and microservices architectures.

To deploy a VMSS, you can use the Azure Cloud Shell. Azure provides scripts for this process, such as creating the resource group, setting the configuration, and specifying autoscaling.

You can also use Terraform for this process, which is an IaC open-source software platform. It allows for defining, provisioning, and managing infrastructure for different cloud providers. It can also handle on-premises environments. You can interact with Terraform using **HashiCorp Configuration Language** (**HCL**) or JSON.

As for working with a VMSS, you can create consistent and repeatable scripts for the deployment by using a state file. This will track changes. Terraform also integrates with the Azure Resource Manager, including source control. This allows for collaboration.

Availability sets

An availability set is a group of VMs that is in a logical form. The purpose is to help provide Azure a way to evaluate an application's ability for redundancy and availability. Microsoft advises having two or more VMs within an availability set. This is to allow it to meet the 99.95% threshold for an Azure SLA, so as to allow VMs to be available during planned maintenance and unexpected outages. A key part of this is that the VMs will be distributed across different fault domains. These are racks in the data center that are separated based on power, cooling, and networking. If one rack fails, only those VMs in the rack are impacted. The others will continue to function properly.

Next, there is an option called an update domain, which is another logical grouping of VMs. However, this is meant for preventing them from being updated at the same time as planned maintenance. Instead, Azure will sequence them (the default is five domains, but it can be as many as 20).

There is no cost for an availability set. Instead, you will be paying for the underlying VMs for it. Yet there are some disadvantages to keep in mind:

- **Regional constraints**: Availability sets only work with VMs in one region or data center. In other words, they do not provide protection when there is a massive failure. Because of this, you might want to use availability zones or Azure Site Recovery.

- **Scaling**: It must be done manually. You should use VMSS for this capability.

- **VMs**: When you set up an availability set, you cannot use existing VMs.

- **Load balancing**: This is not provided automatically. You will need to configure the Azure Load Balancer.

- **Limited protection**: An availability set only guards against hardware problems, not application or OS crashes.

To set up an availability set, you will take these steps:

1. Log in to Azure.
2. Select **Create a resource**.
3. In the search box at the top of the screen, enter: `availability set`.
4. Where it says **Availability Set**, select **Create**.
5. *Figure 4.3* shows the screen for the setup:

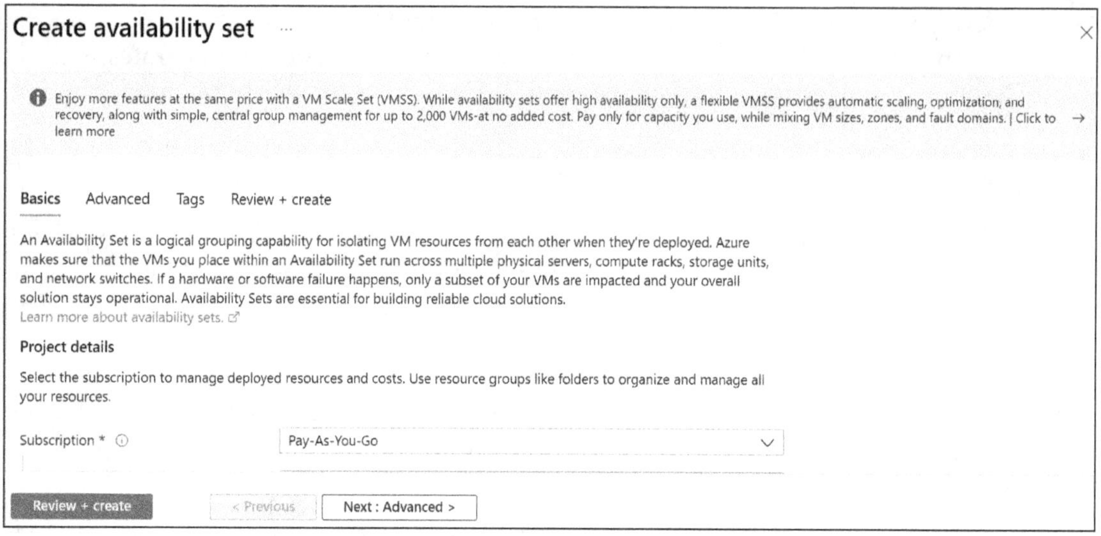

Figure 4.3: Form to create an availability set

6. There are three main sections to fill out: **Basics**, **Advanced**, and **Tags**.

7. For the required configurations, you need to specify the subscription, resource group, name for the availability set, and region. You can also set the number of fault domains and update domains.

8. In the **Advanced** settings, you can establish a proximity placement group. We will explain this in the next section of this chapter.

9. Select **Review + create**.

Proximity placement group

A **proximity placement group** (**PPG**) is a logical grouping of resources, like VMs, that are situated close to the same data center. This helps to lower latency. A PPG can also bolster application performance. This is especially useful for compute intensive programs like games and high-frequency trading.

But PPGs do come with some notable disadvantages. You may not have the option of getting the necessary size and capabilities for VMs in certain regions. Also, it can sometimes be challenging to scale PPGs because of the hardware requirements. Finally, the implementation can be complicated, such as when there are deployments across various zones.

Here are the steps for creating a PPG:

1. Log in to Azure.

2. Select **Create a resource**.

3. In the search box at the top of the screen, enter: **proximity placement group**.

4. *Figure 4.4* shows the screen for the setup:

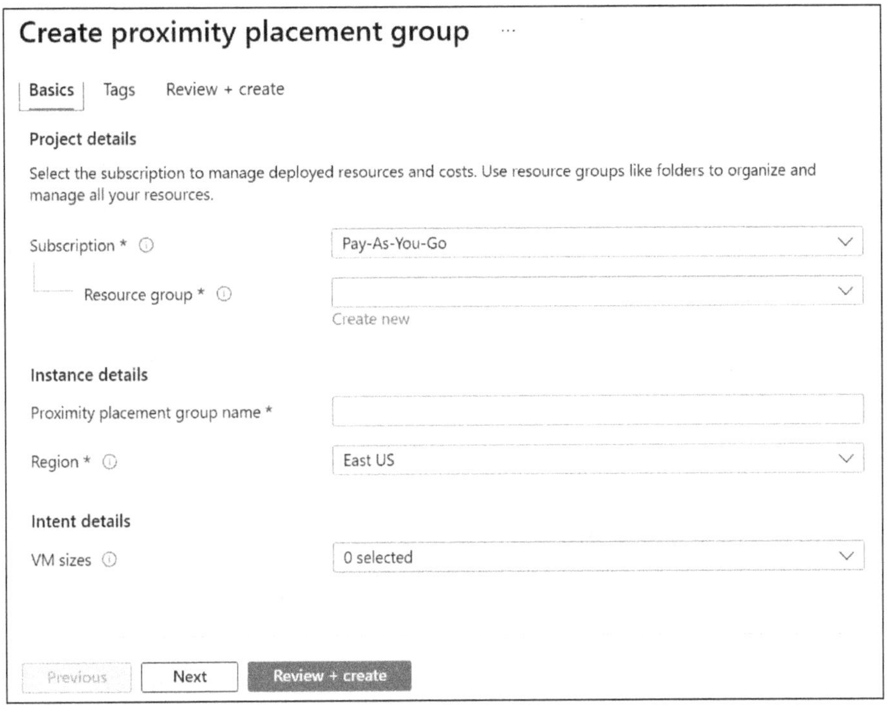

Figure 4.4: *Form to create a proximity placement group*

5. You are required to specify the subscription, resource group, proximity name, and region. You can also select one or more sizes you intend to deploy in the PPG.

6. Select **Review + create**.

To sum up the concepts of VMSSs, availability sets, and PPGs, you can check out *Table 4.1*:

Feature	PPG	Availability sets	VMSS
Main purpose	Minimize latency	High availability and redundancy	Deploy and manage identical, load-balanced VMs
Regional scope	Single region	Single region	Span multiple availability zones
Scaling	Manual	Manual	Automatic
VM limitations	May have size limitations	Cannot use existing VMs	Manage up to 1,000 VMs
Use cases	Compute-intensive applications requiring near real-time responses (gaming, high-frequency trading)	Applications that need high availability within a region	Workloads that need elastic scaling, such as big data analytics, AI, and batch processing

Table 4.1: *Comparisons for PPGs, availability sets, and VMSS*

Azure Virtual Desktop

When the COVID-19 pandemic hit, there was a massive shift towards remote work. This meant that companies had to scramble to adopt software that allowed for collaboration. However, there were challenges, such as data security, scaling, and costs.

One of the solutions that businesses used was the **Azure Virtual Desktop (AVD)**. It is a virtual desktop service that virtualizes a Windows environment that is available from any device or computing platform. This means a user can access their own desktop, using any of the applications. These are some of the main features:

- **OS and software**: You can have a VM with Windows 11 or Windows 10, along with Windows Server 2022, 2019, and 2016. This means there is no learning curve for those who understand how to use these systems.

- **Lower costs**: AVD allows for multi-sessions, where multiple users can use a single VM.

- **Scalability**: It is easy for an administrator to increase or decrease the capacity of the AVD based on the demands for workloads.

- **Administration**: An administrator has a dashboard to manage resources, licenses, and configuration.

- **Compatibility**: You can use the AVD on many platforms besides Windows, such as macOS, iOS, Android, and HTML browsers.

- **Microsoft 365**: The AVD is optimized for this platform, which provides for higher performance.

- **Networking**: You can use the AVD with different types of options, like Azure Private Link and RDP Shortpath. This can help increase security and reliability.

When setting up an AVD, you will need to have a resource group and a virtual network.

Then you will create a host pool, which manages your session hosts:

1. Log in to Azure.
2. In the search box at the top of the screen, enter: `azure virtual desktop`.
3. Select **Create a host pool**.
4. *Figure 4.5* shows the screen for setting up the host pool:

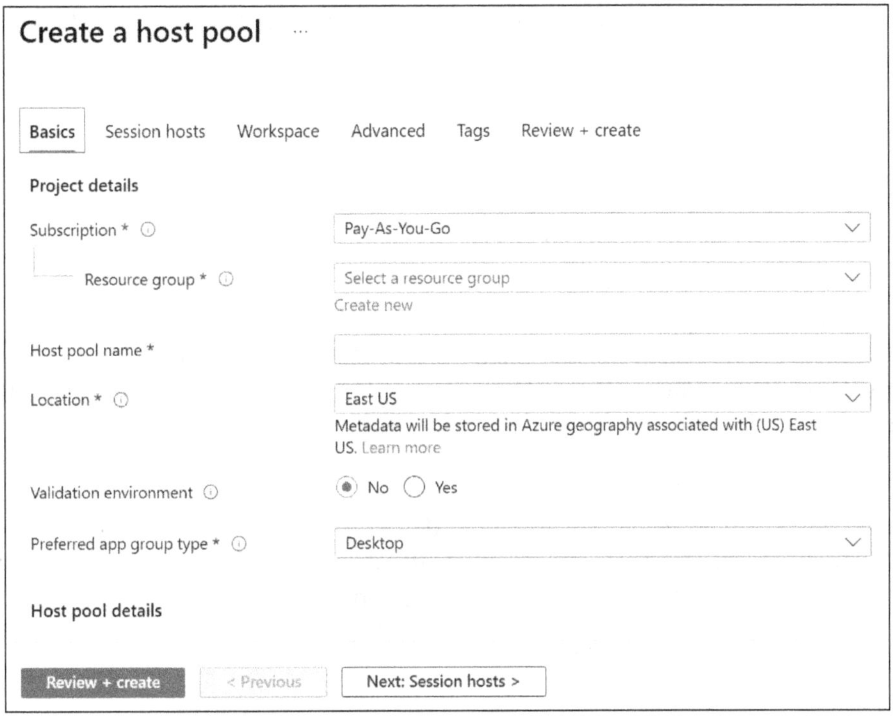

Figure 4.5: Form to create a host pool for an Azure Virtual Desktop

5. You will select the subscription, resource group, and region. You will also need to come up with a unique name for the host pool.

6. If you select the **Session hosts** tab, you can add VMs. You will go through the setup process, such as identifying the resource group, name, type of VM, and so on.

7. If you select the **Workspace** tab, you can create application groups for the host pool. This will allow for more organization of the resources.

To see the benefits of an AVD, let us look at a case study. It is for *Eurowings*, which is Lufthansa Group's low-cost airline. It has over 40 million customers and flies to more than 100 destinations across the world.[1]

The company set out to modernize its systems, with a focus on cloud strategy. The main catalyst for this was the need to update its on-premises systems, a process that would have taken much time and expense.

The company thought that a solution would be to use an AVD solution. This would provide the benefits of a cloud system but would not require ripping out the existing on-premises infrastructure. The result is that the company was able to reduce operating expenses by over

---

1 https://www.microsoft.com/en/customers/story/1643601796669602766-eurowings-travel-transportation-azure-virtual-desktop

50%. The AVD solution also met Eurowings' rigorous security requirements. Then there were the improvements in productivity, such as with employee onboarding times and software updates.

In all, about 5,000 employees use the AVD solution, but Eurowings plans to roll it out to other departments.

Azure App Services

Azure App Services is an application development platform. With it, you can code the software and deploy it. Azure manages the infrastructure in the background. There is no need for a developer to worry about tasks like creating and configuring VMs and networks. Because of this, Azure App Services is considered a PaaS solution.

Here are some of the key features:

- **Language support**: You can develop with a myriad of languages and frameworks like ASP.NET, ASP.NET Core, Java, Tomcat, JBoss EAP, Node.js, PHP, and Python. These can be run in Windows and Linux environments, as well as in containers.
- **Deployment**: This is automated, such as with the packaging of the application and the scaling.
- **Security**: You can easily embed authentication and authorization for an application.

Another benefit of Azure App Services is that you can develop many types of applications. These include the following:

- **Web apps**: These are cloud applications that are deployed using .NET, Python, PHP, Node.js, or Java.
- **Mobile**: You can create the backends for smartphone apps, such as for Android or iOS.
- **APIs**: You can create, host, and manage REST APIs.
- **Logic apps**: These help to automate workflows.
- **Function apps**: These are applications that run on demand and can scale automatically.

Let us see how to use Azure App Services:

1. Log in to Azure.
2. In the search box at the top of the screen, enter: `azure app services`.
3. On the menu at the top of the screen, click **Create**.
4. You will see a drop-down menu with these options: **Web App**, **Static Web App**, **Web APP + Database**, and **WordPress on App Service**.
5. Select **Web App**.

6. *Figure 4.6* shows the screen for setting up the application:

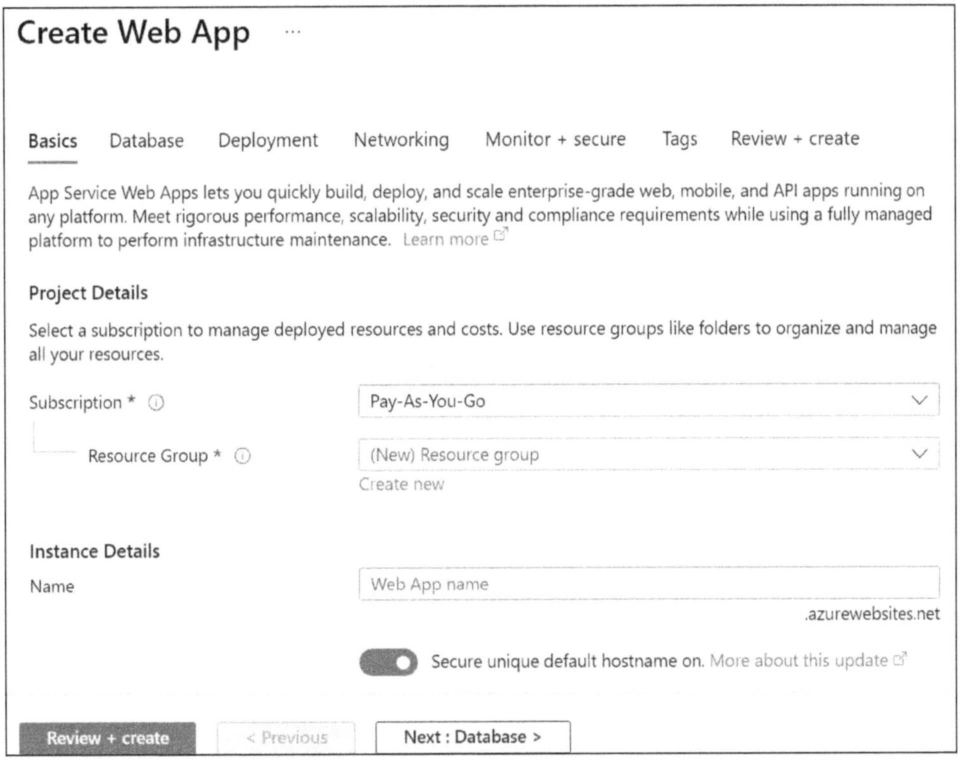

Create Web App ···

Basics   Database   Deployment   Networking   Monitor + secure   Tags   Review + create

App Service Web Apps lets you quickly build, deploy, and scale enterprise-grade web, mobile, and API apps running on any platform. Meet rigorous performance, scalability, security and compliance requirements while using a fully managed platform to perform infrastructure maintenance. Learn more ☐

Project Details

Select a subscription to manage deployed resources and costs. Use resource groups like folders to organize and manage all your resources.

Subscription * ⓘ | Pay-As-You-Go   ∨ |

Resource Group * ⓘ | (New) Resource group   ∨ |
                       Create new

Instance Details

Name | Web App name |
                                              .azurewebsites.net

                     ⬤ Secure unique default hostname on. More about this update ☐

[Review + create]   [< Previous]   [Next : Database >]

Figure 4.6: Form to create a Web App

7. You will specify the subscription, resource group, and region. However, you will need to indicate whether the app will be in a container, and you will specify the language or framework.

8. It is a good idea to create a name for the instance. For example, suppose you use: **todo**. This will mean that the web address will be **todo.azurewebsites.net**.

9. For the **Database** tab, you have options for **SQLAzure** (which is recommended), **PostgreSQL - Flexible Server**, MySQL—Flexible Server, and **Cosmos DB API for MongoDB**. For this, you will create a unique server name and database name.

10. For the **Deployment** tab, you can configure your application for GitHub Actions. This will automate the deployment for your application, which will include updates.

11. For the **Networking** tab, the Web App is enabled for public access to the internet. You can also select or create a virtual network.

12. For the **Monitor + secure** tab, you can enable Azure Monitor as well as Microsoft Defender for Cloud.

13. Select **Review + create**.

Once you create your Web App, there are different ways you can deploy your application. A common approach is to do this through Visual Studio, which has a publish button. You can set this up for your authentication. As for Visual Studio Code, you will need to install an extension.

As mentioned previously, you can deploy the app using GitHub Actions. However, there are some other options available, which are:

- **Azure pipelines**: You can use Azure DevOps for continuous integration and delivery (CI/CD).

- **Packages**: You can package your files in a ZIP archive and upload them to your Web App using the Azure CLI or FTP.

- **Container**: You can use Docker to containerize your application image. This will allow for a consistent development environment.

Azure Functions

In *Chapter 2, The Foundations of Cloud Computing*, we got a high-level overview of Azure Functions, which are serverless, event-driven services. They are generally about executing small blocks of code. When using Azure Functions, developers can spend more time developing and not on the infrastructure.

Another key advantage is the low cost. There is a generous free tier, which allows for up to one million executions per month. When this is used up, the pricing is still reasonable.

These are common use cases for Azure Functions:

- **Notifications**: You can send messages about anomalies or other issues with a system.
- **Scheduled tasks**: You can provide the times for when to conduct a data cleanup or produce a report.
- **API**: You can create the backend for handling HTTP requests and integrations.
- **Image resizing**: You can automate this for Azure Blob Storage, such as for thumbnails.
- **Conversions**: You can convert files into other formats, like Word files or PDFs.
- **Sensor data**: You can process data for IoT devices, such as a motion detector.

This is how to create an Azure Function:

1. Log in to Azure.
2. In the search box at the top of the screen, enter: `function app`.
3. Click **Create Function App**.
4. You will select among five different hosting plans. They are based on features like scaling and resources available.

5. Select the Flex Consumption plan. *Figure 4.7* shows the screen for setting up the Azure Function:

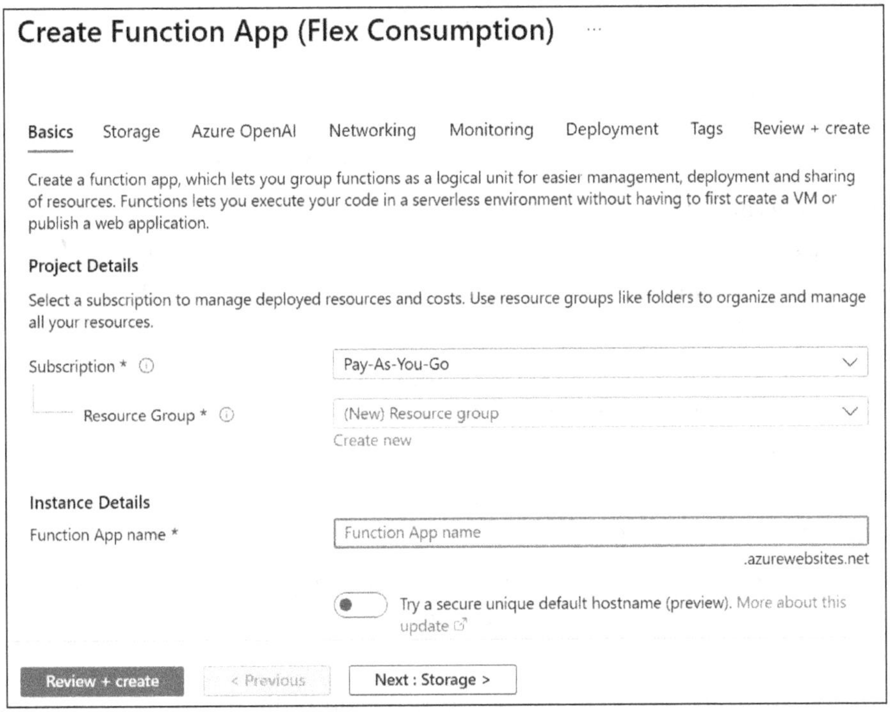

Figure 4.7: *Form to create an Azure Function*

6. You will specify the subscription, resource group, region, and function name.

7. You will select the version, which is the language or framework. The options are .NET, Node.js, Python, Java, and PowerShell Core. You will also select the version for the one you select.

8. As for the other options, you can use Azure Monitor, enable the Azure function for public access, and use virtual network integration. However, the deployment only has basic authentication.

9. For the **Azure OpenAI** tab, you can use OpenAI models and vector databases. With these, you can integrate generative AI capabilities in your applications.

10. Select **Review + create**.

Container services

For modern software development, an application is usually not created from scratch. There is often the use of frameworks, libraries, or modules, which are called dependencies. These include collections of pre-built software blocks that you can use in your own applications.

For example, Microsoft's ASP.NET Core has tools that allow you to create front ends for an application with minimal code. You can then organize these using a **Model-View-Controller (MVC)** design pattern. The front ends are also available for different platforms like Windows, macOS, and Linux.

Next, you can use ASP.NET Core to build the back end, such as for APIs and middleware pipelines. It also has built-in capabilities for security and asynchronous programming. For connecting these various components, you can use a language like C#, F#, or Visual Basic .NET.

While dependencies are powerful, they come with notable drawbacks:

- **Learning curve**: Even though they help to streamline the development of many components, it can still take some time to learn how to use them. They may have unusual structures, configurations, and syntax.

- **Flexibility**: A dependency is often opinionated. This means that they have a rigid approach to handling a task or process, but this can mean limited ability to customize the application.

- **Bloat**: Using dependencies usually means adding unnecessary code, which can lower the performance of the application.

- **Dependence management**: Dependencies are subject to periodic changes. In some cases, they may be unexpected and break your application. Making the change can take time, which can mean that your users suffer.

- **Security**: You are relying on the security precautions of the developer of the dependency. Some may be a small team, perhaps even run by one person. This can make your application vulnerable to breaches.

To help address these problems, it is common to use containerization. This involves packaging the application code with the dependencies and configuration files into a container image. This is a template and is built using a system like *Docker*. The container has everything an application needs to run and can also be deployed across different types of IT environments, such as Windows or Linux.

There is usually an orchestration system for the container. This helps to manage scaling, load balancing, and automated deployment.

Azure has various services for containers, such as **Azure Container Instances (ACI)**, **Azure Kubernetes Service (AKS)**, and Azure Container Apps.

Azure Container Instances

ACI is a fast and simple way to use and manage containers that operate on Linux and Windows. There is no need to have VMs. An ACI can also take less than a minute to set up.

These are the steps to create one.

1. Log in to Azure.

2. On the sidebar, select **Containers** and then click **Create** where it says **Container App**. *Figure 4.8* shows the screen for setting up an ACI:

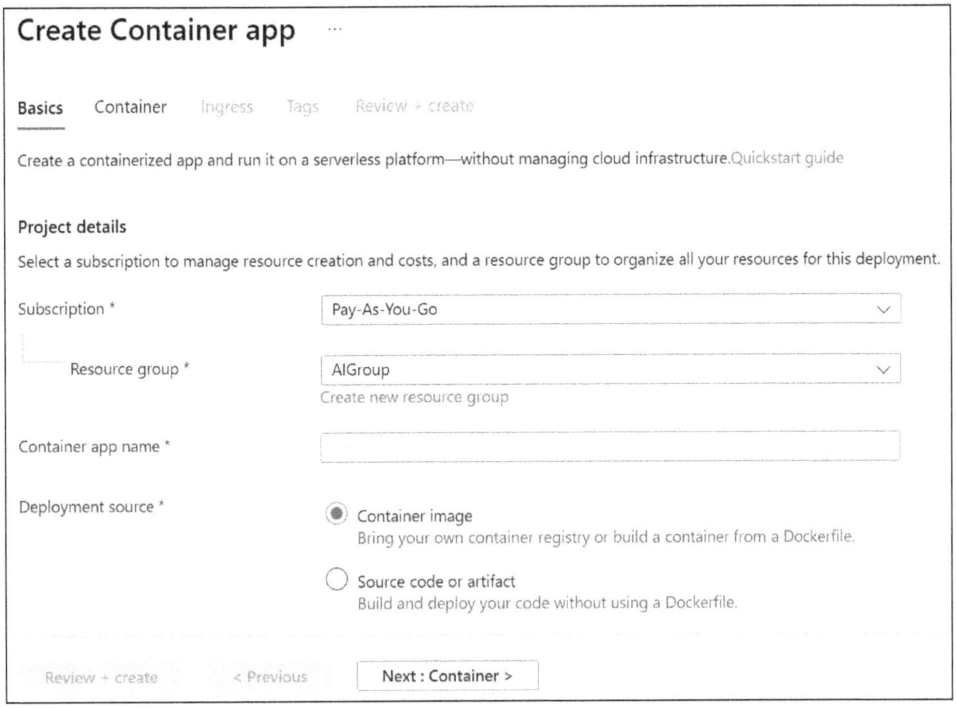

Create Container app   …

Basics   Container   Ingress   Tags   Review + create

Create a containerized app and run it on a serverless platform—without managing cloud infrastructure.Quickstart guide

Project details

Select a subscription to manage resource creation and costs, and a resource group to organize all your resources for this deployment.

Subscription *	Pay-As-You-Go ⌄
Resource group *	AIGroup ⌄
	Create new resource group
Container app name *	
Deployment source *	⦿ Container image
	Bring your own container registry or build a container from a Dockerfile.
	◯ Source code or artifact
	Build and deploy your code without using a Dockerfile.

Review + create   < Previous   **Next : Container >**

Figure 4.8: Form to create an ACI

3. You will specify the subscription, resource group, region, and container name.

4. Deployment source: You have two options. One is for the **Container image**, which is your own container registry or one you build using a Dockerfile. This is a text document that has instructions to create a Docker image. Next, you can select **Source code or artifact**. This is when you are not using a Dockerfile.

5. You can select **Use quickstart image** to create a simple container image. There are templates, such as for an Azure function or a regular container. There will be fixed parameters for the CPU cores, memory size, and enablement of ingress for applications that use HTTP or TCP endpoints, but you can also create a more sophisticated container image.

6. Click **Review + create**.

Azure Kubernetes

Kubernetes is complex. There are intricate configuration settings, such as for the API server and networking systems. Even a slight issue with this can lead to system failure or security exposure. It can also be challenging to manage the resources efficiently.

But AKS helps streamline the process. It is a fully managed service for Kubernetes implementations, allowing for easier ways to handle automation of upgrades, scaling, network configuration, and node provisioning. AKS also comes with a robust system for debugging, logging, monitoring, and **continuous integration and continuous delivery (CI/CD)**. It even allows for deployments to the edge, such as with **Internet of Things (IoT)** resources.

To better understand how AKS works and how it can help an organization, consider a case study of Manulife. This is an insurance and financial services company, based in Toronto, that has been around for over 130 years.

To better serve its millions of customers, the firm knew it had to migrate its IT infrastructure to the cloud. Over a few years, it did this with all its business operations, in Canada, U.S., and Asia, to AKS. This has included more than 250 clusters that run about 3,000 applications and microservices, which are accessible via APIs. The implementation was so successful that Manulife was able to sunset its mainframe systems and run completely on the Azure SQL Managed Instance.

The results of using AKS have been standout. The firm has estimated that development time is about 30% lower, with cost down by roughly 50%.[2]

Being completely on Azure, this opened up other opportunities for Manulife. For example, the firm was able to leverage Azure AI services to help with fraud detection, risk analysis, and customer service. What may have taken months for a data science project can now be done within a few days.

Azure Container Apps

Azure Container Apps is a serverless system to run containerized applications. Much of the infrastructure is managed, such as configuration, orchestration, and deployment. It is similar to ACI except that there is no need for managing Kubernetes.

Azure Container Apps have many use cases. Some examples include API endpoints, event-driven programs, background processing jobs, and microservices. Microservices is where an application is built with small software services that are independent from each other. They communicate with APIs. This allows easier development and maintenance.

When you use Azure Container Apps, the system will automatically handle key processes. They include CPU and memory load, scaling, HTTP traffic, and **Kubernetes Event-driven Autoscaling (KEDA)**. There is also support for **Distributed Apps Runtime (Dapr)**. This is an open-source platform that allows creating microservices, which have secure communications, state management, connectors to databases, file systems, and message queues.

Azure Container Apps comes with a generous free tier. For each month, you get two million requests.

To sum up the concepts of Azure Container Instances, Azure Kubernetes, and Azure Container Apps, you can take a look at *Table 4.2*:

---

2 https://www.microsoft.com/en/customers/story/1629943996414131596-manulife-insurance-azure-kubernetes-service

Feature	ACI	AKS	Azure Container Apps
Description	Easy way to use containers without managing a VM	A fully managed service for Kubernetes Manages deployment and scaling	Serverless system for using containers No need to manage Kubernetes
Scaling	Simple options Fixed parameters for CPU and memory	Scales with advanced orchestration	Automatic scaling According to CPU and memory load
Use cases	Testing and deployment	Kubernetes applications that are enterprise-grade Use of microservices	API endpoints Background jobs Microservices

Table 4.2: Comparisons of Azure Container Instances, Azure Kubernetes, and Azure Container Apps

Azure Container Registry

Azure Container Registry (**ACR**) is a system that allows you to build, store, and manage container images in a central hub. This helps to simplify the container lifecycle, which can be complex. ACR works seamlessly with AKS, Azure App Service, Azure Container Instance, and Azure Red Hat OpenShift, which is an enterprise-grade orchestration system that is built on Kubernetes.

This system is generally for managing Docker container images. But it can also be used for other formats, like *OCI artifacts* and *Helm charts*. ACI also allows for geo-replication, which means that one registry can work across multiple regions.

Conclusion

In this chapter, we learned about the compute services in Azure. We first looked at VMs, how they work, and their use cases. This also included a review of some of the tools to better manage VMs. We then covered systems to build applications on the Azure platform. These included Azure App Services and Azure Functions.

We ended the chapter by learning about containerization. For this, we covered some of the tools for managing this process, like Azure Container Instances, Azure Kubernetes Service, and Azure Container Apps. In the next chapter, we will learn about networking systems and tools for Azure.

Sample questions

The sample questions and answers are as follows:

1. **Why would you use Azure Virtual Machine Scale Sets?**

    a. To provide more security.

    b. To distribute the VMs across multiple regions.

    c.   To lower energy use.

    d.   To get automatic scaling with VMs.

Correct answer: d

Explanation: A key advantage of a VMSS is that it scales the VMSS. This helps to better manage overall costs and improve the user experience.

2. **You want to distribute your VMs across different fault domains, so as to improve availability when there is maintenance. What would you use?**

    a.   Azure Container Instances

    b.   Availability sets

    c.   Azure Functions

    d.   Azure Container Apps

Correct answer: b

Explanation: With an availability set, you can enhance the reliability and availability of your VMs. This can reduce the incidence of downtime when there is maintenance.

3. **What is a key drawback of using a VM?**

    a.   Lack of customization.

    b.   Higher costs compared to on-premises implementations.

    c.   Latency.

    d.   Inability to scale.

Correct answer: c

Explanation: Unlike having access to a physical machine, you need to use the cloud to access a VM. This means there is additional latency.

4. **Why would you use a proximity placement group in Azure?**

    a.   Lower latency.

    b.   Improve high availability.

    c.   To activate the advanced security settings.

    d.   To customize a VM.

Correct answer: a

Explanation: PPGs are located close to each other in a data center, which allows for improved latency.

5. **What is a key advantage of using Azure Virtual Desktop?**

    a.   Passwordless authentication.

  b. Integration with Kubernetes.

  c. Remote access to a virtual desktop.

  d. Streamlined creation of VMs.

Correct answer: c

Explanation: With an AVD system, users can remotely access their virtual desktops. This can be done with various devices.

6. **Among the following compute services in Azure, which one is a platform as-a service?**

  a. Azure App Services.

  b. Azure Functions.

  c. Availability set.

  d. A VM in Azure.

Correct answer: a

Explanation: This is a PaaS system because developers can deploy applications without having to manage the infrastructure.

7. **What is a key benefit of Azure Kubernetes Service?**

  a. It completely automates the application creation process.

  b. It provides tools for testing an application.

  c. It provides templates for application configurations.

  d. It streamlines the management of containerized applications, with built-in orchestration and scaling.

Correct answer: d

Explanation: AKS is a fully managed system for Kubernetes. It helps streamline the complex process of orchestration and scaling.

8. **What is a benefit of using Azure Functions?**

  a. To create a Kubernetes environment.

  b. It is a serverless compute environment.

  c. It does not require authentication.

  d. It streamlines the process of creating VMs.

Correct answer: b

Explanation: This is a serverless compute service. It handles the underlying infrastructure and scales automatically.

9. **What is the difference between an availability zone and an availability set?**

    a. They are synonymous terms.

    b. An availability set protects against regional outages and failures.

    c. An availability zone has its own independent power system, but not for networking.

    d. An Availability Set is a logical grouping of VMs in a single data center.

    Correct answer: d

    Explanation: The distribution of the group is across fault domains and update domains.

10. **What is a key capability of Azure Container Instances?**

    a. You can deploy containers without having to manage VMs.

    b. Integration with VM Scale Sets.

    c. It is stateless.

    d. It is built for Kubernetes clusters.

    Correct answer: a

    Explanation: ACI is a way to allow for a more streamlined implementation of containers, as there is no need to manage the underlying infrastructure.

11. **Among the following, which would you use to build and manage microservices?**

    a. Azure Kubernetes Service.

    b. Availability zones.

    c. Azure Virtual Desktop.

    d. VMs.

    Correct answer: a

    Explanation: With AKS, you can manage container orchestration for microservices.

12. **What is an Azure load balancer?**

    a. A system to protect against security intrusions for a network.

    b. A system to distribute traffic across multiple VMs.

    c. A storage system for container images.

    d. A system to manage the deployment of applications on Azure.

    Correct answer: b

    Explanation: By distributing the traffic, an Azure load balancer helps to enhance availability and performance.

13. **What is the Azure Container Registry?**

    a. A central hub to store and manage container images.

    b. A system that is an alternative to Kubernetes.

    c. An automation platform for cluster deployments.

    d. A system to protect public IP addresses.

    Correct answer: a

    Explanation: For various Azure services, you can use the ACR to store and manage container images.

14. **What is a use case for Azure Functions?**

    a. Running big data workloads.

    b. Configuring VMs.

    c. Managing Azure Virtual Networks.

    d. Handling even-driven tasks, scheduled events.

    Correct answer: d

    Explanation: Azure Functions is for handling specific tasks or functions, such as those triggered by events.

15. **What approach to connecting to a VM offers the most security?**

    a. Remote Desktop Protocol

    b. Azure Bastion

    c. SSH

    d. PowerShell

    Correct answer: b

    Explanation: Azure Bastion is a highly secure system, as it does not require access to a VM using a public IP address.

16. **What is a key advantage of using the Azure Cloud Shell to connect to a VM?**

    a. The security is the highest available.

    b. The access is available only to administrators.

    c. There is no need to use a local CLI.

    d. There is no login required.

    Correct answer: c

    Explanation: Azure Cloud Shell is available in the Azure cloud platform. You can use CLI commands without having to use an application that is installed locally.

17. **Why would you use PowerShell when connecting to a Windows Azure VM?**

    a. To automate updates, configurations, and deployments.

    b. To configure a VM with Linux commands.

    c. To use passwordless access.

    d. To manage the network security groups for a VM.

    Correct answer: a

    Explanation: A common use case for PowerShell in a Windows environment is to automate various tasks.

18. **Which of the following provides a graphical user interface for managing a VM?**

    a. SSH

    b. PowerShell

    c. Remote Desktop Protocol

    d. Azure Kubernetes Service

    Correct answer: c

    Explanation: RDP comes with a GUI for the Windows platform, compared to using a CLI.

19. **With Azure App Services, what type of application can you create?**

    a. REST APIs

    b. Web Apps

    c. Mobile app backends

    d. All of the above

    Correct answer: d

    Explanation: Azure App Services is a versatile system, allowing for the creation of various types of applications.

20. **When using Azure App Services, how can you deploy an application?**

    a. Upload a ZIP package for the application using the Azure CLI or FTP.

    b. Use the Publish option in Visual Studio

    c. Use GitHub Actions

    d. All of the above

    Correct answer: d

    Explanation: All of these options allow for deployment using Azure App Services.

CHAPTER 5
Networking

Introduction

In this chapter, we will cover networking for Azure. This will first include a review of the core fundamentals, like the infrastructure, protocols, and types of networks.

After this, we will look at Azure services for networking. At the core of this is the Azure virtual network. We will also look at systems like the network security group, peering, Azure DNS, Azure VPN Gateway, and ExpressRoute. These allow for more secure, scalable, and reliable networks.

Structure

The chapter covers the following topics:

- Understanding networking
- Azure networking
- Azure Virtual Networks

Objectives

By the end of this chapter, you will have a good understanding of the network services and capabilities in Azure. This will include knowing about the core fundamentals of networking. Next, you will understand the main features of Azure Virtual Networks, like network security groups, peering, the Azure DNS, Azure VPN Gateways, and ExpressRoute. You will learn the skills to configure, secure, and manage Azure Virtual Networks.

Understanding networking

At the dawn of the computer age, from the late 1940s to the 1950s, large mainframe computers mainly used batch processing. They would handle jobs, like for inventory or payroll, in sequential order. This often required lots of complex configuration and programming.

By the late 1950s, there emerged networking, involving connecting computers, storage, printers, and other systems. The data in the network was transferred across telephone lines. In 1958, **American Telephone and Telegraph** (**AT&T**) launched the first modem, called the Bell 101, to handle this process.

This had the benefit of time sharing, where multiple users could use the same computer. This was critical since the systems were expensive and complicated to manage, but it also spurred new innovations like email and file transfers.

The networking technologies would ultimately lead to the creation of ARPANET in 1969. This was a project of the **Advanced Research Projects Agency** (**ARPA**), which was a part of the U.S. Department of Defense, for a nationwide network to assist with sharing resources for universities and research organizations. It would ultimately become the foundation for the public internet.

At the heart of ARPANET was packet switching. This involves dividing data into smaller units or packets before it is transmitted over a network. A packet has a header, which has information like addresses for the source and destination of the data, sequencing details, and error-checking systems. Then there is the payload, which is the data that is transmitted.

When the packets are delivered over the network, they are jumbled, but then reassembled when they reach their destination. This allows for quicker and more efficient data transmission. Moreover, there is no need to make major changes to the underlying infrastructure to scale the transmissions. Keep in mind that packet switching is still how the Internet operates today.

As for a data center, networking is essential. There are connections for servers, applications, and storage. These are both for internal networks, as well as for the internet. This is accomplished by using protocols, which are rules for the sending and receiving of data.

These are common examples in the data center:

- **Ethernet**: Developed in the 1960s, this protocol remains popular today. It is in the form of a cable, which connects to the devices. This provides for high-speed transmissions of data, but the protocol also ensures that the information is being communicated accurately.

- **Transmission Control Protocol/Internet Protocol (TCP/IP)**: This protocol connects network systems to the Internet. This can also be used with private networks. TCP/IP handles complex interactions with routers and switches, which ensures that data packets are transmitted reliably. The current TCP/IP version is **Internet Protocol Version 4 (IPv4)**. However, IPv6 has been gaining more adoption, since it can manage many more IP addresses.

- **Data Center Bridging (DCB)**: These are protocols, developed and maintained by the **Institute of Electrical and Electronics Engineers** (**IEEE**), to improve the performance and reliability of traditional Ethernet networking. A key feature is priority-based flow control, which helps to better manage traffic workloads.

- **Fibre channel**: This protocol is for high-speed networking, with rates up to 128 GBPS. A common use case is to connect servers to shared storage systems.

There are different types of private networks within an enterprise:

- **Local area networks (LANs)**: They are limited to a specific area, such as an office or building, which results in faster speeds.

- **Wide area networks (WANs)**: They are larger and can connect multiple cities. A WAN may even be for a city or country. The speed may not be as quick as a LAN, but there are benefits to having long-distance communications.

- **Software-defined WANs**: They are a virtualized networking system. You can use software to configure, customize, and control the WAN.

  Generally, a cloud platform is an advanced WAN. It can be hosted either via a public or private cloud, with the services made available on demand.

The networking architecture includes switches and routers. The switches are for internal communications with the resources and managing data packets efficiently. As for the routers, these handle data exchange with the data center and external networks like the public internet. They will attempt to find the most optimized pathway.

The networking infrastructure will be secured with firewalls. These are systems, which include both hardware and software, that manage inbound and outbound network traffic. They will do this according to preset security requirements.

When it comes to networking, you will often hear about a concept called client-server architecture. The server manages and provides services like memory, CPU power, and data to the clients or end-users. The clients can communicate with each server but not share the resources.

Another type of network is peer-to-peer architecture. This is where computers have the same privileges. There is no server or central hub to manage the resources. The sharing is handled between computers directly.

Azure networking

Azure's networking platform is one of the largest and most advanced in the world. It is built on a global WAN that connects Microsoft's data centers across more than 60 regions, allowing customers to deploy applications with low latency, high throughput, and maximum resilience. With over 165,000 miles of fiber and undersea cable, Azure's backbone is designed for massive scalability and enterprise-grade performance.[1]

This vast infrastructure supports everything from simple virtual machines to complex hybrid cloud environments. Whether you are running an internal business application or hosting a global customer-facing service, Azure's networking capabilities ensure that your resources can communicate securely, reliably, and efficiently.

In the rest of this chapter, we will look at the core components of Azure networking. This includes **virtual networks** (**VNets**), which form the foundation for private networking in Azure, as well as supporting services like **network security groups** (**NSGs**), VPN gateways, peering, Azure DNS, and ExpressRoute. These tools enable organizations to build highly secure and scalable networks tailored to their unique requirements.

Azure Virtual Networks

An Azure VNet provides access to networking services and capabilities. It allows creating a private network on the Azure platform. With a VNet, you can securely communicate with other private or internet networks.

The default for a VNet is that VMs cannot communicate with each other. They are considered separate entities, which provide for improved security. A VNet is also considered IaaS. The reason is that you have much flexibility in configuring the system.

The following are the steps for creating a VNet.

1. Log in to Azure.
2. In the search box at the top of the screen, enter: `virtual network`.
3. Click **Create virtual network**. You will see the screen in *Figure 5.1*.

---

1 https://learn.microsoft.com/en-us/azure/networking/microsoft-global-network

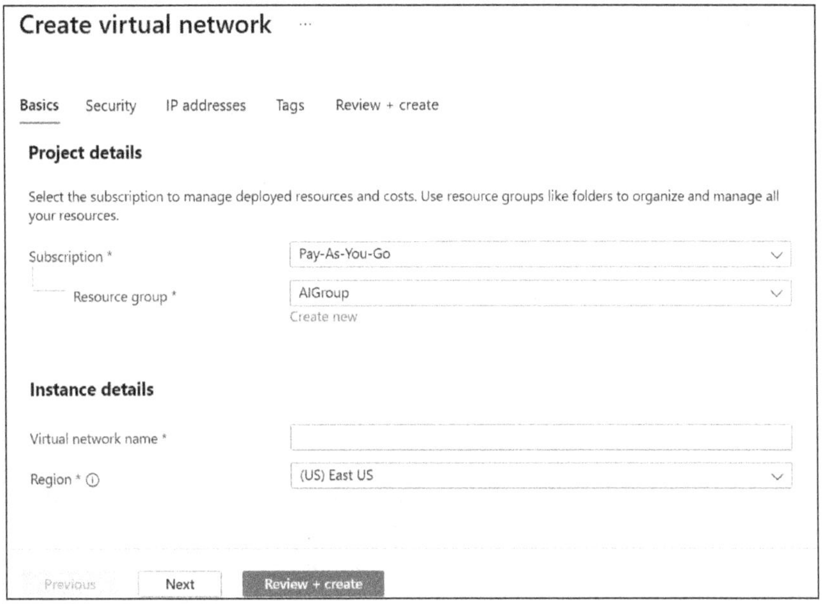

Figure 5.1: *Virtual network setup*

4. You will select the subscription, resource group, and region. You will also need to provide a unique name for the VNet.

5. Select the **Security** tab at the top.

6. You will see four options, all of which charge a fee.

7. Virtual network encryption will encrypt traffic within the VNet. To use this, the VM must have accelerated networking enabled. Moreover, traffic to the public IP is not encrypted.

8. Azure Bastion provides secure RDP/SSH for your VM. There is no need for a public IP address.

9. Azure Firewall is a cloud-based network security system that protects the VNet from unauthorized intrusions.

10. Azure **Distributed Denial-of-Service (DDoS)** network protection provides notification and mitigation for DDoS attacks. This is where a hacker will flood a network with traffic, which can make it inoperable.

11. Select the **IP address** tab at the top of the screen.

12. You will configure the address space for the VNet. You can use either IPv4 or IPv6 addresses, along with subnets. These are private, which means there is no access via the internet. You can also assign a large number of these private addresses to accommodate future growth.

13. Once finished with this process, you will select **Review + create**.

When you create a VNet, you will have at least one subnet, but there are usually more, so long as there are enough IP addresses. A subnet is a way to divide a VNet.

A VM will have at least one subnet. Both are connected with a **network interface card** (**NIC**), which is a hardware device. It is embedded into a motherboard or an expansion card. It can communicate using protocols like *Ethernet*. A VM can have more than one NIC connection. However, a NIC can only connect to a single subnet.

It is possible to assign a public IP to a VM, which will require that this be assigned to the VNet too. However, you need to be careful because this can expose the VNet to security vulnerabilities. Regardless, security is essential for any configuration of your VNet. Azure has a system that helps with this: the NSG.

Network security group

An NSG acts as a filter for network traffic. It does this by using an access control list, which blocks inbound and outbound traffic unless there are matches with certain security rules. You can set these up for the originating IP address or range of addresses for the traffic. The same applies to the source port.

You can then set rules for the destination IP address and port. You can also do this for the type of protocol, like TCP. It is simple to create an NSG, and it can be done through the following steps:

1. Log in to Azure.

2. In the search box at the top of the screen, enter: `network security group`.

3. Click **Create network security group**. You will see the screen in *Figure 5.2*:

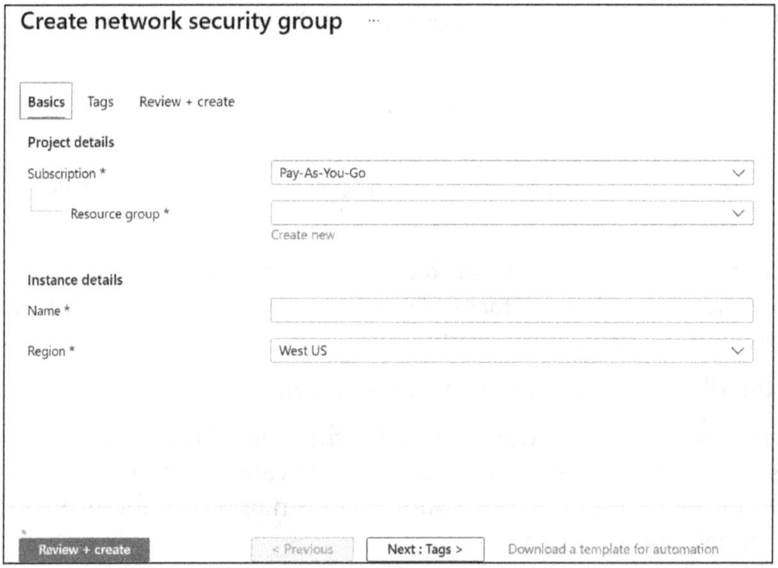

Figure 5.2: NSG setup

4. You will need to select the subscription, resource group, and region. You will also need to create a unique name for the NSG.

5. Click **Review + create**.

Once you have an NSG, you can set up the rules. These are the steps:

1. At the home screen of Azure, select your NSG in the section for **Resources**.

2. On the left side of the screen, you can select the **Activity log**, which shows the inbound and outbound traffic for the VNet. You can also set up access control, establish alerts, and create automations.

3. For the **Settings** tab, you can create the security rules.

4. Click **Inbound security rules**.

5. You can set this for the default rules or create your own by selecting **Add**.

6. When you click **Add**, you will see the screen in *Figure 5.3*:

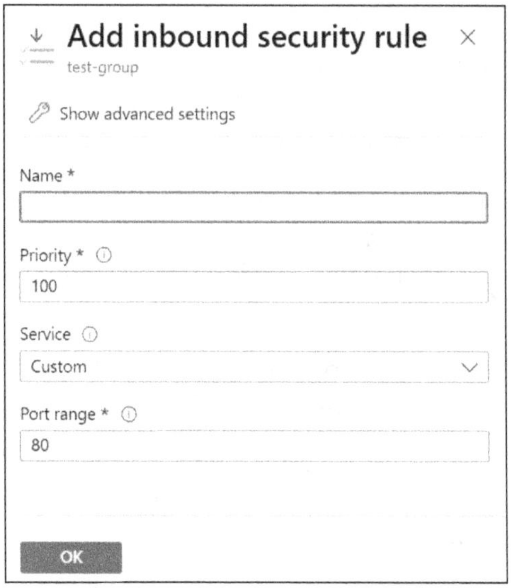

Figure 5.3: Setup for the security rules

7. You will need to create a name for the rule. You will also set the priority for it. The lower the number, the lower the priority. Azure recommends leaving room between the levels, such as 100, 200, 300, etc. Finally, you can set a port or range for them.

Peering and Azure Virtual Network Peering

Azure **Virtual Network (VNet)** peering allows two VNets to connect seamlessly. This makes them appear as a single network for communications. This connection is secure and uses the Microsoft backbone. There is no requirement for public internet routing or gateways.

These are the key points:

- **No overlapping IP ranges**: VNets being peered must have unique address spaces.

- **Low latency and high bandwidth**: Performance is similar to communication within the same VNet.

- **Supports cross-region and cross-subscription peering**: You can peer VNets in different Azure regions (global peering), subscriptions, or even tenants.

These are the setup steps for peering:

1. Log in to the Azure portal.

2. Search for and select **Virtual Networks**.

3. Choose a **VNet** and go to **Peerings**.

4. Click **Add** and then set the peering name. You will then select **Peer VNet**.

Azure DNS

The **Domain Name System** (**DNS**) converts IP addresses into human language. For example, when you enter azure.com in your browser, the DNS will look this up in its registry. It will find that the IP address is 20.49.97.12 and will then connect to the website.

Azure has its own system for internal addresses, which is called Azure DNS. This means you can give them easier-to-remember names. It is common to use this format: *[name].local*. For example, suppose you have a VM that you use for development. You can use this Azure DNS: **http://development.local**.

You can also use a public domain name for your Azure DNS. However, it is not accessible from the internet. It can only be used for Azure's internal systems.

Suppose your company has the public domain name of xyz.com. When you use this, you will be taken to your public website. However, you can have development.xyz.com, which will only be available for authenticated users in your organization.

To create an Azure DNS, you will use either Azure PowerShell or Azure CLI. For the process, you will need to create a DNS zone in Azure, which is a section of the DNS managed by your administrator. Then you will go to your domain registrar's website and update the DNS records, so they point to the Azure DNS.

Azure VPN Gateway

Before describing how the Azure **virtual private network** (**VPN**) gateway works, it is important to have a general understanding of a VPN. This is a system that allows for secure connections. For example, suppose you are at an airport and are using your company's computer. You are accessing the Wi-Fi system. Of course, this is vulnerable to hacks because it is a public network.

You can log into your VPN system with your user ID and password. This may also include **multifactor authentication (MFA)**, where a security code will be sent to another device, like your smartphone.

Suppose you want to visit your company's website at **www.xyz.com**. The following is how your VPN will work:

1. **Routing**: All your internet traffic will be routed to the VPN, not the Wi-Fi system.

2. **Encryption**: The traffic will be encrypted using a sophisticated algorithm, such as AES-256. This will transform the information into a long string of numbers, letters, and special characters. If a hacker captures it, it would not be readable.

3. **VPN server**: This will send your request to **www.xyz.com**, and the IP address will not be visible. Instead, it will be the VPN's IP address. This means that a hacker would not know your location.

4. **Website response:** When **www.xyz.com** sends back the response, it goes to the VPN server. It will then be encrypted and sent to your computer. The VPN will have a private key that will decrypt the data, which will allow the website to be displayed.

As for the Azure VPN Gateway, it is a specialized VNet. It allows for making these two types of connections:

- **Point-to-site**: This connects a computer to a VNet. The connection is initiated from the computer. This is generally used with remote workers, such as with laptops or mobile devices.

- **Site-to-site**: This connects one separate VNet to another, in which the encrypted traffic is passed through a secure virtual tunnel. This is usually when you want to connect the VPNs to those on-premises locations. You can have anywhere from ten to 30 site-to-site connections.

For both, you can get throughput of 100 Mbps to 1.25 Gbps. There is also the option of having a **Border Gateway Protocol (BGP)**, which provides for customizing the routing paths, policies, and rules.

A VNet can only have one Azure VPN Gateway. However, it can still be configured to connect to multiple locations, such as other VNets or on-premises environments. Azure VPN Gateway will have two or more specialized VMs, which have their own subnet called a gateway subnet. They provide for routing the services.

ExpressRoute

If you want faster networking connections between Microsoft data centers and your own on-premises environment, then ExpressRoute is a good option. This makes a connection that does not pass through the public internet. This allows for not only higher speeds, but also more security (which can include encryption of traffic) and reliability. There may also be lower costs.

To sum up what we have covered in this chapter, *Table 5.1* shows details about the various Azure networking services:

Azure networking service	Description	Use case	Features
Network security group	Filters network traffic using access control lists.	Provide security by controlling traffic within Azure VNets	• Inbound and outbound traffic filtering • Custom security rules
Peering	Allows communication between subnets of different VNets.	Connect VNets or extend to on-premises environments securely	• ASN requirement • IPv4 and IPv6 support
Azure DNS	Allows for easier-to-remember names for internal IP addresses.	Manage domain name resolution using an external DNS provider.	• Integration with Azure services • Secure internal DNS resolution
Azure VPN Gateway	Allows for secure connections using VPN tunnels	Point-to-site and site-to-site connections	• Encryption of traffic • Supports multiple VPN connections • Configured for routing and policies
ExpressRoute	Private connection between on-premises infrastructure and Microsoft data centers	Useful for financial institutions, large enterprises, and latency-sensitive applications	• Security with optional encryption • Cost-effective for high-bandwidth needs

Table 5.1: Comparisons of Azure networking services

Conclusion

In this chapter, we looked at networking for the Azure platform. We learned about the core infrastructure and protocols. We also covered the myriad of services available, including network security groups, peering, the Azure DNS, Azure VPN Gateways, and ExpressRoute. They are essential for making Azure more secure, scalable, and reliable. In the next chapter, we will look at storage in Azure.

Sample questions

Read the following questions to assess your understanding:

1. **In what way does packet switching improve data transmission in a network?**

    a. It allows data to be sent in reverse order.

    b. It reduces network bottlenecks and congestion by breaking data into smaller packets.

c. It encrypts data to and from the network.

d. It provides automatic error checking.

Correct answer: b

Explanation: Packet switching is at the core of networks like the internet. It breaks down data traffic into smaller packets. They are then reassembled when they reach their destination. This process allows for lower latency and improved efficiency.

2. **What is a network protocol?**

    a. It is a policy for enforcing security rules.

    b. It manages power consumption.

    c. It is a type of virtualization.

    d. It is a collection of rules and standards for the transmission of data for networks.

Correct answer: d

Explanation: A network needs protocols to manage the processes. It will include rules for data transmission and reception.

3. **What is the purpose of the server in the client-server architecture?**

    a. To share resources and services such as memory, CPU power, and data with the clients.

    b. To allow for peering of the network.

    c. To provide access to virtual private networks.

    d. To manage legacy systems like mainframes.

Correct answer: a

Explanation: The client-server architecture is a model that is about managing resources and services, allowing for network communications.

4. **What is a primary difference between a public domain name and an internal Azure DNS name?**

    a. You configure a public domain with PowerShell, and you use the Azure CLI for the Azure DNS domain.

    b. You can only access an Azure DNS name within Azure, whereas a public domain is accessible via the internet.

    c. A public domain can have any name, whereas the Azure DNS is limited to no more than ten characters.

    d. The Azure DNS is more efficient when accessing the internet.

Correct answer: b

Explanation: You can only use the Azure DNS name within your Azure private network. A public domain, on the other hand, is available on the public internet.

5. **What is the purpose of a firewall in a network?**

   a. To set user authentication.

   b. To optimize the network performance.

   c. To control inbound and outbound traffic in a network.

   d. To allow for high-speed connections.

   Correct answer: c

   Explanation: A firewall can be software or hardware. It is configured to control inbound and outbound traffic of a network. The purpose is to improve security.

6. **What is the difference between a local area network (LAN) and a wide area network (WAN)?**

   a. A LAN covers a larger geographical space than a WAN.

   b. A WAN typically has lower latency than a LAN.

   c. A LAN is limited to a specific area, like a building, while a WAN connects multiple locations over larger distances.

   d. A WAN is a physical network, while a LAN is solely based on software.

   Correct answer: c

   Explanation: A LAN is for small locations and areas, such as offices. A WAN, on the other hand, is for larger networks. It can even be for cities or countries.

7. **What is the key advantage of Azure ExpressRoute?**

   a. It is an alternative to a firewall.

   b. It is for managing mobile devices.

   c. It replaces the TCP/IP protocol.

   d. It creates a connection between Microsoft data centers and on-premises environments.

   Correct answer: d

   Explanation: With ExpressRoute, you can create a connection between Microsoft data centers and on-premises environments. This means that the data does not pass through the public internet. This allows for higher speeds and security. There may also be lower costs.

8. **What is Ethernet in networking?**

   a. A system that manages firewalls.

   b. A protocol for high-speed, wired data transmission between devices.

    c. A protocol for encrypting data.

    d. A system to monitor networks.

Correct answer: b

Explanation: Ethernet is a widely used protocol for networking. It helps to provide high-speed data transmissions.

9. **What is a key benefit of Fibre Channel in networking?**

    a. Connecting on-premises systems to the cloud.

    b. Supporting high-speed networking between servers and storage systems.

    c. Connecting mobile devices to the cloud.

    d. Allowing for LAN connections.

Correct answer: b

Explanation: Fibre Channel is a system that provides for high-speed networking. It connects servers to shared storage, and the speeds are up to 128 Gbps.

10. **What is the main difference between point-to-site (P2S) and site-to-site (S2S) connections in Azure VPN Gateway?**

    a. P2S connects a device to a VNet, whereas S2S connects entire networks.

    b. P2S connects to a firewall, while S2S does not.

    c. S2S is exclusively for cloud connections, whereas P2S is for on-premises environments.

    d. P2S connections are encrypted, while S2S connections are not.

Correct answer: a

Explanation: A P2S connection provides for a device, such as a laptop or smartphone, to make a secure connection to a VNet. This is often used for scenarios like remote working. As for S2S, this connects a complete network through a virtual tunnel.

11. **What is a VPN?**

    a. It lowers latency by avoiding network firewalls.

    b. It blocks access to certain websites.

    c. It replaces the need for **internet service providers (ISPs)**.

    d. It allows for secure and encrypted connections over potentially unsafe networks.

Correct answer: b

Explanation: With a VPN, a user can securely access a private network while using a public network, like the Internet, when using a Wi-Fi connection. This is done by using encryption of traffic.

12. **What is the role of Azure VNet Peering?**

 a. It connects subnets within the same VNet.

 b. It assigns public IP addresses.

 c. It enables secure, private communication between different VNets.

 d. It provides firewall protection.

Correct answer: c

Explanation: VNet peering connects separate VNets, allowing resources in each to communicate securely and efficiently using Azure's backbone network. No public internet or additional gateways are required.

13. **What is required when setting up Azure VNet Peering?**

 a. No overlapping IP address ranges between the VNets.

 b. Installation of IPv6 addresses only.

 c. A Fibre Channel connection.

 d. An **autonomous system number (ASN)**.

Correct answer: a

Explanation: To establish VNet peering, the VNets cannot have overlapping IP address ranges. ASN is not required for VNet peering—it applies only to advanced services like ExpressRoute or Azure Peering Service.

14. **What does an NSG do in Azure?**

 a. It assigns dynamic and static IP addresses for VMs.

 b. It filters network traffic based on predefined security rules.

 c. It encrypts data that flows through a network.

 d. It is a replacement for a firewall.

Correct answer: b

Explanation: With an NSG, you can filter network traffic by using an access control list. You can do this for blocking inbound and outbound traffic in a network, according to your own rules and policies.

15. **How is the priority of security rules set for an NSG?**

 a. All rules have the same priority.

 b. They are based on Azure standards.

 c. Rules are evaluated based on their priority number, with lower numbers taking precedence.

 d. They are only for role permissions.

Correct answer: c

Explanation: You assign priority numbers for the NSG. It is usually recommended to have gaps between priority levels, like 100, 200, and 300. This allows for changes in the future.

16. **What is the role of a VNet?**
    a. To create a private network that securely communicates with other private or internet networks.
    b. To enable a virtual firewall.
    c. To operate a LAN.
    d. To create a virtual machine.

Correct answer: a

Explanation: With a VNet, you can create a private network within Azure, which provides for secure communication between private and public networks.

17. **Why are VMs in an Azure VNet kept separate from each other by default?**
    a. For disaster recovery.
    b. To provide better security.
    c. For lowering storage costs.
    d. To use IPv6 protocols.

Correct answer: b

Explanation: The default option for a VNet is to keep the VMs separate. This prohibits unauthorized access, unless there is a specific configuration for it.

18. **What role does a subnet provide for an Azure VNet?**
    a. It allows for a direct connection to the public internet.
    b. It provides encryption of data traffic.
    c. It divides a VNet with a range of private IP addresses.
    d. It allows for authentication.

Correct answer: c

Explanation: A subnet subdivides a VNet, with each having a range of IP addresses. This helps to better manage resources for security and scalability.

19. **What is a key benefit of IPv6 compared to IPv4?**
    a. IPv6 is significantly faster than IPv4.
    b. IPv6 does not need routers and switches.

    c.   IPv6 allows for a much larger number of IP addresses.

    d.   IPv6 automatically connects to a firewall.

Correct answer: c

Explanation: A key issue with IPv4 is the limitations on the number of IP addresses, but with IPv6, this has been addressed.

20. **What is a key benefit of Data Center Bridging (DCB)?**

    a.   It is integrated with a firewall.

    b.   It improves traffic management by implementing priority-based flow control.

    c.   It encrypts all data flows.

    d.   It does not require switches or routers.

Correct answer: b

Explanation: DCB improves Ethernet networking by using priority-based flow control. This helps manage network traffic more efficiently and ensures better performance and reliability.

Join our Discord space

Join our Discord workspace for latest updates, offers, tech happenings around the world, new releases, and sessions with the authors:

https://discord.bpbonline.com

CHAPTER 6
Storage

Introduction

In this chapter, we will look at storage capabilities in Azure. We will start by getting an overview of this topic, such as the Azure storage account. We will then review the ways data is protected through redundancy. There is an elaborate section on different storage tiers, which vary in terms of access and retention of the data.

This chapter will look at blob storage, which is at the core of Azure storage. We will also look at other options, including AzCopy, Azure Files, and Azure Migrate. These allow for more efficient management of complex storage requirements, such as those in on-premises environments or involving enormous amounts of data.

Structure

This chapter covers the following topics:

- Overview
- Redundancy
- Storage tiers
- Blob storage

- Creating an Azure storage account
- AzCopy
- Azure Files
- Azure Migrate

Objectives

By the end of this chapter, you will have a good understanding of the storage options for Azure. This will include setting up an Azure storage account and using blob storage. You will also understand how to manage complex data storage needs, such as for on-premises environments or where there are substantial amounts of data. This will involve using tools like AzCopy, Azure Files, and Azure Migrate.

You will also gain hands-on skills such as creating containers, uploading and managing files in blob storage, and using command-line tools for efficient data transfer. Moreover, you will learn how to plan and execute cloud migrations with Azure Migrate and implement hybrid storage solutions using Azure File Sync.

Overview

IDC estimates that the amount of data generated in 2025 will come up to 175 **zettabytes** (**ZBs**), up from 33 ZBs in 2018.[1] Nearly half of this will be stored in cloud platforms. A ZB is equal to one trillion gigabytes. To put this into perspective, it is about the size of 250 billion DVDs.

The growth of data is expected to remain strong. Some of the drivers of this include:

- **Artificial intelligence**: Training models, especially those from OpenAI, Microsoft, and Amazon, require enormous amounts of data. Some of them include much of the internet. More models are also trained on images and video, which means using enormous amounts of data.

- **Mobile**: Smartphones are a part of the daily lives of billions of people. These devices are also consuming huge amounts of data, especially with video.

- **IoT**: This is another category seeing strong growth. Sensors are becoming ubiquitous for collecting data about homes, offices, and factories.

- **Streaming**: Services like Netflix, Peacock, and Disney++ have millions of people who watch movies on the internet.

With the flood of data, there is a need for storage, but this can be costly. Handling large volumes means using sophisticated systems like direct-attached storage, **network-attached storage** (**NAS**), and **storage area networks** (**SANs**), but with a cloud platform like Azure, you can affordably access storage on demand. It is seemingly endless. The Azure storage account has

---

1 https://edgedelta.com/company/blog/data-market-size-and-forecast

various solutions, which are considered IaaS. This is generally for working with applications or backup.

An Azure storage account will have a unique namespace where you can manage different kinds of data, such as:

- Blobs
- Files
- Queues
- Tables

For the AZ-900 exam, you will need to know about the first two. They are a part of **General-Purpose v2** (**GPv2**), which is the most common. This type of Azure storage account can store up to 5 petabytes of data, which is equivalent to 5 million GBs. The fee is fairly low, usually 2 cents per GB per month or lower.

You can use GPv2 for data lakes. These are massive storage systems that can store exabytes of data, which are usually for sophisticated use cases like AI or data analytics. While a GPv2 account is powerful, you may still need a system that has even higher performance. There are several premium Azure storage accounts for this. They use advanced **solid-state disks** (**SSDs**), which provide low latency. With an Azure storage account, there are several options to consider. They include redundancy and storage tiers.

Redundancy

To protect your data, Azure automatically maintains multiple copies. The exact replication approach depends on the redundancy option you choose. This involves trade-offs for cost, performance, and availability. The redundancy setting applies at the storage account level. This means that all data in the account follows the same replication method.

There are two categories of redundancy: within a primary region and across a secondary region. Primary region redundancy means all copies of your data stay within the same Azure region. These are the options:

- **Locally redundant storage (LRS)**: Stores three copies of your data within a single data center in one region. This is the lowest-cost option but offers the least protection against regional failures.

- **Zone-redundant storage (ZRS)**: Spreads three copies of your data across three availability zones within one region. This improves availability (11 nines, or 99.999999999%) because the copies are in physically separate datacenters in that region.

Next, with secondary region redundancy, this replicates your primary storage (LRS or ZRS) to a paired Azure region, located hundreds of miles away. This provides added protection in case of a regional outage. These are the options:

- **Geo-redundant storage (GRS)**: This is LRS combined with replication to a secondary region. Data is first stored locally in triplicate within one data center (LRS), then asynchronously copied to a secondary region.

- **Geo-zone-redundant storage (GZRS)**: This is ZRS combined with replication to a secondary region. Data is replicated across three zones in the primary region (ZRS) and then asynchronously copied to a secondary region.

Azure storage also includes automatic disk-level failover within a region. If a disk fails, Azure transparently restores service from the remaining replicas. This means your data remains safe and available without any action required.

Storage tiers

While Azure storage is relatively inexpensive, the costs can still add up when the volumes of data increase. To manage this, you can adjust for the level of access to the data and how long the information should be retained.

Azure has four storage tiers for this:

- **Hot tier**: This is the default option. It optimizes the costs based on the frequency with which the data is stored or modified. The cost to store the data is higher, but the costs for accessing the data are lower. The hot tier tends to be more cost-effective for data that is used often.

- **Cool tier**: The costs for storage are much lower than those for the hot tier, but the access costs are higher. The data should be stored for a minimum of 30 days. Otherwise, Azure will impose a penalty. This will also be the case with the cold and archive tiers.

- **Cold tier**: This is when access to the data is minimal. However, if there is a need to retrieve the information, the process will be quick. Compared to the cool tier, the cold tier has lower storage costs and higher access costs. The data should be stored for at least 90 days.

- **Archive**: This is for data that is rarely accessed. If there is a retrieval, the process can take days. The archive option is usually for data that must be retained for legal or compliance reasons. Azure requires that the information be stored for a minimum of 180 days.

Blob storage

Binary large object (BLOB) storage is the most popular in Azure. It is used for storing large amounts of unstructured data. This is information that does not have a predefined organization or format. Examples include videos, social media posts, blogs, Slack, and emails.

Structured data, on the other hand, has a clear structure or schema. Often, there will be tables that have rows and columns, such as with a relational database or spreadsheet. This type of data tends to be easier to process compared to unstructured data.

With a blob, you can store any type of file, such as JPG, PDF, CSV, or TXT. These are some of the use cases:

- Streaming video
- Hosting images, such as for a website
- Providing access to documents
- Storing log files
- Backing up data

You can configure a blob to be accessed privately or through the public internet. With private access, you can use the Azure Storage REST API, Azure CLI, or Azure PowerShell. There are also libraries for programming languages like Java, Python, .NET, Node.js, and Go. You can also use the SSH File Transfer Protocol for secure access to blobs.

There is a hierarchical structure with a blob, which you can find in *Figure 6.1*:

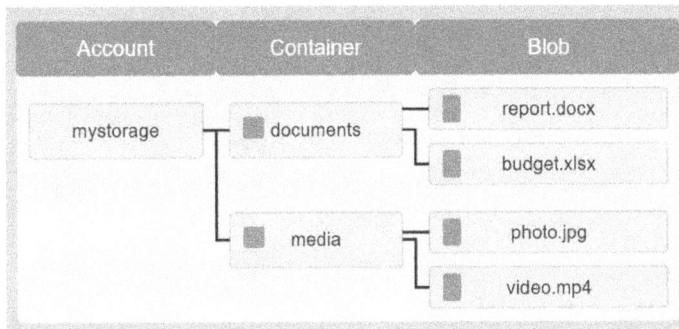

Figure 6.1: Blob hierarchical structure

At the top, there is the storage account. This will have one or more containers. In *Figure 6.1*, the containers are for documents and media. Then, within each of them, there are files, which are the blobs. However, a blob can only have one container.

To access a blob, you can use a URL. An example is:

https://mystorage.blob.core.windows.net/documents/report.docx

There are three types of blobs:

- **Block blobs**: These store text and binary data. Each block blob can store up to 190.7 TBs.
- **Append blobs**: These are connected block blobs. These are usually for logs of VMs.
- **Page blobs**: These will store a group of files up to 8TBs, which are randomly accessed. These are used as virtual hard drive files.

Creating an Azure storage account

We will create an Azure storage account. These are the steps:

1. Log in to the Azure portal.

2. Click **Create a resource**.

3. On the left sidebar, select **Storage**.

4. Click **Create**, which is under the heading of **Storage Account**.

5. *Figure 6.2* shows the form to create a storage account:

> **Create a storage account** ···
>
> __Basics__   Advanced   Networking   Data protection   Encryption   Tags   Review + create
>
> Azure Storage is a Microsoft-managed service providing cloud storage that is highly available, secure, durable, scalable, and redundant. Azure Storage includes Azure Blobs (objects), Azure Data Lake Storage Gen2, Azure Files, Azure Queues, and Azure Tables. The cost of your storage account depends on the usage and the options you choose below. Learn more about Azure storage accounts ⬈
>
> **Project details**
>
> Select the subscription in which to create the new storage account. Choose a new or existing resource group to organize and manage your storage account together with other resources.
>
> Subscription *   Pay-As-You-Go ⌄
>
> Resource group *   AIGroup ⌄
> Create new
>
> **Instance details**
>
> Storage account name * ⓘ   _____
>
> Region * ⓘ   (US) West US ⌄
>
> Previous | Next | Review + create

Figure 6.2: Form to create a storage account

6. Select the subscription, resource group, and region. Generally, you want a closer region for a lower cost.

7. Create a unique name for the storage account.

8. Select a primary service, which is either Azure blob or data lake, Azure Files, or tables and queues. Select Azure Blob.

9. For the performance option, you can either select **Standard** or **Premium**, which has lower latency but has a higher cost. Select **Standard**.

10. The options for **Redundancy** depend on whether you select **Standard** or **Premium**. If you choose **Standard**, you have a choice between **LRS** or **GRS**. If you select **Premium**, then you can only have **LRS**. Also, you can select the account type: **block blobs, file shares, or page blobs**.

11. If you select **Advanced**, there are many configuration options. You can set parameters for security and access protocols.

12. For the **Data protection** tab, you have options for recovery of data if there is accidental or erroneous deletion or modification. There is also version tracking for blobs and access control.

13. In the **Encryption** tab, you can choose the type of encryption for your blobs.

14. Select **Review + create**.

The data protection capabilities are powerful. Therefore, we will take a deeper look at these. The following are the options:

- **Enable point-in-time restore for containers**: You can revert to an earlier version of the blob.

- **Enable soft delete for blobs**: You can recover blobs that were marked for deletion. This also includes those that were overwritten.

- **Enable soft delete for containers**: You can recover containers that were marked for deletion.

- **Enable soft delete for file shares**: This allows the recovery of file shares that you marked for deletion.

For the last three options, you can specify the days to retain the blobs, containers, or file shares. The default is seven days.

Another useful capability is to enable version-level immutability support. This allows you to create a time-based retention policy at the account level for all blob versions.

For the Azure storage account we created, you will get a screen with some details about it. These include an ID number and start time, but the next step is to click on **Go to resource**. *Figure 6.3* shows the dashboard:

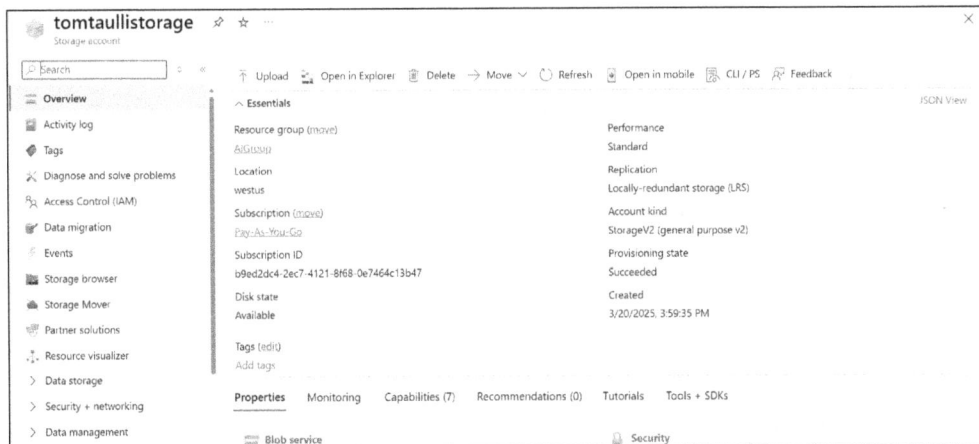

Figure 6.3: *Dashboard for an Azure storage account*

We can create a container by taking these steps:

1. Select **Data storage** on the left sidebar.

2. Click **Containers**.

3. Choose **+ Container**.

4. Enter a name: `first-container`.

5. You can make the container anonymous. For example, you could do this for security if you have images for your website.

6. If you click the **Advanced** tab, there are other security features, such as encryption.

7. Select **Create**.

8. *Figure 6.4* shows the container:

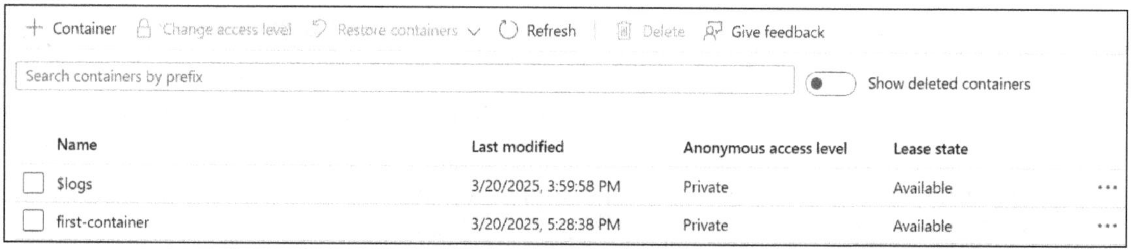

Figure 6.4: The listing of containers

9. Click **first-container**.

10. Click **Upload**.

11. *Figure 6.5* shows a form that allows you to upload files to the container:

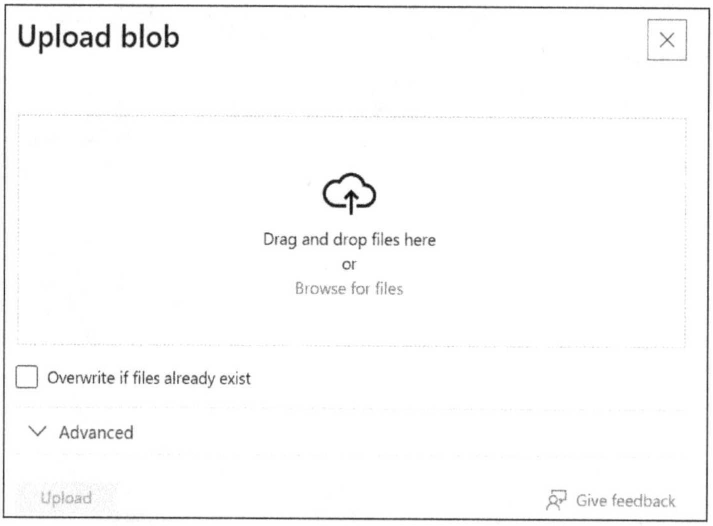

Figure 6.5: A form to select files for a container

12. You can drag and drop files to the form or click **Browse for files**.

13. If you select the **Advanced** tab, you can configure the files for blob type, storage tier, and encryption.

14. Click **Upload**.

15. Click on one of the files you have uploaded.

16. You will get a profile for it, which you can see in *Figure 6.6*:

4 - Role of Data.doc ...
Blob

🖫 Save   ✕ Discard   ↓ Download   ○ Refresh   🗑 Delete   ⇄ Change tier   𝒶 Acquire lease   𝒶 Break lease   𝒶 Give feedback

| Overview | Versions | Snapshots | Edit | Generate SAS |

Properties

URL	https://tomtaullistorage...
LAST MODIFIED	3/20/2025, 5:38:30 PM
CREATION TIME	3/20/2025, 5:38:30 PM
VERSION ID	-
TYPE	Block blob
SIZE	179 KiB
ACCESS TIER	Hot (Inferred)
ACCESS TIER LAST MODIFIED	N/A
ARCHIVE STATUS	-
REHYDRATE PRIORITY	-
SERVER ENCRYPTED	true
ETAG	0x8DD6810B3D690A0
VERSION-LEVEL IMMUTABILITY POLICY	Disabled
CACHE-CONTROL	

Figure 6.6: A form to select files for a container

17. The URL is the address from which you can access this file. On the icon on the right side, this will copy it to your clipboard. However, if you run this in your browser, you will get an error. You will need to create a **shared access signature** (**SAS**) token to allow access, which will be appended to the URL. You can configure this for expiration times and access constraints.

When managing your files, you will usually use the Storage Browser, which is accessible in the Azure portal. These are the steps to use it:

1. In your storage account, select **Storage Browser** in the left sidebar.

2. Click **Blob containers**.

3. You will see your containers. You can click on one of them to view your files, shown as follows:

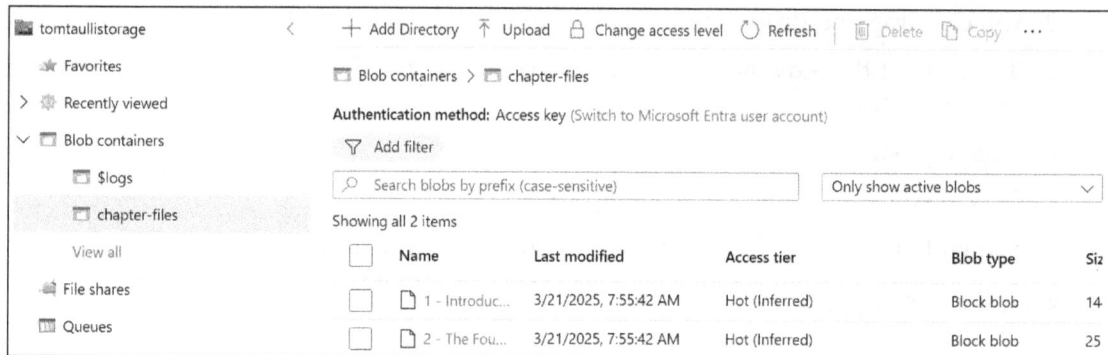

Figure 6.7: The Storage Browser

The Storage Browser is similar to the File Explorer in Windows. You can create and delete directories, add filters for viewing files, rename files, and search the blobs. You can also change the access level for users.

AzCopy

As you use your Azure storage account, you will create various containers and many files. If you want to transfer files from one container to another, one approach is to use the browser. You will first download the files to your local computer and then upload them to the other container.

However, this process can be time-consuming if you are transferring a large number of files. It can also add to the costs. The reason is that you will be charged for the bandwidth used.

A better option is to use AzCopy, which is a **command-line interface** (**CLI**) system for file transfers. You can download AzCopy on your computer. It is available for operating systems like Windows, Linux, and MacOS. You can also use the Azure Cloud Shell.

Regardless of which you choose, you will need to create a SAS token for both the source of the files in the container and the destination container. AzCopy not only transfers files but also entire directories in one operation. You can also create scripts that automate the process.

Azure Files

An on-premises file server is a network that centralizes the storage and management of files. It is based on a client-server architecture, where the server stores the files and the client can access them through a **local area network** (**LAN**). It can be configured to control access, such as based on roles.

Azure Files is a cloud-based version of a file server. Some of the benefits of this system include:

- **Fully managed**: You do not have to set up and manage the hardware or OS, such as with patching for security updates.

- **Configuration**: You can use PowerShell or AzureShell to create, mount, and manage **Azure File.**

- **Sharing**: Azure Files supports **Server Message Block (SMB)** and **Network File System (NFS)** protocols. This allows you to share files across applications and VMs.

- **Development**: Azure Files has APIs, which you can use to develop applications that use the storage system. In fact, this system is a common way for lift and shift migration to the cloud.

- **Cross-platform compatibility**: You can use Azure Files on Windows, Linux, and macOS.

- **Protection**: Azure Files automatically has the benefits of redundancy, data recovery, and failover features.

Another capability is Azure File Sync. This is where you have a hybrid environment, with both cloud and on-premises storage. This system will synchronize the files, such as when there are modifications, new files uploaded, files deleted, or files moved.

A strategy for this is to use cloud tiering. You will have frequently used files cached on your local server, and the others in the cloud. This provides a more cost-effective approach to file management.

Azure Migrate

Migration is the process of taking an organization's IT resources, like data and applications, and moving them to the cloud. This can allow for lower costs, more scale, higher performance, and enhanced security.

However, the migration process can often be challenging, especially for large organizations. They will usually have old technology that can be difficult to transfer to the cloud. Another issue is that there are complex dependencies among various systems. Even a small change can have a major impact, such as with a disruption of certain functions or features. This can lead to higher costs and poor customer experiences.

A research report from McKinsey highlights the potential risks of migrations. It found that 75% of them were over budget and 37% were behind schedule.[2]

To help improve the migration process, there is the Azure Migrate tool, which is free. It helps transfer many types of IT assets like servers, databases, web applications, storage, and file servers.

Azure Migrate has three main steps:

1. **Discover**: Azure Migrate will identify the workloads in your IT environment. Microsoft recommends the Azure Migrate appliance for this, which analyzes your on-premises

2 https://curiositysoftware.medium.com/the-research-is-clear-too-many-migration-projects-fail-cff52b32e340

resources, with support for VMware and Hyper-V virtualization setups, as well as physical servers. It can also assess other cloud provider environments. This is done using a PowerShell script on a Windows server.

2. **Assess**: Azure Migrate will evaluate what resources are ready for migration to Azure. This will involve estimates for the types of cloud assets that are needed for setup, like VMs, and the configurations. There will also be a dependency analysis and cost estimate for the migration.

3. **Migrate**: This is where you perform the migration to Azure.

For a migration, there may be enormous amounts of data, but uploading this information could be expensive and time-consuming.

Microsoft has a suite of products that allow for a more streamlined transfer of data. This involves sending a physical storage system to your organization. You will connect this to your network, and the information will be transferred to it. The process will use encryption. You will then send the system back to Microsoft, where the information will be uploaded to your storage account, and the storage system will be wiped.

These are the three types of storage systems:

- **Data Box**: This has a storage capacity of 100 TB.

- **Data Box Disk**: This is an SSD, which holds up to 40 TB.

- **Data Box Heavy**: This has a storage capacity of 1 PB. A Data Box Heavy is large, weighing roughly 500 pounds. It has rollers at the bottom of the system to allow it to be moved. It is 26 inches wide, 48 inches long, and 28 inches high.

To sum up the concepts of blob storage, AzCopy, Azure Files, and Azure Migrate, you can refer to *Table 6.1*:

Feature	Blob Storage	AzCopy	Azure Files	Azure Migrate
Purpose	Store large amounts of unstructured data like images, videos, logs, and documents.	Transfer files efficiently to and from Azure storage accounts.	File sharing system that acts like a traditional file server.	Tool for discovering, assessing, and migrating on-premises workloads to Azure.
Common use cases	Hosting media files, streaming, backup, storing logs, and website images.	Transfer between containers, bulk file moves, and scripted data migration.	File sharing across platforms, lift-and-shift apps, and hybrid cloud storage.	Cloud migration, dependency mapping, on-prem discovery.
Access management	Private and public access via SAS tokens or secure protocols.	Requires SAS token for source and destination containers.	Role-based access, encryption, and hybrid sync.	Permissions based on Azure roles.

Table 6.1: Comparisons of Azure storage options

Conclusion

In this chapter, we covered the topics for Azure storage that you will find on the exam. We learned about the Azure storage account and how to set it up. We then reviewed how to use blob storage to store different types of files. We also learned how to use tools like AzCopy, Azure Files, and Azure Migrate for complex IT environments. In the next chapter, we will look at core security capabilities for Azure, such as identity and access solutions.

Sample questions

1. **What is the role of the GPv2 Azure storage account?**

    a. To manage user authentication.

    b. To host websites.

    c. To store and manage blobs and files for applications and backups.

    d. To operate VMs.

    Correct answer: c

    Explanation: With a GPv2 storage account, you can store blobs and files. This is an effective solution for applications and backup systems. This is the most common storage account in Azure.

2. **Why is Azure storage a cost-effective method for managing large amounts of data?**

    a. It uses SSDs.

    b. It offers a flat-rate subscription business model.

    c. It allows scalable, on-demand storage with low cost per GB.

    d. It specialized for the needs of file servers.

    Correct answer: c

    Explanation: Azure storage offers affordable, on-demand storage with rates as low as 2 cents per GB per month. This makes it a scalable and cost-efficient option for large data volumes.

3. **What is a good option for an Azure storage account when you need very low latency?**

    a. GPv2 account

    b. Standard storage account

    c. Archive storage tier

    d. Premium storage account with SSDs

    Correct answer: d

Explanation: The premium storage account is for low-latency requirements. This type of storage uses sophisticated SSDs.

4. **What is a ZB?**

    a. One trillion gigabytes

    b. One million petabytes

    c. One billion gigabytes

    d. One billion megabytes

Correct answer: a

Explanation: A ZB is equal to one trillion gigabytes.

5. **What is a common use case for a data lake in Azure?**

    a. Hosting static websites

    b. Running VMs

    c. Performing AI and data analytics on massive datasets

    d. Sending notifications

Correct answer: c

Explanation: Data lakes store massive amounts of data. Generally, they are for intensive use cases like AI or big data analytics.

6. **What is the main trade-off when selecting a redundancy option in Azure Storage?**

    a. CPU speed versus the amount of RAM

    b. Cost versus availability

    c. The latency versus the billing cycle

    d. Storage capacity versus CPU speed

Correct answer: b

Explanation: When evaluating redundancy, there is a trade-off between the cost of storage and the availability. For example, LRS has a lower cost but also lower availability when compared to ZRS or GZRS.

7. **This redundancy type stores data across three availability zones in a primary region.**

    a. **Locally redundant storage (LRS)**

    b. **Geo-redundant storage (GRS)**

    c. **Zone-redundant storage (ZRS)**

    d. **Geo-zone-redundant storage (GZRS)**

Correct answer: c

Explanation: **Zone-redundant storage (ZRS)** copies data across three availability zones. This is done within the primary region.

8. **Why would an organization use more than one Azure storage account?**

   a. To use load balancing

   b. To use ZRS

   c. To get a discount

   d. To apply different redundancy settings for different data types

Correct answer: d

Explanation: An Azure account must use the same type of data. This is why an organization would use multiple accounts. This can allow for getting levels of redundancy and availability.

9. **What is the key difference between GRS and GZRS?**

   a. GZRS uses LRS while GRS uses ZRS

   b. GZRS includes zone-redundancy in the primary region before geo-replication

   c. GZRS only works with queues

   d. GRS stores data in multiple secondary regions

Correct answer: b

Explanation: GZRS allows zone-redundancy in the primary region by using ZRS, and then replicates that data to a secondary region.

10. **What is a key advantage of using the hot storage in Azure?**

    a. You get the lowest costs for data that is rarely accessed

    b. You get fast retrieval and minimal access costs for frequently used data

    c. It allows for long-term legal compliance and infrequent access

    d. It allows for archiving data

Correct answer: b

Explanation: If you have data that requires frequent access and modifications, then the hot tier is a good option. The storage costs are higher, but the access costs are generally lower.

11. **When should you use cool storage?**

    a. When you need a high level of security for your data.

    b. When you want daily access to data.

    c.   When you have data that is accessed infrequently.

    d.   When the data must be retained for at least 10 years.

Correct answer: c

Explanation: Cool storage is a good option when you have infrequently accessed data. For Azure, the minimum is 30 days. If you do not meet this requirement, you will pay a penalty.

12. **What best describes archive storage in Azure?**

    a.   Storage that meets the requirements for the U.S. federal government

    b.   Storage for a minimum of 30 days

    c.   Access for streaming videos

    d.   Storage for a minimum of 180 days

Correct answer: d

Explanation: Archive storage is for data that is rarely accessed. This is usually for data that must meet compliance or regulatory requirements. For Azure, the data for archive storage must be stored for a minimum of 180 days.

13. **Blob storage in Azure usually stores this type of data.**

    a.   Only structured data, such as from spreadsheets or databases

    b.   Large amounts of unstructured data

    c.   Only code files

    d.   Azure billing information

Correct answer: b

Explanation: With Azure Blob Storage, you can store unstructured data. This is information that does not have a predefined structure or format. Examples of unstructured data include email, blogs, videos, images, and logs.

14. **The following is correct about blob storage containers in Azure.**

    a.   A blob can be placed in multiple containers.

    b.   Containers organize blobs within a storage account.

    c.   Containers are used only for structured data.

    d.   Each blob must be in its own storage account.

Correct answer: b

Explanation: You will set up a blob in your Azure storage account. It can only belong to one container.

15. **You would use this protocol for secure access to a blob in Azure.**

    a. FTP

    b. HCP

    c. SMTP

    d. **SSH File Transfer Protocol (SFTP)**

    Correct answer: d

    Explanation: If you want a high degree of security when accessing a blob in Azure, you can use the **SSH File Transfer Protocol (SFTP)**.

16. **Which type of Azure blob is a virtual hard drive?**

    a. Block blob

    b. Page blob

    c. Append blob

    d. Extract blob

    Correct answer: b

    Explanation: A page blob allows for random access for reading and writing operations. This makes it similar to a physical hard drive.

17. **This allows you to recover a blob in Azure that was accidentally overwritten or deleted.**

    a. Hard delete

    b. Non delete

    c. Version-level immutability

    d. Soft delete

    Correct answer: d

    Explanation: With soft delete, you can recover deleted or overwritten blobs. This is for a certain retention period.

18. **In the Azure portal, what tool for managing blobs and containers is similar to the Windows File Explorer?**

    a. Azure File Sync

    b. **Shared Access Signature (SAS)**

    c. Azure Explorer

    d. Storage Browser

    Correct answer: d

Explanation: With the Storage Browser, you can manage containers and blobs. Some of the features include renaming files, creating directories, and adjusting access levels.

19. **Why would you use AzCopy versus the Azure portal when transferring a large number of files between containers?**

    a. It reduces RAM usage on virtual machines.

    b. It eliminates the need to pay for file storage.

    c. It avoids unnecessary bandwidth charges and is faster.

    d. It is the most secure option.

Correct answer: c

Explanation: AzCopy makes direct transfers with containers. This means not paying for bandwidth charges. The process is also much faster when compared to using the Azure portal.

20. **What is the purpose of Azure File Sync with cloud tiering?**

    a. To eliminate the need for local storage.

    b. To provide maximum security for files.

    c. To cache frequently used files locally while storing less-used files in the cloud.

    d. To optimize blob storage.

Correct answer: c

Explanation: Cloud tiering is a technique used with Azure File Sync. It is for frequently accessed files that are cached on local systems, which increases performance. As for less-accessed files, these remain in the cloud. This provides for a more cost-effective solution for storage.

Join our Discord space

Join our Discord workspace for latest updates, offers, tech happenings around the world, new releases, and sessions with the authors:

https://discord.bpbonline.com

CHAPTER 7
Identity, Access, and Security

Introduction

This chapter will review identity, access, and security capabilities for Azure. We will begin by understanding the overview of security, such as the various threats like ransomware and phishing. This will be followed by understanding identity, which is about authentication and authorization of users into a network or application. The Microsoft Entra ID handles these capabilities.

Furthermore, we will cover the different types of security services for Azure. These include Azure **Active Directory** (**AD**) Conditional Access, multifactor authentication, role-based access control, and Microsoft Defender for Cloud. We will also look at important security concepts like the Zero Trust model, passwordless, and defense in depth.

Structure

This chapter covers the following topics:

- The importance of security
- Identity
- Microsoft Entra ID
- Authentication and authorization

- The Zero Trust model
- Defense in depth
- Microsoft Defender for cloud

Objectives

By the end of this chapter, you will gain practical skills for implementing and managing identity, access, and security features on the Azure platform. You will learn how to use Microsoft Entra ID for secure authentication and authorization, configure conditional access policies, implement multifactor and passwordless authentication, and manage user roles through RBAC. Moreover, you will understand how to apply security strategies like the Zero Trust model and defense in depth, and use tools such as Microsoft Defender for Cloud.

The importance of security

The cybersecurity field emerged in the 1960s when computers were networked. The reason behind this was that it was possible to send software to other systems.

In 1971, *Bob Thomas* created the first worm, which is malware that copies itself across networks. It displayed the image, *I'm the creeper: catch me if you can*. It was relatively harmless, though. Thomas created the program as an experiment, not as a way to be malicious. His goal was to test the ability to replicate software.

Ray Tomlinson would then develop software called the **Reaper**, which deleted Creeper. This was the first antivirus software system.

Since then, the cybersecurity field has grown significantly in size and importance. In 2024, *Grand View Research* estimated the value of the market at $245.62 billion and predicted that it would grow to $500.70 billion by 2030.[1]

The cybersecurity landscape has seen a proliferation of risks. According to *Microsoft*, its customers are subjected to more than 600 million cybersecurity attacks every day. The company notes: *These cyberattacks are continuing at a breathtaking scale, and as they increasingly put human health at risk, the stakes for stopping them could not be higher.*[2]

There are many types of cybersecurity threats. Most involve malware, which is short for malicious software. It accesses unauthorized systems to make them inoperable, destroy data, wipe critical information, or steal sensitive data.

There are a variety of types of malware, such as:

- **Ransomware**: This will lock a software system or device. To gain access, you will have to pay a ransom to the hacker. In 2024, the average demand was $5.2 million,

---

1 https://www.grandviewresearch.com/industry-analysis/cyber-security-market
2 https://cdn-dynmedia-1.microsoft.com/is/content/microsoftcorp/microsoft/final/en-us/microsoft-brand/documents/Microsoft%20Digital%20Defense%20Report%202024%20%281%29.pdf

according to the *US Department of the Treasury's* **Office of Foreign Assets Control (OFAC)**.[3] Ransomware is often delivered through a worm or a Trojan horse, which is malware that tricks people into downloading it on their system.

- **Phishing**: Phishing uses emails, text messages, or phone calls to get people to take action. For example, it could involve requesting information like credit card details or a social security number. There is also **Domain Name System** (**DNS**) spoofing. This is where the hacker will spoof a website, such as a form to enter payment information.

- **Denial-of-service (DoS) attack**: A hacker will send a huge volume of requests to a website or application. This will slow down the service, making it difficult or impossible to access.

- **Man-in-the-middle attack**: A hacker will eavesdrop on a network connection and capture the traffic, which may include sensitive data. This is common for unsecured Wi-Fi networks.

- **Zero-day exploits**: This is when a hacker uncovers a vulnerability in a system. It could be because issues have not been addressed with a patch or upgrade. *Zero-day* means that the organization has no time to deal with the problem. A famous example of this vulnerability was known as **Log4Shell**. In late 2021, it infected about 10% of the world's digital infrastructure.[4]

- **Password attack**: Using automation systems, a hacker will try to guess the login credentials of users. This may also be done by using social engineering. This is where a hacker tries to trick a person into divulging information.

- **Injection attacks**: This is embedding malicious code into a program or website. It allows for using remote commands, such as reading or modifying databases.

In some cases, cyberattacks can be extremely advanced. Often, these are from nation-states, which have access to teams of hackers.

In *Chapter 2, The Foundations of Cloud Computing*, we learned about the ways Microsoft has invested in security for the Azure platform. We saw that there was not only the use of sophisticated technologies like firewalls but also physical security, such as concrete walls and biometric access systems for data centers.

However, we will focus on the core security capabilities in Azure in this chapter.

Identity

Identity is crucial for an organized society. It can help provide access, such as with a driver's license or passport. The same applies to computer systems, but the concept of identity is broader than this. It not only includes people, but also applications and devices.

---

3 https://www.trmlabs.com/resources/blog/ransomware-in-2024-latest-trends-mounting-threats-and-the-government-response?utm_source=chatgpt.com
4 https://www.ibm.com/think/topics/log4shell

Identity is often a key part of security. You do not want a person or application to access a system if they are not authorized to do so. This can lead to the types of vulnerability that we discussed earlier in this chapter.

The most common approach for identity in a computer system is to use a user ID and a password. The user ID is usually your name, nickname, or email. As for a password, you will probably need to have one of a certain length and use a mix of letters in both uppercase and lowercase, as well as special characters and numbers. This will make it much more difficult for a hacker to guess it.

However, there are other best practices. They are as follows:

- **Length**: You should go beyond the minimum required. A good rule of thumb is for a password to be at least 15 characters.

- **Words**: Do not use words you can find in a dictionary. You should also avoid using the names of people, products, or organizations.

- **New passwords**: When you make an update, it should not have any similarity to your previous password, whatsoever.

- **Unique**: You should have a different password for each account. In case a hacker breaches one password, they will not be able to get into your other accounts.

- **Communication**: Do not send a password via email or instant messaging. There will likely not be sufficient security.

- **Written passwords**: You should not have them easily accessible, such as sticky notes on your computer. Keep your written passwords in a hidden area.

While long and complex passwords can be effective for security, they can be impossible to memorize. In this case, you can use a password manager. This will securely store your passwords, using encryption and multifactor authentication. The password manager can be activated in your applications to allow for seamless logins.

Identity for applications is usually provided by using digital certificates. They use public keys and digital signatures to verify the authenticity of the system. An application may also have a version number or serial number, which is visible on a network. The same is the case with devices.

A login system for an application has a common structure:

- **Input form**: A user will enter their username and password.

- **Client-side processing**: There will be validation of the input, such as to determine if it is the correct format (say for a phone number), and it meets the minimum password requirements.

- **Data transmission**: The login information will be sent securely using the HTTPS protocol.

- **Authentication**: The login information will be processed in the server. It will look up the username in the database and compare the password, which involves using hashing. The reason is that the passwords in the database will be encrypted.

- **Session management**: When the user is authenticated, a session will be created. This will use a token to track the activity of the user.

This process is complicated and requires sophisticated security procedures, due to which many organizations rely on identity providers. They will provide the services necessary for registering, authenticating, and managing users.

Microsoft has two types of identity provider solutions. One is Windows AD, which is for on-premises environments and runs on Windows Server. The data is stored as objects, say for a user, group, printer, and so on.

Next, there is Microsoft Entra ID, which was previously named **Azure Active Directory** (**Azure AD**). This is a cloud-based identity solution. This will be one of our focus areas in this chapter.

Microsoft Entra ID

More than 720,000 organizations use Microsoft Entra ID. It is common for many users to not even know they are using the service.[5]

For eight consecutive years, *Gartner* has named Microsoft Entra ID as a leader in its *Magic Quadrant* for access management.[6] Some of the reasons include affordable pricing, a strong ecosystem of partners, product innovation, and tight integration with Microsoft 365. Nevertheless, a key benefit of using Microsoft Entra ID is its strong foundation of security. For example, it uses cutting-edge AI systems to detect potential threats in real-time.

There are other benefits, such as:

- **Ease-of-use**: Microsoft Entra ID allows for different ways for users to log into a system. They can create their own user IDs and passwords or use their corporate credentials. Users can even use social media logins, such as with *Facebook, Google,* or *Outlook*.

- **Self-service capabilities**: A user can reset their user ID and password without having the assistance of IT personnel. This can help reduce the workload for the help desk.

- **Reduced development time**: Implementing Microsoft Entra ID is straightforward. It involves embedding a few lines of code in an application. This will not only access Azure for the login but also create the input forms.

- **Centralized administration**: With a dashboard, an administrator can easily manage users. Some of the functions include enrolling new users, setting permissions, and revoking users.

---

5 https://www.microsoft.com/en-us/security/business/identity-access/microsoft-entra-id
6 https://www.gartner.com/doc/reprints?id=1-2JFXRFAU&ct=241125&st=sb

- **Single sign-on (SSO)**: This means you can use a single username and password for more than one service or application. This can reduce the wasted time of the re-login process. There is also integration with many Azure services, such as VMs and storage.

A use case of Microsoft Entra ID is *BT Group*, a global telecommunications company. Its roots go back to 1846, when it started as a telegraph operator in the *United Kingdom*. Today, the company has operations in about 180 countries.

The consumer division, called **Everything Everywhere** (**EE**), wanted to reimagine its customer authentication experience. It has 25 million customers and provides broadband, landline, mobile, gaming, TV, and entertainment services. However, the registration process was cumbersome and often required re-entering information, leading to high levels of abandonment.

To provide for a more cohesive experience, EE implemented Microsoft Entra ID, which included various security solutions like Conditional Access and Microsoft Sentinel. Within a few weeks, the system showed significant improvements. There was a major drop in registration abandonment, and the security software thwarted about 100,000 attacks.[7] In this process, EE onboarded over five million customers.

Another key validator happened a year later, when the company broadcast the *Champions League* and the *Europa League* final. Microsoft Entra ID was able to seamlessly process over a million IDs within four minutes.

Authentication and authorization

It is common to confuse the concepts of authentication and authorization. However, it is important to know the differences.

Authentication involves proving the identity of a user. This can be done with a user ID and password, as well as facial recognition, thumbprints, and biometrics. Traditionally, when authenticating the user, the default will be to grant full access to the system, but this can pose potential security issues. If a hacker obtains the credentials, they can get wider access and do more damage.

This is why the best practice is to limit access, which is done with authorization. This is usually based on a person's role. The idea is to limit the authorization as much as possible, without hindering a user's ability to do their job.

Microsoft Entra ID has several ways for using authorization, some of which include:

- Azure AD Conditional Access
- Multifactor authentication

---

7 https://www.microsoft.com/en/customers/story/1703698973431043259-bt-group-telecommunications-microsoft-entra-id?culture=en-us&country=us

- Passwordless
- Role-based access control

Azure AD Conditional Access

Suppose a user logs into your organization's Microsoft Entra ID system. They did this through their company laptop and while inside the office. This is likely to be low-risk access, and there should be user authorization for the same.

However, suppose we change the circumstances. The user, instead, logs into the system while in another country at 3 AM local time. These are known as identity signals. While there could be legitimate reasons for this, they would still raise some red flags.

For these types of situations, you can use Azure AD Conditional Access, which allows for detecting identity signals. You can then set policies for them. *Table 7.1* highlights the examples for the same:

Note: **This is for a financial services firm.**

Condition	Description
• **Users**: Admins and finance team • **Grant**: Require multifactor authentication	Prevents account takeovers of high-privilege users, especially those accessing sensitive customer financial data.
• **Client app**: Block IMAP, POP3, SMTP • **Grant**: Block access	Stops attackers from bypassing **multifactor authentication** (**MFA**) by using older protocols that do not support modern authentication.
• **Location**: Include office IP ranges • **Grant**: Allow access only from trusted locations	Ensures customer and investment data cannot be accessed from personal or insecure remote networks.
• **Device state**: Require compliant or hybrid Azure AD joined devices • **Grant**: Grant access only if the device is compliant	Protects sensitive trading platforms and financial models from unauthorized or insecure devices.

Table 7.1: Policies for Azure AD Conditional Access

Each of the conditions is an if-then structure. So, the first one states that if the user is an admin and signs in from a new device, then there must be multifactor authentication. Microsoft Entra ID will enforce all the conditions in real-time, allowing for a seamless experience for logins.

Multifactor authentication

We mentioned **multifactor authentication** (**MFA**) several times in this chapter. This highlights the importance of this technique for security. MFA is also a key topic on the AZ-900 exam.

The definition for this is: there must be two or more factors or pieces of evidence in order to allow a user to log into a system. A factor is not a username. The reason is that this is something that may be known, such as your name, nickname, or email. In fact, it is common for a web service to display a person's username in an application.

Microsoft has provided a way to think about a factor. It is about a three-part classification system:

- **Something you know**: The most common is your password or PIN. Another example is a passphrase, which is a longer version of a password. It can also be a security question/answer. For example, *Who was your best friend in high school?* or *What is the name of your first pet?*

- **Something you have**: This is often a physical device, such as a smartphone. A text of the passcode will be sent to it. This could also be an authentication app, such as Microsoft Authenticator. When you attempt to log in to it, a passcode will appear for a short period of time. Another example of something you know is a smart card or ID badge.

- **Something you are**: This is a person's biometric characteristic. It could be a face, fingerprint, iris, voice, or palm.

By combining at least two of these factors, the security of a system will significantly improve. A study from Microsoft found that MFA reduced the risk of compromised accounts by 99.22%.[8] Another study, from *Google, New York University*, and the *University of California*, San Diego, showed that it warded off 100% of automated bots and 96% of phishing attacks.[9]

Microsoft Entra ID requires that all global administrators use MFA. The feature is also available for free for all users. Microsoft Entra ID supports all the factors mentioned earlier, as well as the following:

- **Voice call**: Microsoft will call your phone and tell you the passcode.

- **Passkey (FIDO2)**: This is a specialized device that usually connects to a computer or mobile device through USB-A, USB-C, or **near field communication** (**NFC**). It uses encryption, with the private key on your device and the public key in Microsoft Entra ID.

- **OATH hardware token**: This is a device that generates **time-based one-time passwords** (**TOTP**). It meets the requirements of the **initiative for open authentication** (**OATH**) standard, which includes open protocols for strong authentication.

- OATH software token: This is an application that generates **one-time passwords** (**OTPs**).

---

8 https://www.microsoft.com/en-us/research/publication/how-effective-is-multifactor-authentication-at-deterring-cyberattacks/
9 https://watech.wa.gov/ocs/news/research-shows-multi-factor-authentication-works

Passwordless

Using MFA can be inconvenient. You may have to take a couple of steps using a passcode to log into a system. Then again, this helps to explain why MFA provides much higher levels of security.

There does not necessarily need to be a tradeoff between strong security and convenience. This is possible with passwordless. As the name implies, you skip the step of entering a password or passcode. It will instead rely on using biometric approaches, like facial recognition or retinal scans.

This data remains on the device and is not sent to Microsoft Entra ID. This helps provide more privacy for the user but also reduces security risks. The reason behind this is that if there is a breach, not all the data will be exposed.

Passwordless often uses cryptography. The public key is provided for the setup, and the private key is stored on the user's device.

Windows Entra ID provides passwordless capabilities in various forms, such as with the Microsoft Authenticator app (which is available on iOS and Android devices) and FIDO2 Security Keys. There is also *Windows Hello for Business*, which is for Windows PCs. Then there is the ability to use **certificate-based authentication** (**CBA**). This authenticates users with X.509 certificates and integrates with public key infrastructure systems.

Role-based access control

RBAC in Azure lets you manage authorization by assigning permissions to specific roles. A role is a set of permissions (such as read, write, or delete actions) that you can scope to management groups, subscriptions, resource groups, or individual resources. Scoping follows a parent–child hierarchy. That is, a role assigned at a higher level (subscription) cascades down to all child resources.

Azure provides hundreds of built-in roles, with three broad categories:

- **Reader**: View-only access. The user can read resources but not make changes.
- **Contributor**: Create and manage resources, but cannot grant access to others.
- **Owner**: Full access, including the ability to delegate permissions.

You can also define custom roles with your own permissions and scope, but this requires a premium edition of Microsoft Entra ID. Custom roles are powerful but add complexity, so the best practice is to rely primarily on built-in roles unless there's a special need.

Azure RBAC follows several important behaviors. First, group inheritance is transitive, meaning if a user belongs to Group A, which is itself a member of Group B, the user automatically inherits Group B's permissions. Second, role assignments are additive. This means that when a user is given multiple roles, the permissions are combined. For example, if someone has both the Reader and Contributor roles, they effectively gain contributor rights.

To ensure security and simplicity, Azure recommends following the principle of least privilege, granting only the minimum permissions required to complete a task. Roles can be assigned in several ways, including through the Azure portal, Azure PowerShell using the `New-AzRoleAssignment` command, the Azure CLI, or programmatically with REST APIs and SDKs.

The Zero Trust model

The traditional approach to network security is called the perimeter-based security model. It is also referred to as the castle-and-moat architecture. This is where there are security systems like firewalls that detect and prevent intrusions into a corporate network. The presumption is that threats are external, while the corporate network is assumed to be trustworthy.

However, this model has major drawbacks, which have been worsened because of trends like remote work, cloud computing, and the proliferation of mobile devices. There are more opportunities for threats to emerge within the corporate network, which can lead to significant damage.

To address these issues, a new approach has emerged: *The Zero Trust model*. It provides for the following:

- **Assume a breach**: This means there must be a more proactive approach to managing the corporate network. There should be end-to-end encryption, continuous monitoring of potential threats, and segmentation of the resources.

- **Verify explicitly**: At all times, there needs to be authentication and authorization for requests to the corporate network. This is for all data points, whether for the user identity, location, device health, or workload.

- **Use the least privilege access**: You need to be restrictive with access. It should only be enough for a user's role. In some cases, there may be a need for access to administrative capabilities. But this can be done using techniques like **just-in-time and just-enough-access (JIT/JEA)**. They provide for temporary permission to take an action, say for 15 to 30 minutes.

With the Zero Trust model, you should establish a comprehensive policy, which will require the help of a security expert. Azure recommends that there be conditional access and MFA. The policy should have the following factors:

- Inventory of the network assets, including the applications, data, and users.

- Ensure the systems are updated.

- Use patch management.

- Develop procedures for how to react to security events, like breaches.

Defense in depth

Defense in depth ensures multiple layers of security. Suppose you only have a firewall to protect your corporate network. This would provide a high level of security, but if there is a breach, then the corporate network will be exposed.

You can see this in *Figure 7.1*:

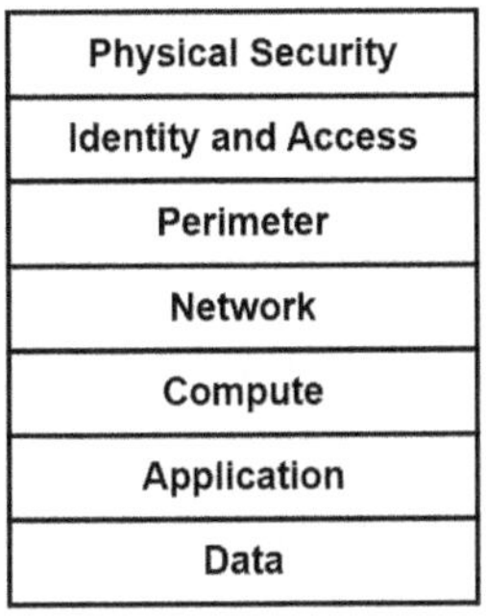

Physical Security
Identity and Access
Perimeter
Network
Compute
Application
Data

Figure 7.1: Layers of security in the defense in depth model

We have already covered topics for these security layers, such as NSG, MFA, and RBAC. But these only scratch the surface of available solutions. Here are some others:

- **Secure access service edge (SASE)**: This is a cloud system that provides network security protections, including Zero Trust access and data protection.

- **Security information and event management (SIEM)**: This process secures security data across an organization. It helps with monitoring, incident response, compliance reporting, and threat detection.

- **API management**: This allows for creating, deploying, and securing APIs. It provides for managing authentication, authorization, and traffic monitoring.

- **Application security testing**: This analyzes applications for security issues. There are various approaches, such as code analysis, simulated attacks, and real-time monitoring.

While defense in depth can greatly improve security, it can be challenging to manage the different solutions. It can also be costly in terms of the various subscriptions and licenses. This is why more companies have been consolidating their security offerings to a smaller number of vendors. The approach can even improve overall security because of the higher levels of integration with the functions.

Microsoft Defender for Cloud

Microsoft Defender for Cloud is a **Cloud-Native Application Protection Platform (CNAPP)**. It not only works with Azure, but also AWS and Google Cloud. Integration with source control systems like GitHub and GitLab is also available.

The protection services are comprehensive:

- **Development Security Operations (DevSecOps)**: This integrates security into the entire software development lifecycle.

- **Cloud security posture management (CSPM)**: This provides security protection and remediation for cloud infrastructure. It is also proactive, in which the system will provide early detection of potential threats.

- **Cloud Workload Protection Platform (CWPP)**: This protects workloads in cloud environments, like VMs, containers, and serverless functions.

Microsoft Defender for Cloud has a security posture indicator. This shows the number of critical recommendations, attack paths, and overdue recommendations. This provides an overview of the security for your cloud environment.

A regulatory compliance function is also present, which will show if your resources meet the standards. Then there is an inventory section, which catalogs all your IT assets in the cloud.

To see a real-world example of Microsoft Defender for Cloud, consider the case study of Danfoss. Founded over 100 years ago, the company is a leader in inventing and manufacturing energy-efficient solutions for automotive, industrial, marine, construction, and power-generation industries.

Over the past decade, the company has been focused on digital transformation, and that has been key to its growth and innovation. However, the company's on-premises security platform became a challenge. There were more manual security reviews, and the number of security alerts was weighing on the IT staff.

Danfoss needed a cloud-based solution that could integrate with its SAP system. After an extensive evaluation, the company adopted core Microsoft technologies, including Defender for Cloud. The migration was fairly streamlined, even though there were 20 large applications and thousands of devices. This included systems inside the company's manufacturing facilities.

By using Microsoft security systems, Danfoss was able to mitigate 80% of phishing and compromised identity events automatically.[10] They were also able to reduce false positives and repetitive tasks by 50-60%.

Conclusion

In this chapter, we covered the core concepts and capabilities of identity, access, and security for Azure. This included a review of the main identity system, Microsoft Entra ID, as well as Azure AD Conditional Access, MFA, RBAC, and Microsoft Defender for Cloud. We also covered security approaches like the Zero Trust model, passwordless, and defense in depth.

In the next chapter, we will learn about cost management for Azure.

---

10 **https://www.microsoft.com/en/customers/story/22786-danfoss-microsoft-sentinel**

Sample questions

1. **Which type of security threat is about tricking a person into disclosing sensitive personal information through emails or other types of online messages?**

    a. Phishing

    b. Password attack

    c. Zero-day exploit

    d. Injection attack

    Correct answer: a

    Explanation: Phishing attacks are a common security threat. They involve using a message in an email or other online message to trick a person into revealing sensitive personal information, like a Social Security number or credit card information.

2. **How does ransomware work?**

    a. The attacker spoofs an email

    b. The attacker floods a website with huge amounts of traffic

    c. The attacker locks a system to demand money for regaining access

    d. The attacker injects malware into an application

    Correct answer: c

    Explanation: Ransomware is when an attacker will infiltrate a system and make it inaccessible. To open it up, the victim will be required to make a payment.

3. **What does identity mean for a cloud platform like Azure?**

    a. It identifies VMs

    b. It describes a system that restricts unauthorized access

    c. It finds malware in a system

    d. It is a method for inventorying IT assets for security purposes

    Correct answer: b

    Explanation: Identity is a key concept for security. It is a way to authorize users to access a system, like Azure. It can also be used to restrict access to certain resources.

4. **The following are best practices for creating strong passwords, except:**

    a. Using a combination of uppercase and lowercase characters, numbers, and special characters

    b. Using different passwords for multiple accounts

    c.   Avoiding easily guessable information

    d.   Using at least eight characters

Correct answer: d

Explanation: A password should be long, say 15 characters or more.

5. **How does a password manager work?**

    a.   It changes passwords every 15 minutes

    b.   It securely stores and manages multiple passwords

    c.   It shares passwords for authorized users

    d.   It completely eliminates the need for passwords

Correct answer: b

Explanation: A password manager provides convenience, as it securely stores and manages multiple passwords. This means that a user will not have to memorize complex passwords.

6. **What is Microsoft Entra ID?**

    a.   A hardware-based firewall

    b.   A cloud-based identity and access management service

    c.   An anti-phishing system

    d.   A Zero Trust application

Correct answer: b

Explanation: Microsoft Entra ID is a key security solution for Azure. It provides comprehensive identity services, such as identity and access management.

7. **This Microsoft Entra ID feature allows users to access multiple applications with a single set of login credentials:**

    a.   Multi-factor authentication

    b.   Azure identity management

    c.   Conditional Access

    d.   SSO

Correct answer: d

Explanation: **Single sign-on (SSO)** is when the user is authenticated once. After this, they can access multiple applications without needing to log in for each one.

8. **What is the difference between authentication and authorization in a system like Azure?**

   a. Authentication verifies a user's identity, while authorization determines their access rights.

   b. Authentication grants access to resources, whereas authorization verifies user identities.

   c. Authentication and authorization explain the same thing.

   d. Authentication is optional in security systems, but authorization is mandatory.

   Correct answer: a

   Explanation: Authentication is about verifying a user, such as with passwords or biometrics. As for authorization, this is what resources a user is permitted to have access to.

9. **Among the following, which would likely be an Azure AD Conditional Access policy requiring MFA?**

   a. A user logging in from a trusted office location during regular business hours.

   b. A user logging into the system from an unrecognized device in a foreign country at 1 AM local time.

   c. An administrator accessing the system from their company laptop within the corporate network.

   d. A user signing in from a recognized device within a trusted IP range.

   Correct answer: b

   Explanation: Azure AD Conditional Access will evaluate signals like login location, device, and time. This can detect unusual activities, which may pose security risks. This would certainly be the case if a user logs into a system from an unrecognized device in a foreign country at 1 AM local time.

10. **For the following, which is an example of a signal from the Azure AD Conditional Access system?**

    a. User's personal website

    b. User's email signature

    c. File types accessed by the user

    d. Location of the sign in

    Correct answer: d

    Explanation: Azure AD Conditional Access evaluates a variety of signals, such as the location of a sign-in.

11. **This authentication approach is considered "something you have" for multifactor authentication**:

    a. Password

    b. Security question

    c. Smart card

    d. Fingerprint

    Correct answer: c

    Explanation: The concept of *something you have* is about a physical object a user has for authentication, like a smart card, a mobile device with an authentication app, or a security token.

12. **What is the reason for using MFA?**

    a. To eliminate the login process

    b. To store passwords

    c. To improve security by requiring multiple forms of verification

    d. To give users the option of their preferred authentication approach

    Correct answer: c

    Explanation: MFA greatly increases security by requiring users to provide multiple forms of verification.

13. **This is an example of something you are in multifactor authentication**:

    a. Biometric data like a retina scan

    b. Personal identification number

    c. Email address

    d. One-time passcode sent through SMS

    Correct answer: a

    Explanation: The concept of something you are is about biometric approaches that are unique to an individual, like retina scans, fingerprints, or facial recognition.

14. **This is not a category of authentication factors used in multifactor authentication (MFA)**:

    a. Something you know

    b. Something you have

    c. Something you are

    d. Something you create

    Correct answer: d

Explanation: The three factors include something you know (e.g., a password), something you have (e.g., a smartphone or security token), and something you are (e.g., biometric characteristics like fingerprints or facial recognition). As for "Something you create," this is not an authentication factor.

15. **What is the key advantage of passwordless authentication over traditional password-based methods?**

    a. Passwords are easier to remember

    b. Reduced risk of phishing attacks

    c. Users can share credentials easily

    d. It eliminates the need for any form of user authentication

    Correct answer: b

    Explanation: Passwordless authentication reduces the risk of phishing attacks because a user does not have to enter a password. Rather, there are more secure approaches used, like biometrics or security keys.

16. **This is not a built-in role in Azure RBAC:**

    a. Reader

    b. Contributor

    c. Administrator

    d. Owner

    Correct answer: c

    Explanation: The three built-in roles in Azure RBAC are owner, contributor, and reader. The Administrator role is not one of them.

17. **This is the scope in Azure RBAC:**

    a. The level for the granting of resources, such as a management group, subscription, resource group, or resource.

    b. A limited set of permissions assigned to a role.

    c. User intrusion activities within Azure.

    d. There is no scope.

    Correct answer: a

    Explanation: Scope in Azure RBAC describes the level of access to resources. This can be for the management group, subscription, resource group, or resource level.

18. **This is not a key principle of the Zero Trust security model**:

    a. Assume breach

    b. Verify explicitly

    c. Use least privileged access

    d. Grant no access by default

Correct answer: d

Explanation: The zero-trust security model is based on a few key principles: assuming a breach, verifying explicitly, and using least privilege access. However, this does not include preventing any access by default to a network.

19. **What is the main purpose of using defense in depth**?

    a. To rely only on hardware-based firewalls for network security

    b. To establish multiple layers of security controls

    c. To focus only on external security threats and intrusions

    d. To simplify the security infrastructure by consolidating the number of security tools

Correct answer: b

Explanation: Defense in depth is a concept where there are multiple layers of security, in terms of physical, technical, and administrative approaches. Thus, if one layer fails, there will be others to provide backup support.

20. **What is the main purpose of Microsoft Defender for Cloud**?

    a. A tool for managing VMs for different cloud platforms.

    b. A platform that provides unified security management and threat protection across cloud platforms.

    c. A service that only monitors network traffic within Azure environments.

    d. A software suite for developing cloud-native applications without security features.

Correct answer: b

Explanation: Microsoft Defender for Cloud is a cloud application that provides comprehensive security services for different cloud environments, including Azure, AWS, and Google Cloud.

CHAPTER 8

Cost Management for Azure

Introduction

In this chapter, we will cover cost management for the Azure platform. We will start by looking at the importance of this task. This will be followed by learning about the best practices. Furthermore, we will look at the Azure services for cost management. These include the TCO calculator, Azure Cost Management tools, and resource tags.

Structure

This chapter covers the following topics:

- Importance of cost management
- Best practices
- TCO calculator
- Azure Cost Management tools
- Resource tags

Objectives

By the end of this chapter, you will gain practical skills for understanding techniques for cost management with the Azure platform. This will also include understanding the capabilities and benefits of tools like the TCO calculator, the Azure Cost Management tools, and resource tags.

Importance of cost management

A key benefit of migrating an IT environment to the cloud is lower costs. The savings can be significant, as there is no need to buy and manage infrastructure resources in a private data center. Yet the cloud can still be expensive. For example, suppose you create a **virtual machine** (**VM**) in Azure. You use that pay-as-you-go model and will pay $0.097 per hour, which is based on the configuration of the stem.

However, there are associated costs like:

- Storage
- Bandwidth
- Disaster recovery
- Monitoring
- Security
- Software licenses
- IP addresses
- Support plans

These costs can quickly accumulate, which is why it is important to use cost management with Azure. It involves using tools and strategies to plan, evaluate, and control the budget. This can not only lead to lower costs but also more predictability with monthly bills, more efficiency, reduced waste, and better forecasting.

Best practices

Cost management is not an easy process. You will need to spend considerable time on the analysis. But there are some best practices to consider to help improve the effectiveness:

- **Understand the pricing**: Every resource in Azure has a pricing page. Make sure you read them. Often, you will find nuances in the costs of the resource. For example, Azure Blob Storage has a fee for how much data you store, but also for the frequency with which you perform operations, like reading, writing, or copying the files. Then there are costs for outbound data transfer.

- **Use resources closest to your users**: This can provide considerable discounts. Another benefit is lower latency, such as faster load time for a website. However, there are limitations to this best practice, as the resource may not be available in a closer region. Another reason is that you may be required to place the resource in a region because of regulatory requirements. This is often a major consideration for organizations that have global operations.

- **Select the right purchase option**: A resource may have different pricing models. For example, selecting Azure reservations means that if you commit to one-or three-year terms, you can get major discounts. This is when an organization has stable, predictable workloads that require consistent compute capacity. Another potential option is spot VMs, which have unused capacity. The discounts can also be substantial. Spot VMs are generally for fault-tolerant or non-critical tasks that can withstand deallocation.

- **Leverage existing assets**: If you already have licenses for software, such as Windows Server or SQL Server, you can use these as part of your Azure implementation. This is done by using the Hybrid Benefit program. This means not having to pay extra fees for more licenses.

- **Organize resources**: A way to help lower costs is to think about the organizational structure of your Azure implementation. This means providing a clear view of management groups, subscriptions, and resource groups. You will be able to evaluate the use of the resources better, allowing for taking effective actions in lowering costs.

Azure has various tools that can help with cost management. One is the pricing calculator, which we covered in *Chapter 2, The Foundations of Cloud Computing.*

However, for the rest of the chapter, we will look at the other tools.

TCO calculator

In *Chapter 4, Compute Services*, we learned about the concept of TCO. This assesses the total costs of purchasing, deploying, operating, and maintaining IT assets. It is for the entire lifecycle. TCO provides a way to get a comprehensive view of the true financial impact of an IT investment.

Azure has the Azure TCO Calculator to estimate the cost savings and benefits of a migration from on-premises to the Azure cloud. You can find it at **https://azure.microsoft.com/en-us/ pricing/tco/calculator/**.

This is something that will take considerable preparation to use, especially if you have a large IT environment. The reason is that you need to input details about your on-premises assets. If you do not provide enough details, you will likely get inaccurate results.

You can see the Azure TCO calculator in *Figure 8.1*:

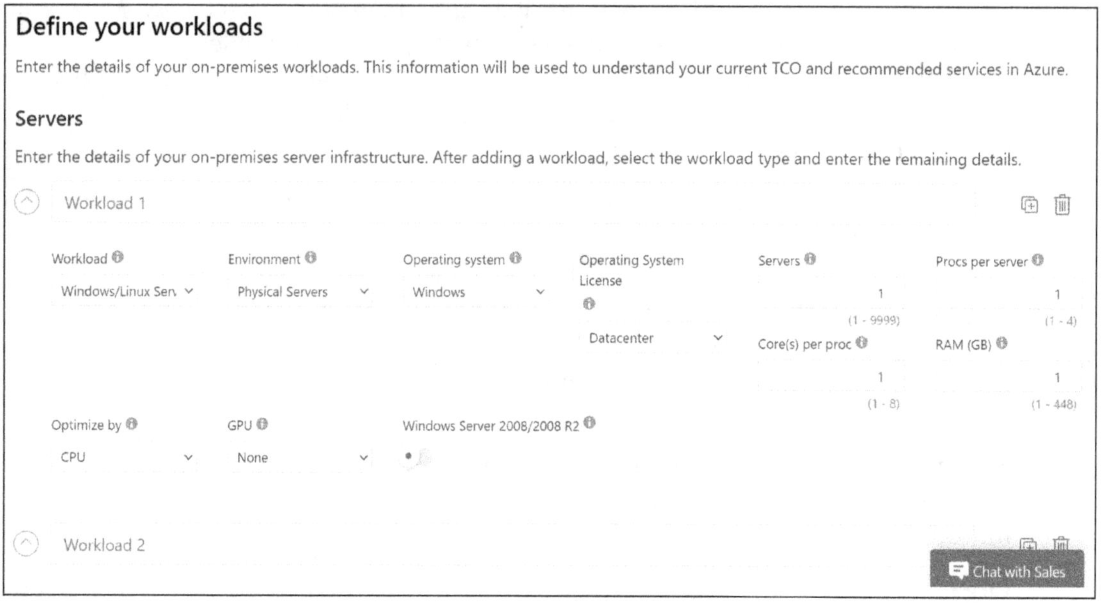

Figure 8.1: Input form for your on-premises assets

The Define your workloads section has four sub-sections. They are as follows:

- **Servers**: For each, you will specify the workload, such as Windows or Linux, environment, OS, RAM, core, and GPU or CPU.

- **Databases**: The options for source databases are MySQL, PostgreSQL, SQL Server APS, and Oracle Exadata. Then you indicate the destination databases, which include SQL database, SQL database managed instance, and SQL Server VM.

- **Storage**: The storage types are local disk/SAN, NAS/file share, and blob. They are for either a hard disk drive or an SSD. You will also specify the storage capacity and backup options.

- **Networking**: You will enter the amount of the network bandwidth for outbound transfers. You will also indicate the destination region.

Once you are finished with this process, you will select **Next** to go to the **Adjust assumptions** section, which you can see in *Figure 8.2*:

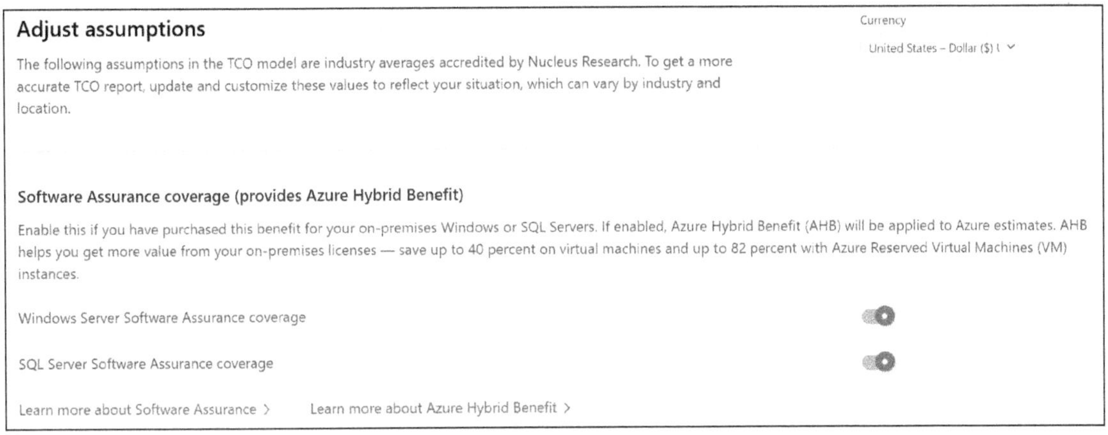

Figure 8.2: *Adjust the assumptions for the TCO calculator*

These include the factors that Azure will use to forecast the TCO for the cloud migration. The default settings are based on industry standards from *Nucleus Research*.

The factors are for the following categories:

- **Software assurance coverage**: This is when you purchased on-premises versions for Windows or SQL Servers. It will mean you can get significant discounts on VMs, which can be up to 82%.

- **Geo-redundant storage (GRS)**: This will factor in the cost benefits of replicating your data to a secondary region.

- **VM costs**: This means that the TCO calculator will not recommend B-series VMs.

- **Electricity costs**: You can set the price per kWh.

- **Storage costs**: You can adjust these for various options, like local disk, NAS/file storage, blobs, and tape.

- **IT labor costs**: You can estimate the number of physical servers and VMs that a full-time administrator can manage. You can also specify the hourly rate.

- **Other assumptions**: You can provide details on many parts of your IT environment, like the costs for software, virtualization, networking, databases, and data warehouses.

When finished, you will click **Next**, and you will be taken to the **View Report** section, which you can see in *Figure 8.3*:

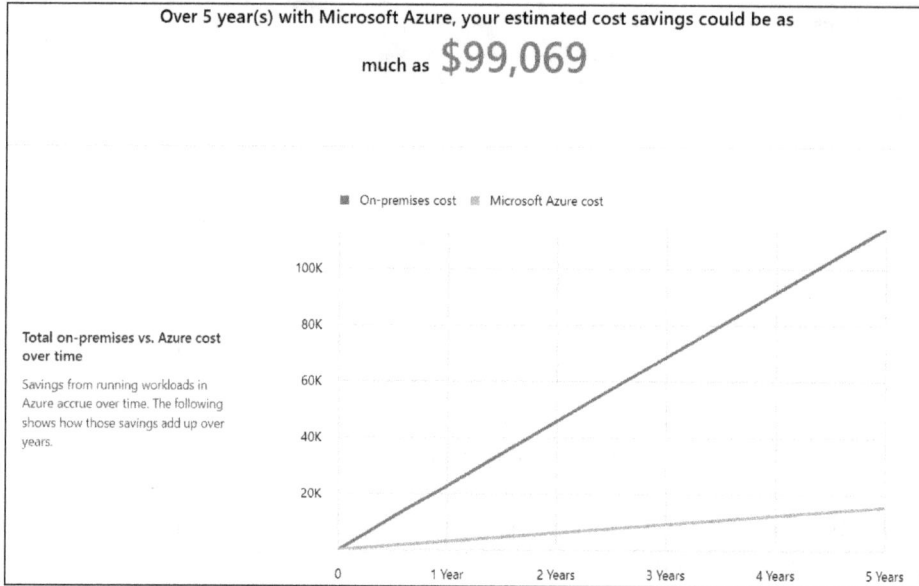

Figure 8.3: *The report in the TCO calculator*

This shows the cost advantages of moving to Azure, according to a five-year estimate. You can also change the factors like the region, licensing program, and timeframe.

Azure Cost Management tools

Azure will track extensive details about the costs of using the platform. You can find them by searching for *cost management*. This will take you to a dashboard, which you can find in *Figure 8.4*:

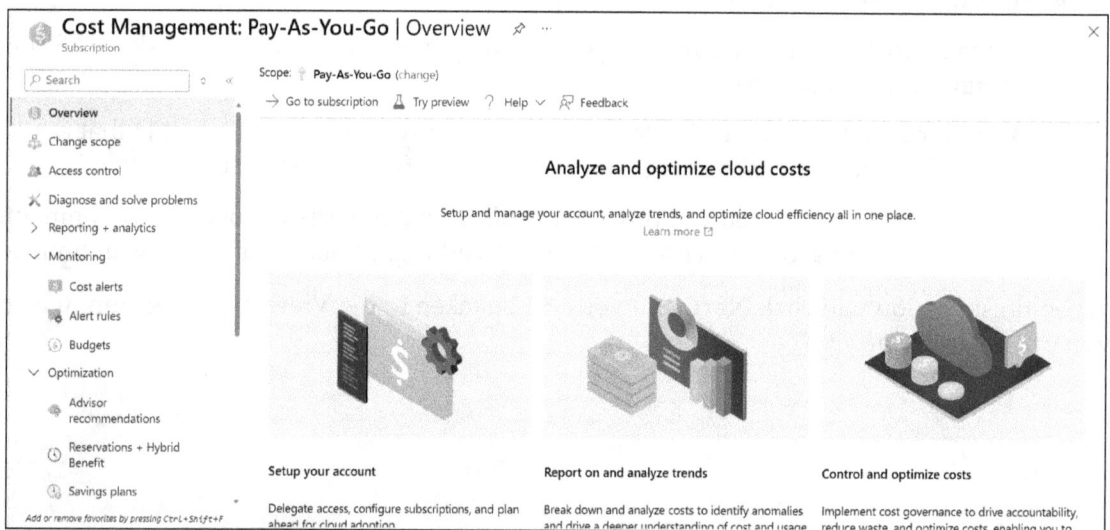

Figure 8.4: *Dashboard for the cost management tools in Azure*

Here are some of the features:

- **Spending**: You can use the cost analysis tool to visualize expenses over time, such as on a monthly or quarterly basis. This can help identify trends, issues, or cost spikes. This can help us understand the underlying causes, like usage, pricing changes, or the use of new resources.

- **Budget**: You can create one that is based on your requirements. Once completed, Azure will monitor the spending in real-time and issue alerts when the levels hit certain thresholds.

- **Forecasting**: This is based on past usage data in Azure. It can help anticipate any increases to take proactive actions with the budget.

- **Reports**: You can customize them, such as for certain metrics, services, or departments, and have them sent based on certain schedules or triggers.

- **Data exports**: You can export the cost and usage data for integration with other software tools. One is Microsoft's Power BI, which allows for creating sophisticated dashboards, automated reports, and data analytics.

Resource tags

A resource tag is metadata in the form of a key-value pair. It is a way to identify a resource, resource group, or subscription in Azure. This allows for better organization, allowing for bulk operations, setting access controls, and creating reports. You can also use resource tags for search. For example, they can enable an administrator to quickly identify all resources belonging to a specific department or project, such as applying security policies.

The following steps will help you create a tag:

1. Log in to **Azure**.
2. Click + **Create a resource**.
3. Select **Create** for a storage account.
4. On the menu above, select **Tags**. *Figure 8.5* shows what you will see:

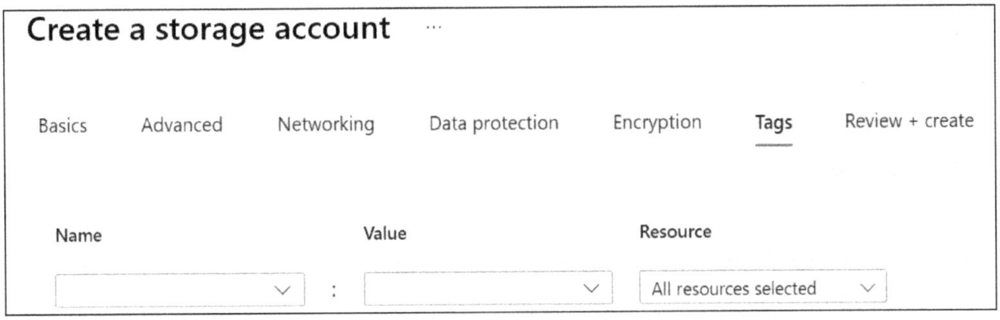

Figure 8.5: Form to add tags

5. Suppose you want to categorize this storage account based on the department of your organization. You can enter **department** where it says **Name**. You can then specify which one. You can enter **marketing**. You can also create more than one tag for a resource.

With resource tags, you can do the following:

- **Cost allocation**: You can create reports that segment costs based on factors like departments, projects, and business units. This helps provide better tracking and accountability. This can also allow for allocating shared costs, like for networking or storage, across different entities.

- **Search**: You can locate resources based on the tags. For example, they can be according to attributes like the application or the owner of the resource. This can allow for bulk operations, setting access controls, and creating reports.

Conclusion

In this chapter, we covered cost management for the Azure platform. We learned about the best practices, such as evaluating pricing, using resources closest to users, and leveraging existing assets.

We also looked at several of the Azure services for cost management, such as the TCO calculator, Azure Cost Management tools, and resource tags. In the next chapter, we will cover governance and compliance in Azure.

Sample questions

1. **What is the major benefit of migrating an IT environment to the cloud?**

   a. Increased manual management and control

   b. Unlimited free services

   c. Lower costs due to reduced infrastructure needs

   d. Only lower costs for VMs

   Correct answer: c

   Explanation: A key benefit of moving to the cloud is lower costs. There is no need to purchase or maintain infrastructure in a private data center.

2. **This Azure pricing model provides discounts if you agree to use a resource for one or three years:**

   a. Azure reservations

   b. Spot instances

    c. Usage model

    d. Premium tier

Correct answer: a

Explanation: Azure reservations require customers to commit to one or three-year terms. For this, they can receive significant discounts.

3. **Besides the hourly usage rate, what costs can accumulate when using an Azure VM?**

    a. Network traffic within the VM resource

    b. Data storage and outbound data transfer

    c. One-time setup fee

    d. Access to public IP websites

Correct answer: b

Explanation: With a VM, there may be additional charges for storage, outbound data transfers, and other services like security and monitoring.

4. **What is a potential limitation when deploying Azure resources close to users for cost savings?**

    a. It always results in higher latency

    b. It may violate regional compliance or regulatory requirements

    c. It disables security monitoring and management features

    d. It significantly increases spot pricing

Correct answer: b

Explanation: Generally, deploying resources closer to users will be a good option. But in certain cases, this may not be available because of compliance and regulatory requirements.

5. **What is the key advantage of using Azure spot VMs?**

    a. Guaranteed resource availability and scalability

    b. Higher levels of security features

    c. Access to unused capacity at a lower price

    d. Built-in disaster recovery and backup

Correct answer: c

Explanation: Azure spot VMs offer discounted pricing. This is for unused compute capacity on the platform. However, there is a downside as a VM may be deallocated if Azure needs the capacity back.

6. **What is the purpose of the Azure TCO calculator?**

   a. To configure VM specifications using the Azure console

   b. To estimate the cost savings of migrating from on-premises to Azure

   c. To calculate monthly Azure invoices only

   d. To monitor security vulnerabilities and threats

   Correct answer: b

   Explanation: The Azure TCO Calculator will estimate the total cost savings and financial benefits of moving from an on-premises IT setup to the Azure cloud.

7. **Why might the TCO calculator require significant preparation before use?**

   a. It only supports one type of VM

   b. It requires manual Azure subscription verification

   c. It needs detailed information about on-premises assets

   d. It must be installed locally

   Correct answer: c

   Explanation: To get an accurate comparison, you must enter comprehensive details about your current on-premises environment. This can potentially take considerable time to collect.

8. **This is a benefit of selecting software assurance coverage when using the TCO Calculator:**

   a. It provides unlimited Azure credits for smaller organizations

   b. It allows access to private regions

   c. It does not require licensing agreements

   d. It can reduce VM costs by up to 82%

   Correct answer: c

   Explanation: Software assurance coverage can provide significant cost savings, up to 82% for VMs.

9. **This Azure tool allows you to visualize your spending trends over time and identify cost spikes:**

   a. Azure Monitor

   b. Cost analysis

   c. Azure Policy

   d. Usage insights

   Correct answer: b

Explanation: The cost analysis tool in Azure helps visualize expenses over time, say on a monthly or quarterly basis. This can allow for spotting trends, anomalies, or unexpected increases in costs.

10. **What happens when you create a budget in Azure Cost Management?**

    a. Azure automatically reallocates funds

    b. Azure issues refunds if overspending occurs

    c. Azure monitors real-time spending and sends alerts at set thresholds

    d. Azure disables resources once the budget is exceeded

Correct answer: c

Explanation: After you set up a budget, Azure continuously monitors your spending and will send notifications when spending reaches certain thresholds.

11. **What is a resource tag in Azure?**

    a. A key-value pair used for organizing resources

    b. A script that automates VM creation and management

    c. An encrypted security token for Azure resources

    d. A log file generated during deployment

Correct answer: a

Explanation: A resource tag in Azure is a key-value pair. It helps organize and categorize resources, resource groups, or subscriptions. This can allow for better management and tracking.

12. **How can resource tags help with cost allocation in Azure?**

    a. They provide a discount on shared resources

    b. They enable encryption of data

    c. They allow costs to be segmented by department or project

    d. They automate the billing cycle

Correct answer: c

Explanation: Resource tags allow organizations to segment and track costs by categories such as department or project. This helps to improve cost allocation and accountability.

CHAPTER 9

Governance and Compliance in Azure

Introduction

This chapter covers governance and compliance in Azure, which are important for ensuring that cloud environments are secure, well-managed, and aligned with both internal policies and external regulations. We begin with a high-level overview of what governance and compliance mean in the context of cloud computing. Governance involves the people, processes, and policies that guide the use of technology within an organization, while compliance focuses on adhering to laws, regulations, and industry standards such as GDPR, HIPAA, or PCI-DSS.

From there, we take a closer look at the tools Azure provides to help organizations establish and enforce a strong governance and compliance framework. You will learn how to use Azure Policy to create and apply rules across cloud resources, which provides consistency and control. We will also cover resource locks, which protect key resources from being altered or deleted unintentionally. Finally, we explore Microsoft Purview, which is Azure's platform for data governance. It includes features for classification, auditing, data lifecycle management, and risk mitigation.

Structure

This chapter covers the following topics:

- Overview of governance and compliance for Azure

- Azure Policy
- Resource locks
- Microsoft Purview

Objectives

By the end of this chapter, you will have a clear understanding of how to design and implement a governance and compliance strategy using Azure tools. You will develop practical skills in defining governance policies that align with your organization's business goals, structuring rules around resource usage, and ensuring those rules are consistently enforced across your cloud environment.

You will also gain experience in using Azure Policy to apply built-in and custom rules that monitor and remediate non-compliant resources automatically. You will learn how to protect critical infrastructure using resource locks, minimizing the risk of accidental deletions or unauthorized modifications.

In addition, you will see how to use Microsoft Purview to manage sensitive data, track access, maintain audit trails, and apply data classification and lifecycle policies. These skills will help you ensure regulatory compliance, support internal accountability, and build trust with stakeholders by maintaining visibility and control over your cloud assets.

Overview of governance and compliance

Governance and compliance are key for effective management of cloud environments. Governance is about people, processes, and policies that are focused on selecting, implementing, and monitoring technology across a business.

Compliance, on the other hand, is about adhering to external rules, laws, and regulatory requirements. These are from sources like industry bodies, governments, or international standards organizations. Compliance ensures that the organization's use of technology meets legal obligations, such as for data privacy laws like the **General Data Protection Regulation (GDPR)** or industry regulations like the **Health Insurance Portability and Accountability Act (HIPAA)** or the **Payment Card Industry Data Security Standard (PCI-DSS)**.

When combined, governance and compliance create a powerful system of checks and balances. They help to protect the business, manage risks, and foster trust with customers and stakeholders.

Governance and compliance generally start at the top of an organization. This includes senior leadership teams like the board of directors and executives. They will define the high-level rules and objectives. Then there will be groups, like IT governance and security committees, to implement and manage them. For example, a security committee might meet quarterly to evaluate new threats, approve new technologies or upgrades, and review incidents and controls.

The following are examples of governance rules:

- All resources must include tags for the cost center, owner, and environment.
- **Virtual machines** (**VMs**) must be managed and use premium storage for production workloads.
- Public IP addresses must not be assigned directly to VMs.
- Only approved Azure regions may be used for resource deployments.
- All storage accounts must have encryption enabled using customer-managed keys.

You might document these rules in an internal wiki or knowledge base, but documentation alone is not enough. Without enforcement, rules are easily ignored. This can lead to data breaches, downtime, or poor system performance.

Azure provides several built-in tools to help organizations enforce governance. These include:

- Azure Policy
- Resource locks
- Microsoft Purview

Azure Policy

In *Chapter 2, The Foundations of Cloud Computing*, we briefly looked at Azure Policy. This helps to create and enforce governance rules across an organization. They are all encrypted at rest. If you use Azure Arc, you can apply these governance rules to other cloud providers like AWS and Google Cloud. This is especially important for larger enterprises that often have complex IT environments.

Azure Policy comes with over 1,000 predefined governance rules. However, you can also create your own. This is done by using JSON format, which can use functions, parameters, conditions, and logical operators. It is similar to a programming language. For example, you can use JSON to enforce a resource tag, such as for a cost center or revenue.

See the following steps to know how to use Azure Policy:

1. Log in to Azure.
2. In the search box at the top of the screen, enter: `policy`
3. Click **Policy**. You will see the dashboard in *Figure 9.1*. This will provide an overview of the compliance of your resources. Where there are problems, you can drill in on them and make fixes.

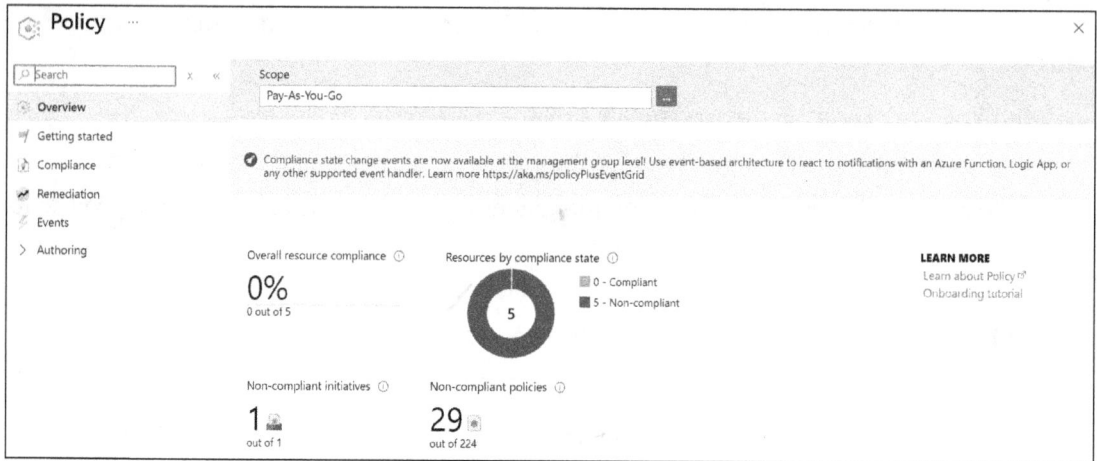

Figure 9.1: Dashboard for Azure Policy

4. To create a rule, you will go to the **Authoring** section on the sidebar and select **Definitions**. *Figure 9.2* shows a listing of the available built-in rules, as there are many of them, and you will probably want to use the filter and search features.

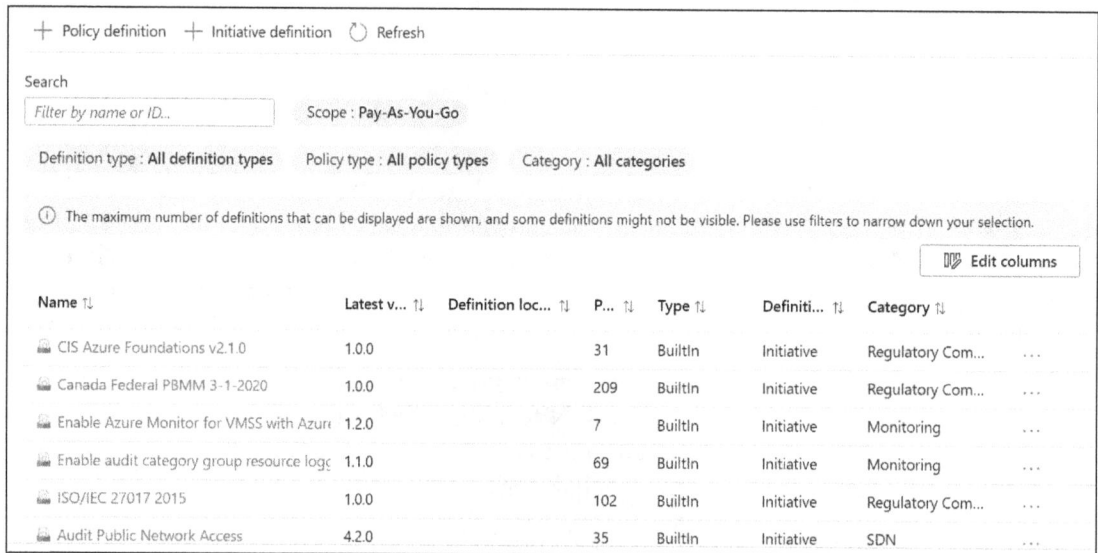

Figure 9.2: The definitions section of Azure Policy

5. In the search box, enter `backup`.

You will see a list of built-in rules. An example is: Configure backup on virtual machines without a given tag to a new recovery services vault with a default policy. Select this one. *Figure 9.3* shows the screen for this:

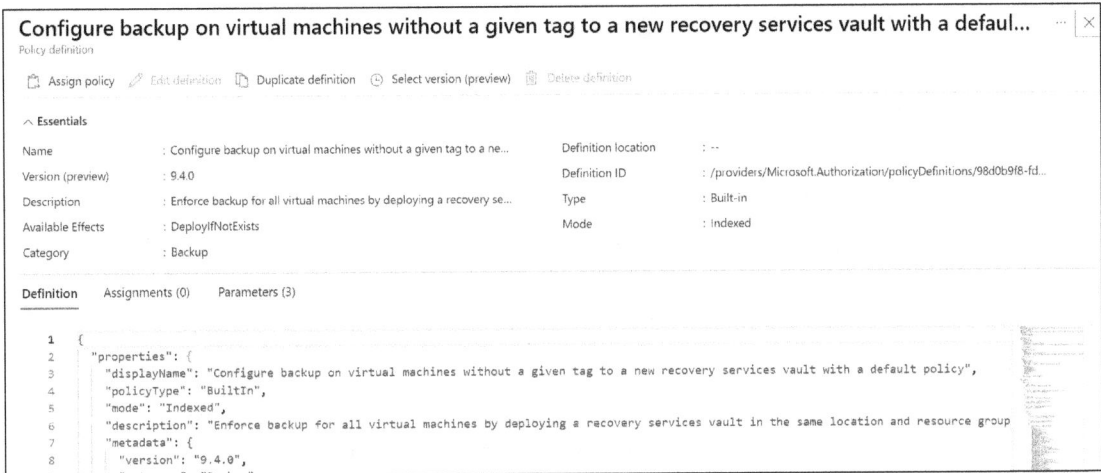

Figure 9.3: Definition of a built-in rule

6. You will see details about the rule, including the version number, description, category, location, and type. At the bottom, there is also the JSON format. You can copy and paste this into an editor, where you can customize it.

7. At the top left of the screen, select **Assign policy**. *Figure 9.4* shows the screen for this:

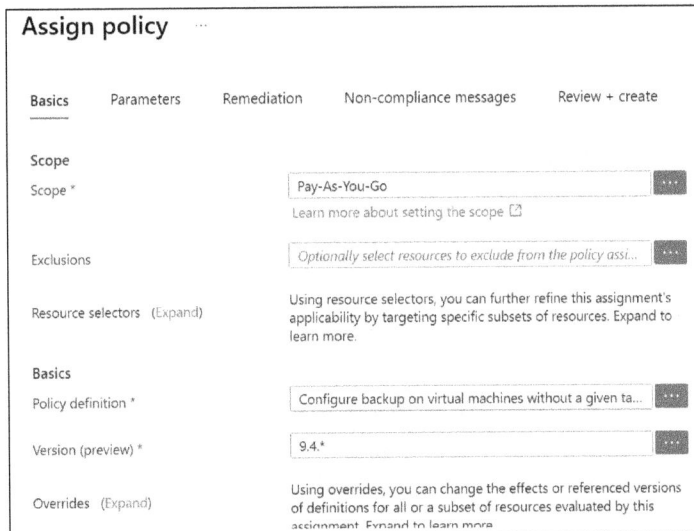

Figure 9.4: The screen for assigning a rule

8. You will set up the scope for this rule, which includes the subscription and resource group. You can also create exclusions for these.

9. The default is that a rule will only apply to newly created resources, but you can change this by going to the **Remediation** tab. You will select **Create a remediation task**.

10. In the **Non-compliance messages** tab, you can create a message that appears when a user violates a rule.

11. Select **Review + create**.

Resource locks

In *Chapter 3, Architectural Components and Services of Azure*, we briefly looked at resource locks. They prevent accidental or unauthorized changes to subscriptions, resource groups, or individual resources. This capability is critical for governance and compliance.

There are two types of resource locks:

- **ReadOnly lock:** This lock restricts users from viewing the resource only. They can see that the resource exists and view its properties, but cannot make any changes. Consider using a ReadOnly lock on critical, immutable infrastructure components like a production **virtual network** (**VNet**) or a core database server after its initial deployment.

- **CanNotDelete lock:** Users can read and modify the resource but are prevented from deleting it. This is suitable for resources that need regular updates but are too important to be accidentally removed, such as storage accounts used for centralized logging or critical VM disks that might have snapshots updated periodically but should never be deleted.

Setting a resource lock is straightforward. You will go to the resource or resource group and select **Locks** from the **Settings** area. You will then click **Add** to create a new lock. You will specify the type and name. You can also create scripts for automating resource locks by using Azure CLI, PowerShell, or ARM templates.

You can use RBAC with resource blocks. For example, you can set them based on user roles like owner or administrator. You can even use custom roles.

By combining RBAC and resource blocks, you can provide for a strong governance and compliance framework. It will both protect unintended changes and manage access to the resources.

Microsoft Purview

In the summer of 2024, the **Securities and Exchange Commission** (**SEC**) announced settlements with various Wall Street firms like *Edward Jones, Raymond James*, and *Ameriprise Financial*. This was for a $392.75 million settlement for violations of unauthorized communication among employees.[1] They were using applications like *WhatsApp, iMessage*, and *Signal* without complying with regulations.

This example highlights the potential impact of the lack of governance and compliance.

However, Azure has an extensive platform that can help to mitigate these types of risks, i.e., Microsoft Purview, which is a data governance platform that helps with the following:

---

1 https://www.wealthmanagement.com/regulation-compliance/sec-charges-26-firms-for-off-channel-communications-violations

- **Information protection:** This allows for classification and labels for sensitive data. This helps to provide appropriate management of information.

- **Data loss prevention:** This identifies and prevents unauthorized sharing of sensitive data.

- **Insider risk management:** This helps to detect and minimize threats from insiders in an organization. It is done by analyzing activities and communications.

- **Audit:** This includes extensive audit logs for monitoring user activities.

- **eDiscovery:** This helps to streamline the identification and retrieval of legal and compliance records.

- **Data map:** This scans and segments data across an organization.

- **Unified catalog:** This is a searchable knowledge base of data assets.

- **Data lifecycle management:** This manages data retention and deletion for organizational policies and regulatory requirements.

A common use case for Microsoft Purview is GDPR compliance for sensitive customer data. For example, Information Protection can classify and label the data, data loss prevention can then identify and prevent unauthorized sharing of that data, and Audit can provide logs to track all access attempts for compliance reporting.

Regardless, Microsoft Purview works across on-premises, SaaS, and multicloud environments. There are also deep integrations with Microsoft services like Microsoft 365, Azure, and Microsoft Fabric, as well as third-party platforms such as Amazon S3 and Snowflake.

Another key to Microsoft Purview is its use of AI. It leverages this powerful technology to automate metadata tagging, suggest data classifications, and provide natural language search capabilities.

Conclusion

In this chapter, we looked at the foundational elements of governance and compliance in Azure. These are two important factors for managing secure, efficient, and accountable cloud environments. We began with an overview that highlighted the roles of governance, which involve internal policies and oversight, and compliance. This focuses on adhering to external legal and regulatory standards such as the GDPR, the HIPAA, and the PCI-DSS.

We then reviewed Azure's built-in tools that support these efforts. With Azure Policy, you learned how to define, assign, and manage rules that keep your resources aligned with organizational and regulatory standards. We also examined how resource locks can safeguard critical infrastructure from unintended changes, and how Microsoft Purview delivers a powerful suite of capabilities for data classification, protection, and lifecycle management.

In the next chapter, we will build on these principles by exploring how to deploy and monitor Azure resources effectively.

Sample questions

1. **What is the main role of governance in cloud environments?**

    a. Enforcing global regulations

    b. Managing infrastructure security only

    c. Establishing people, processes, and policies for managing technology

    d. Limiting user access to data sources

    Correct answer: c

    Explanation: Governance is about defining and managing the people, processes, and policies for technology use across a business.

2. **What is the main difference between compliance and governance?**

    a. Governance is optional, compliance is not

    b. Compliance focuses on external rules, while governance is about internal controls

    c. Compliance is only for data protection, governance is for user training

    d. Governance deals with AI systems only

    Correct answer: b

    Explanation: Governance handles internal processes and controls, while compliance ensures alignment with external laws and regulations.

3. **The following is an example of a governance rule in Azure**:

    a. Only U.S. citizens can access resources

    b. Resources must be stored on a local server for security purposes

    c. All resources must include tags for cost center, owner, and environment

    d. Encryption must use the default Microsoft keys

    Correct answer: c

    Explanation: Using resource tags for cost center, owner, and environment is a common governance policy. This helps to improve resource management.

4. **What Azure tool would you use to define and enforce organizational policies?**

    a. Azure Firewall

    b. Azure Monitor

    c. Azure Security Center

    d. Azure Policy

    Correct answer: d

    Explanation: Azure Policy allows organizations to create, assign, and manage policies that enforce rules.

5. **Which best describes a ReadOnly lock in Azure?**

   a. Users can view the resource, but cannot make any changes

   b. Users can delete the resource but not modify it

   c. Users can modify but not delete a resource

   d. Users have full access

   Correct answer: a

   Explanation: A ReadOnly lock restricts users from making any changes to a resource. Rather, they can only view its properties.

6. **What is the role of the Remediation tab when assigning an Azure Policy?**

   a. To delete non-compliant resources

   b. To create a remediation task that applies the policy to existing resources

   c. To remove all existing policies

   d. To encrypt the policy with a private key

   Correct answer: b

   Explanation: The Remediation tab allows organizations to apply policy enforcement to existing resources through remediation tasks.

7. **What is a key advantage of Microsoft Purview's data loss prevention feature?**

   a. It reduces latency

   b. It reduces cloud storage costs

   c. It prevents unauthorized sharing of sensitive data

   d. It removes unused data automatically

   Correct answer: c

   Explanation: Data loss prevention in Microsoft Purview helps prevent the unauthorized sharing or exposure of sensitive information.

8. **What is the main reason for using resource locks in Azure?**

   a. To speed up deployment

   b. To hide unused resources

   c. To restrict billing access

   d. To prevent accidental or unauthorized changes

   Correct answer: d

   Explanation: Resource locks are used to prevent users from deleting or modifying critical resources.

9. **What file format is used to define custom Azure Policies?**

    a. XML

    b. YAML

    c. CSV

    d. JSON

    Correct answer: d

    Explanation: Custom Azure Policies are written in JSON. This can create functions, parameters, and logical operators.

10. **Which of the following best describes the CanNotDelete lock in Azure?**

    a. It prevents users from accessing the resource

    b. It stops users from modifying the resource

    c. It allows changes but blocks deletion

    d. It encrypts the resource

    Correct answer: c

    Explanation: A CanNotDelete lock allows users to modify a resource but prevents it from being deleted.

11. **Which Azure governance tool allows policies to be enforced across multiple cloud providers like AWS and Google Cloud?**

    a. Azure Key Vault

    b. Azure Arc

    c. Azure Active Directory

    d. Microsoft Defender for Cloud

    Correct answer: b

    Explanation: Azure Arc allows organizations to extend Azure Policy governance to non-Azure environments like AWS and Google Cloud.

12. **What Microsoft Purview feature helps discover sensitive data across the organization?**

    a. Information protection

    b. Unified catalog

    c. Azure Firewall

    d. Microsoft Sentinel

    Correct answer: a

    Explanation: The information protection feature enables automatic classification and labeling of sensitive data.

CHAPTER 10

Deployment and Monitoring of Azure Resources

Introduction

Effectively deploying and monitoring resources in the cloud is important for maintaining operational efficiency, ensuring security, and delivering reliable services. Microsoft Azure offers a variety of tools that help IT professionals manage the lifecycle of their cloud infrastructure, from initial deployment to ongoing monitoring and optimization.

This chapter looks at the essential capabilities Azure provides for deploying both native and third-party resources using the Azure portal. It also explores the more advanced management strategies, such as IaC, Azure Arc for hybrid and multi-cloud environments, and ARM templates for repeatable and scalable deployments. In addition, the chapter examines powerful monitoring services like Azure Advisor, Azure Service Health, and Azure Monitor, which help identify issues, optimize performance, and maintain system health. Whether you are managing a single application or a complex environment across cloud and on-premises systems, these tools provide the visibility and control needed to ensure your Azure workloads are secure, resilient, and cost-effective.

Structure

This chapter covers the following topics:

- Overview of deploying Azure resources

- Azure Advisor
- Azure Service Health
- Azure Monitor

Objectives

By the end of this chapter, you will have a practical understanding of how to manage Azure resources using a range of deployment and monitoring tools. You will be able to deploy services through the Azure portal and extend your capabilities using automation technologies such as ARM templates and IaC. You will also learn how to manage complex environments that span on-premises and multi-cloud systems with Azure Arc. Moreover, you will be able to evaluate and improve the health and performance of your resources using Azure's built-in monitoring tools, Azure Advisor, Azure Service Health, and Azure Monitor, equipping you with the knowledge to build scalable, reliable, and secure cloud solutions.

Overview of deploying Azure resources

The Azure portal is a powerful tool. Throughout this book, we have used it to demonstrate how to deploy different services. You can also use the Azure portal for third-party resources. You can go to the marketplace to see a list of them, as shown in the following *Figure 10.1*:

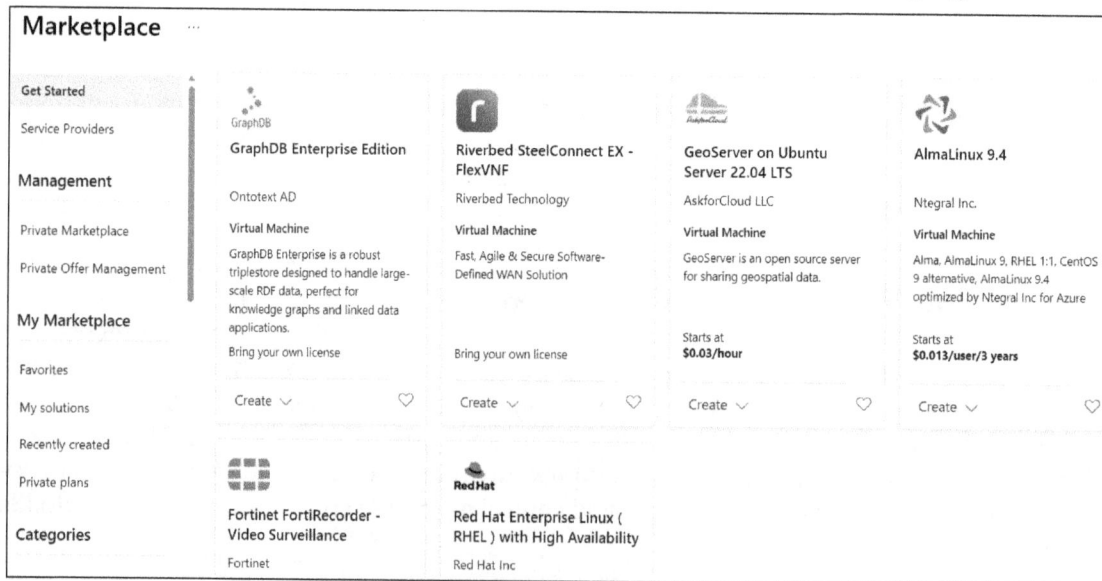

Figure 10.1: Listing of third-party resources in Azure

There are thousands of categories available, like security, compute, web, storage, and databases. Some of the common vendors include Oracle, Palo Alto Networks, Datadog, and VMware.

A key advantage of the Azure portal is its ease of use. You can also customize the interface. At the top of the screen, select the gear icon and then click **Appearance + startup views**.

The following *Figure 10.2* shows the customization options:

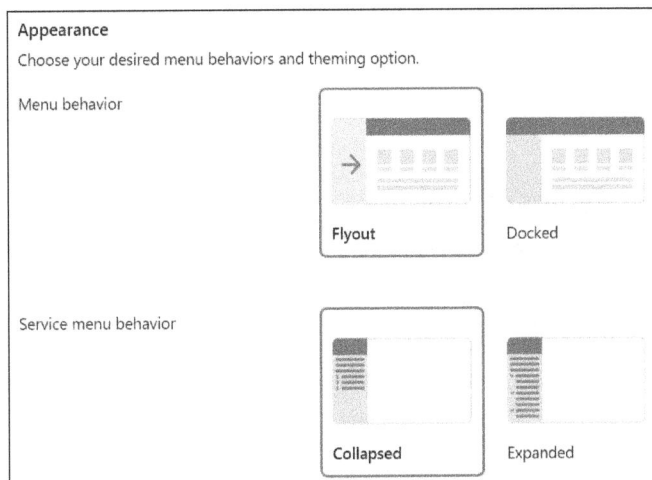

Figure 10.2: The customization options for the Azure portal

You can have menus that use flyouts or are docked. You can also set the theme, such as light or dark.

However, the Azure portal can be limited, as you cannot create automations. Instead, there are other tools that can provide more sophisticated approaches. One is the CLI, such as Bash and PowerShell. In *Chapter 4, Compute Services*, we learned how to use these tools.

However, there are others that can be helpful, which we will cover in this chapter:

- Azure Arc
- IaC
- ARM templates

Azure Arc

In *Chapter 9, Governance and Compliance in Azure*, we briefly covered Azure Arc. This service allows you to manage infrastructure and applications in on-premises, multi-cloud, and edge environments.

Azure Arc can centralize management by enabling you to apply Azure Policy to your on-premises Windows and Linux servers. This ensures consistent security configurations and compliance across your hybrid environment, just as you would for your Azure VMs.

To use this service, you will go to the search box at the top of Azure and enter **Azure Arc**. You will see the following, similar to *Figure 10.3*:

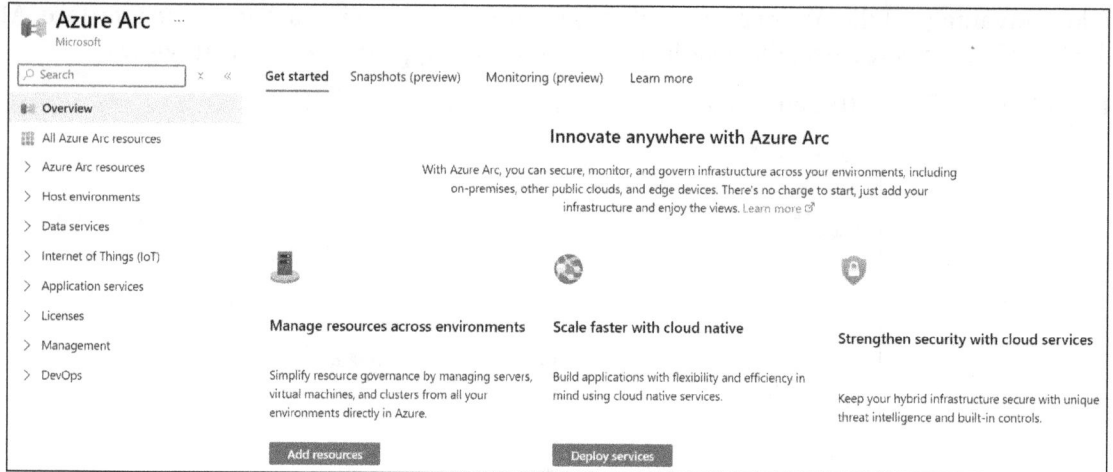

Figure 10.3: *Azure Arc*

These are its main capabilities:

- **Consistent operations**: You can manage Windows and Linux servers, both physical and virtual, using Azure tools like Azure Policy and Azure Monitor.

- **Kubernetes integration**: You can connect Kubernetes clusters from any environment to Azure. This allows for centralized management and governance.

- **VM extensions**: You can deploy extensions such as the Azure Monitor agent to collect telemetry data, perform performance analysis, and monitor logs.

- **Custom scripts**: You can use VM extensions to run custom scripts for tasks like software installation or configuration changes.

- **Certificate management**: Integrate with Azure Key Vault to manage and automatically renew certificates on your servers.

- **Monitoring**: You can use Azure Monitor to gain insights into cluster performance and health.

Azure Arc does not charge for connecting and managing your existing infrastructure. You only pay for the Azure services you use, such as monitoring or security solutions.

Infrastructure as code

Software developers will back up their code by using a version control system like Git or GitHub. This will involve merging changes into a repository.

However, the process for backing up cloud infrastructure like VMs, web applications, databases, and network configurations is not as straightforward. One approach is to manually recreate these resources through the Azure portal. However, this can be time-consuming and prone to error.

A better approach is IaC, which we briefly covered in *Chapter 2, The Foundation of Cloud Computing*. This allows you to define your infrastructure using code, such as automating the provisioning and management of your cloud resources. This is done with scripts or configuration files.

For example, suppose you have a production environment with several VMs, a load balancer, and a database. Using IaC, you can create a configuration file that defines all these resources. If you need to replicate this environment for testing or disaster recovery, you can simply run the configuration file to provision an identical setup.

You can also store the configuration files in a version control system. This will track changes over time, allow for collaboration with team members, and provide for rolling back to previous configurations if necessary.

However, it is important to be aware of configuration drift. This happens when the state of your infrastructure diverges from the defined state in your configuration files. This can happen if someone makes manual changes through the cloud provider's portal without updating the IaC files. Over time, drift can lead to inconsistencies, which can make it difficult to manage and reproduce your infrastructure reliably.

To address this, you can implement **Desired State Configuration** (**DSC**) tools. They will continuously monitor and enforce the defined state of your infrastructure. You can also use Azure Policy, such as to enforce desired states during or after deployment. Generally, by using IaC, you bring the same rigor and efficiency to your infrastructure management as you do to your application development.

Azure Resource Manager templates

Suppose you are setting up a consistent environment for a customer-facing web app across different Azure subscriptions, one for development, one for staging, and one for production. Instead of manually creating resources in the Azure portal each time, which can be error-prone and time-consuming, you define everything in a code file. This is what IaC allows you to do.

In Azure, a powerful way to implement this is by using ARM templates. ARM is the engine that handles all the resource creation, updates, and deletions in Azure, no matter whether you use the Azure portal, PowerShell, CLI, Bicep, or REST APIs. Think of it as the control center that standardizes every deployment.

With an ARM template, you describe your resources like web apps, databases, or API gateways in a JSON format. You say what you want, not how to build it.

Once this template is saved, you can commit it to a Git repository and reuse it to spin up identical environments with different parameters, like different app names or locations, without rewriting your infrastructure from scratch. It is scalable, auditable, and repeatable. If a deployment fails, you can roll back or re-deploy it.

We will look at a demo of how an ARM template is created, using the following steps:

1. Log in to Azure.

2. Select **Create a resource**.

3. Where it says **Storage account**, select **Create**.

4. Choose your subscription and resource group.

5. Enter a unique storage account name.

6. Select a region.

7. Select the **Review + create** tab. The following *Figure 10.4* shows the screen:

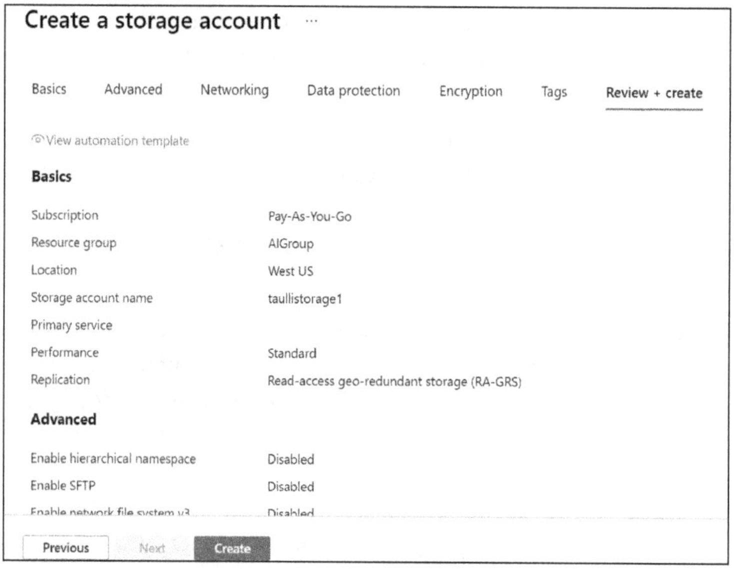

Figure 10.4: The Review + create tab for the storage account

8. At the top of the screen, select **View automation template**. The following *Figure 10.5* shows the ARM template:

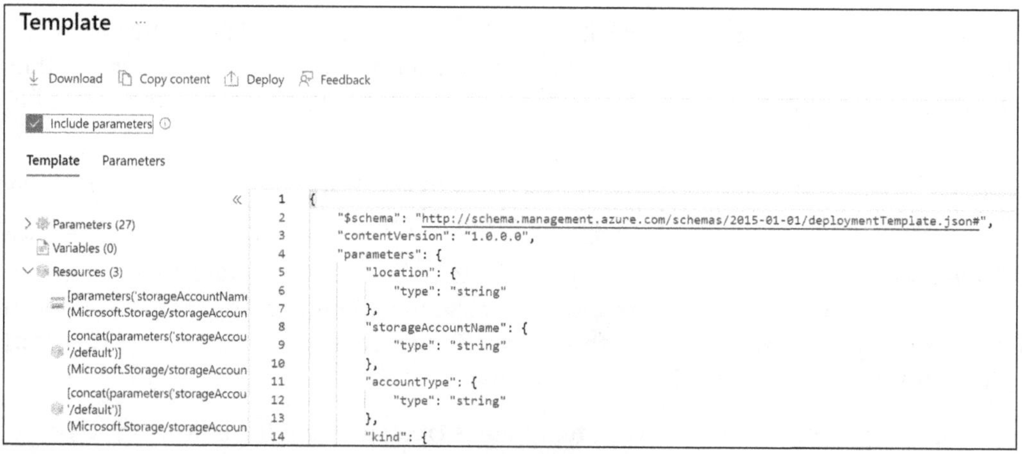

Figure 10.5: The ARM template

The ARM template is machine-readable. but it is still understandable. For example, the storage account name is not hardcoded. It is represented as a parameter, making the template reusable.

You can download the ARM template as a ZIP file, which can be saved to your local system and deployed using Azure PowerShell or the Azure CLI. If you want to deploy the same template multiple times, for instance, to spin up 100 storage accounts with different names, you can write a script that loops through and updates the name parameter for each instance.

Another deployment option is to save the template in Azure's Template Specs. This turns the template into a reusable asset within Azure.

After saving it, you can go to the resource group, find the new template spec, and deploy it directly. However, when deploying from the spec, the parameter values may not be pre-filled. You will need to re-enter them or upload a parameters file.

Azure Advisor

Azure Advisor is a free service that provides tailored suggestions and recommendations to enhance your cloud environment. To access this service, you will log into Azure and in the search box, enter: **advisor**. The following *Figure 10.6* shows the dashboard:

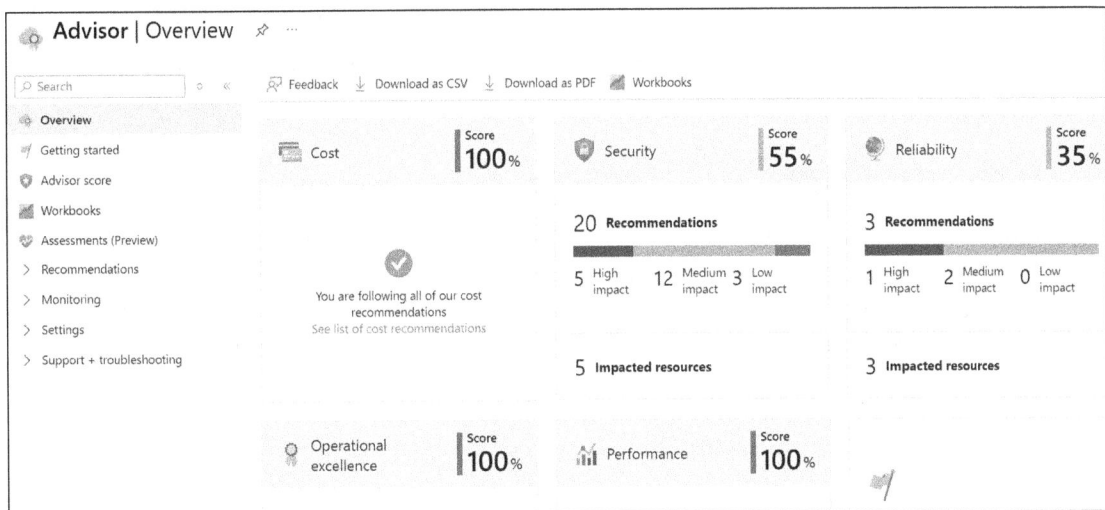

Figure 10.6: Azure Advisor

These are the different categories present in Azure Advisor:

- **Cost**: Azure Advisor identifies opportunities to reduce expenses by analyzing underused resources. For example, if you have a VM that is consistently operating at only 10% CPU usage, Azure Advisor might recommend resizing it to a smaller instance or shutting it down during off-peak hours to save costs.

- **Security**: These recommendations focus on identifying vulnerabilities and strengthening your environment's defenses. An example would be if you have a storage account that allows anonymous access. Azure Advisor would suggest configuring access policies to restrict public access, which would protect your data from unauthorized users.

- **Reliability**: To ensure high availability and fault tolerance, Azure Advisor provides suggestions to bolster your system's resilience. For example, if your application is deployed in a single region, Azure Advisor might recommend setting up geo-redundant storage or deploying resources across multiple regions to mitigate the risk of regional outages.

- **Operational excellence**: These are recommendations for streamlining processes and maintaining best practices. For instance, if you are using outdated API versions in your application, Azure Advisor could advise updating to the latest versions to benefit from improved features and support.

- **Performance**: To improve the responsiveness and efficiency of your applications, Azure Advisor suggests performance-related improvements. An example is if your database queries are experiencing high latency, Azure Advisor might recommend creating appropriate indexes or partitioning your data to accelerate query performance.

Accessing Azure Advisor is quite straightforward through the Azure portal, and its recommendations are optional. You can choose to implement, postpone, or dismiss them based on your specific needs.

Azure Service Health

Azure Service Health is a monitoring tool that provides personalized alerts and guidance when there are service issues. Unlike tools that monitor your specific resources, Service Health focuses on the broader Azure platform across the globe. It provides insights into service incidents, planned maintenance, and health advisories that could impact your applications.

Here are some key features of Azure Service Health:

- **Personalized alerts**: Set up alerts for specific regions and services relevant to your applications.

- **Real-time updates**: Receive timely information about service incidents, maintenance, and health advisories.

- **Historical data**: Access a history of past incidents to analyze trends and prepare for future events.

The following are the steps for setting up alerts:

1. Log in to Azure.

2. In the search box at the top, enter: **service health**. Click the link.

3. The following *Figure 10.7* shows the dashboard:

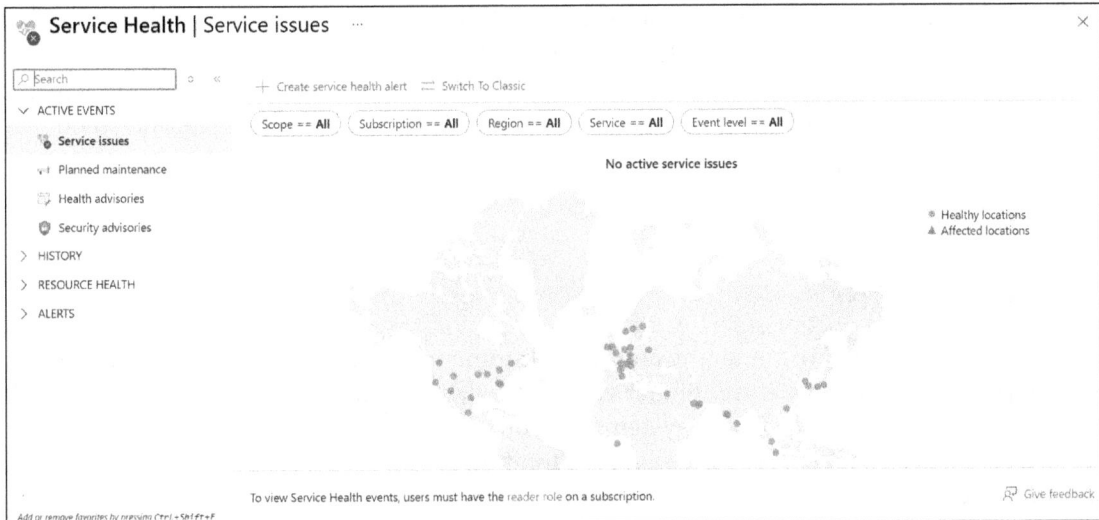

Figure 10.7: Dashboard for Azure Service Health

4. You will see an image of the globe, which will show any locations that have active service issues. On the left sidebar, you can also check if there are security or health advisories, as well as planned maintenance.

5. At the top of the screen, select **+ Create service health alert**. The following *Figure 10.8* shows the screen for this:

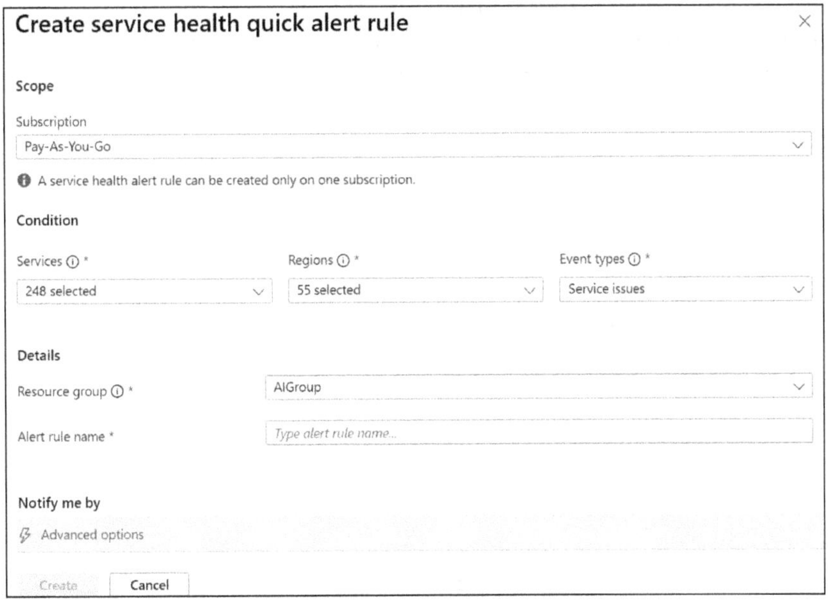

Figure 10.8: Setting a service health alert

6. You will need to select a resource group and create a name for the alert.

7. You will need to set the conditions for the alert. One is for services, of which there are 248 available. The default is the selection of all of them. This is often the recommended approach. Next, you will select the regions you want to monitor. Finally, you can specify the service issues like planned maintenance, health advisories, and so on.

8. You will then select the name and email of the person who will receive the alert.

9. Select **Create**.

Azure Monitor

Monitoring is a vital part of managing any IT environment. This is for whether you are working with applications, infrastructure, or networks. It helps you understand the overall health, behavior, and performance of your systems, so you can optimize operations, detect problems early, and ensure reliable service delivery. Monitoring involves gathering data, analyzing patterns, and triggering alerts or responses when certain thresholds are reached. This lets you proactively manage your resources rather than reacting after an issue has occurred.

Azure Monitor is Microsoft's comprehensive solution for monitoring applications and services across Azure, on-premises systems, and other cloud platforms. As soon as you add resources to your Azure subscription, Azure Monitor begins collecting data. It offers tools to gather metrics and logs, apply data filters, and store information with configurable retention policies. Its integration with services like Event Hubs and APIs makes it flexible enough to monitor multiple layers of your tech stack.

You can access Azure Monitor by entering the following in the search box in the Azure platform: monitor. The following *Figure 10.9* shows the dashboard for this:

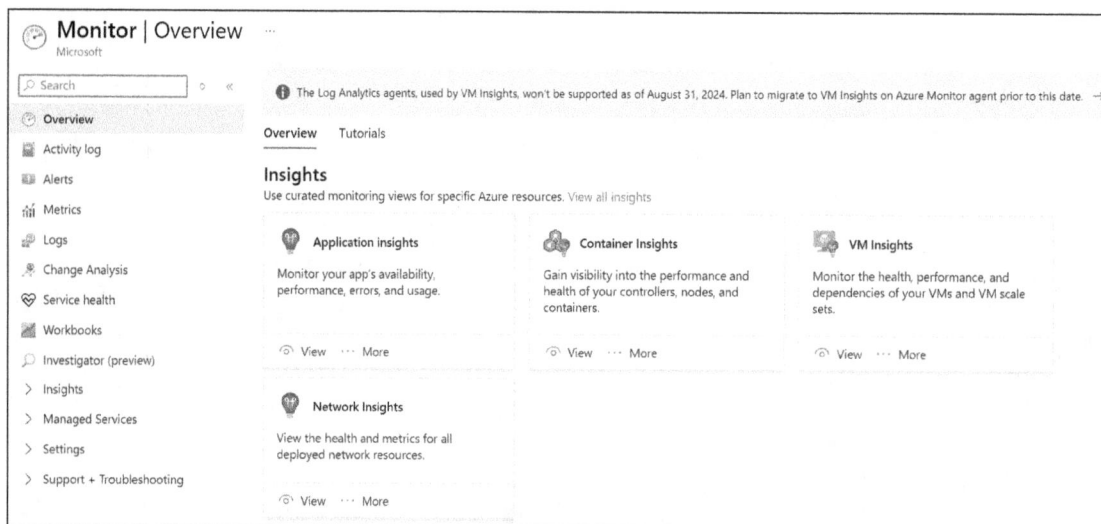

Figure 10.9: The dashboard for Azure Monitor

A key advantage of Azure Monitor is its support for analysis and response. The platform features a user-friendly portal interface and supports **Kusto Query Language** (**KQL**) for querying large volumes of data efficiently. Azure Monitor also enables autoscaling based on workload, uses machine learning to detect anomalies, and supports alerting mechanisms that can send messages or trigger automated actions.

Visual tools are another advantage of Azure Monitor. You can use workbooks to build dynamic reports using data from multiple sources, dashboards to unify different types of monitoring data into a single view, and third-party tools like Power BI and Grafana for deeper analytics and sharing insights with broader audiences.

Metrics and logs play a central role in Azure Monitor's capabilities. Metrics are numerical indicators such as CPU usage or transaction rates, which are useful for real-time tracking. Logs, on the other hand, are detailed textual records that capture the sequence of events in a system. They help with diagnostics and forensic analysis.

To help provide an in-depth analysis, Azure Monitor offers Insights that are tailored for specific resource types. For example, Application Insights tracks app performance and user behavior, while Container Insights monitors Kubernetes environments.

Azure Monitor also supports actions based on monitoring data. These include autoscaling, advanced alert rules, and integration with **IT service management** (**ITSM**) tools. Features under AIOps use machine learning to identify trends, predict failures, and automate parts of IT management. With all of these capabilities, Azure Monitor enables organizations to maintain efficient, secure, and responsive operations across diverse environments.

Conclusion

Deploying and monitoring Azure resources requires more than just familiarity with the portal; it demands an understanding of the broader ecosystem of tools that support scalability, automation, and operational excellence. In this chapter, you explored how to provision resources using the Azure portal and to use more advanced and scalable approaches, such as IaC and ARM templates, to streamline deployments and maintain consistency across environments.

You also examined Azure Arc, a powerful solution for extending Azure's capabilities beyond its own cloud. This allows you to bring Azure governance, management, and monitoring to on-premises and multi-cloud systems. On the monitoring front, tools like Azure Advisor, Azure Service Health, and Azure Monitor give you the insights needed to proactively manage your infrastructure, reduce costs, and prevent downtime.

Together, these tools form a comprehensive foundation for building and maintaining a well-architected Azure environment. In the next chapter, we will cover strategies for passing the AZ-900 exam.

Sample questions

1. **Which of the following is a customization option available in the Azure portal?**

    a. Creating AI copilots

    b. Changing the font type

    c. Setting light or dark themes

    d. Embedding videos into the dashboard

    Correct answer: c

    Explanation: The Azure portal allows users to customize the interface. This includes selecting themes like light or dark.

2. **What is a drawback of the Azure portal?**

    a. It does not support third-party integrations

    b. It does not allow access to storage services

    c. It cannot be used for deploying compute services

    d. It lacks automation capabilities

    Correct answer: d

    Explanation: While the Azure portal is user-friendly, it does not support automation. Instead, you will need to use tools like CLI and ARM templates for this.

3. **Which tool is recommended when automation is required beyond what the Azure portal provides?**

    a. Azure DevOps Boards

    b. Azure Resource Graph

    c. Azure CLI, like Bash or PowerShell

    d. Azure Key Vault

    Correct answer: c

    Explanation: For automation tasks that the Azure portal cannot handle, CLI tools like Bash and PowerShell are recommended.

4. **What is the main purpose of Azure Arc?**

    a. To migrate virtual machines to Azure

    b. To manage infrastructure and applications across on-premises, multi-cloud, and edge environments

    c. To run Azure VMs without an internet connection

    d. To provide storage backups to local servers

Correct answer: b

Explanation: Azure Arc extends Azure's management capabilities to on-premises, multi-cloud, and edge environments.

5. **How does Azure Arc handle costs?**
   a. Charges a monthly subscription fee for each connected VM
   b. Requires a license for each VM
   c. Is free to connect and manage, but charges apply for Azure services used
   d. Charges only for Kubernetes clusters

Correct answer: c

Explanation: Azure Arc itself does not charge for management. Instead, you pay only for the Azure services used, like monitoring or security.

6. **What is a key benefit of using IaC in Azure?**
   a. It eliminates the need for network configuration
   b. It allows infrastructure to be defined, provisioned, and replicated using code
   c. It automatically optimizes cloud spending
   d. It enables manual resource creation in the Azure portal

Correct answer: b

Explanation: IaC allows users to define infrastructure with code. This makes it easier to provision and replicate environments.

7. **How can developers track changes to IaC configuration files?**
   a. By using Visual Studio
   b. By storing them in Azure Key Vault
   c. By manually documenting updates
   d. By using a version control system like Git

Correct answer: d

Explanation: Configuration files can be stored in version control systems. This allows for tracking, collaboration, and rollback.

8. **What is the primary role of the ARM in Azure?**
   a. Monitoring application performance
   b. Backing up data to local servers
   c. Standardizing and managing resource deployments
   d. Creating user accounts and permissions

Correct answer: c

Explanation: ARM acts as the central control plane for all resource deployment, updates, and deletions in Azure.

9. **What format is used to define infrastructure in an ARM template?**

   a. YAML

   b. XML

   c. JSON

   d. Markup

Correct answer: c

Explanation: ARM templates use a declarative JSON format to define Azure resources and configurations.

10. **Which of the following is an advantage of storing ARM templates in a version control system like Git?**

    a. It encrypts the template data

    b. It allows you to connect directly to VMs

    c. It enables tracking, collaboration, and rollback

    d. It reduces Azure storage costs

Correct answer: c

Explanation: Version control helps teams manage changes, collaborate on updates, and roll back to previous configurations if needed.

11. **What is the primary purpose of Azure Advisor?**

    a. To provide personalized recommendations to optimize your Azure environment

    b. To track user login activity

    c. To schedule VM backups automatically

    d. To manage Azure billing accounts

Correct answer: a

Explanation: Azure Advisor offers tailored suggestions across cost, security, performance, reliability, and operational excellence.

12. **Which Azure Advisor category focuses on ensuring high availability and disaster recovery readiness?**

    a. Security

    b. Reliability

　　c.　Cost

　　d.　Performance

Correct answer: b

Explanation: Reliability recommendations help build fault-tolerant systems by advising actions.

13. **What is the primary focus of Azure Service Health?**

　　a.　Monitoring your deployed virtual machines

　　b.　Managing billing and subscription costs

　　c.　Providing personalized alerts about platform-level Azure issues

　　d.　Enforcing security compliance policies

Correct answer: c

Explanation: Azure Service Health notifies users of issues, maintenance, or advisories at the broader Azure platform level.

14. **What is Azure Monitor?**

　　a.　A backup service for Azure storage

　　b.　Microsoft's centralized solution for monitoring applications and infrastructure

　　c.　A billing dashboard for Azure subscriptions

　　d.　A user access control service

Correct answer: b

Explanation: Azure Monitor is a comprehensive platform for collecting, analyzing, and acting on telemetry data from Azure, on-premises, and other cloud services.

Join our Discord space

Join our Discord workspace for latest updates, offers, tech happenings around the world, new releases, and sessions with the authors:

https://discord.bpbonline.com

CHAPTER 11
Strategies for the Exam

Introduction

This chapter provides strategies to help you succeed on the AZ-900 exam. It begins with tips on staying calm and reviewing your work, then walks you through techniques like pacing yourself, reading questions carefully, and using the process of elimination. The chapter also introduces a high-level overview of core exam topics, including cloud computing concepts, Azure services, security, pricing, and governance, to reinforce what you should focus on during your final review.

Structure

This chapter covers the following topics:

- Keep a clear head and review your work
- Pace yourself
- Take time to read the questions closely
- Narrow down your options
- Topics on the exam

Objectives

By the end of this chapter, you will be equipped with strategies to approach the AZ-900 exam with confidence and clarity. You will learn techniques to manage your time effectively, minimize test anxiety, read questions carefully, and apply logical reasoning to eliminate incorrect answers. You will also review essential topic areas to focus your study efforts and maximize your exam performance.

Keep a clear head and review your work

Staying relaxed during the exam can make a big difference. It is normal to feel anxious when a difficult question pops up or when the clock seems to be moving too fast. However, letting stress take over can cloud your thinking and lead to avoidable errors. If you start feeling overwhelmed, pause for a moment. Take a few slow, deep breaths to help steady your thoughts. Even a short break can reset your focus and help you move forward with more clarity.

If you finish the test with a little time left, refrain from rushing to submit it. Use the extra minutes to revisit questions you flagged or felt unsure about. A second look can often help you catch mistakes or rethink a response you were not certain about. Even small tweaks can make a difference in your score.

Pace yourself

Time management is key during the AZ-900 exam. Begin with the questions you are confident about. Doing this helps build momentum and keeps your confidence up. If you get a tough question, do not get stuck. Mark it and move on. Focus on making one full pass through the exam and answering what you can. Then, go back to the more challenging questions once you have covered the rest. This approach helps you use your time efficiently and avoid unnecessary pressure.

Take time to read the questions closely

Slowing down to read each question carefully can have a real impact on how you perform on the exam. Many questions include small but critical words like *not, except,* or *only*—that can completely change the meaning. These words are easy to skim past, especially under time pressure, but missing them can lead you to choose the wrong answer.

For example, you might get a question like: *Which of the following is not a responsibility of the customer under the shared responsibility model in Azure?* If you miss the word *not,* you could end up picking something that actually is the customer's responsibility, like configuring data encryption, and lose points on your final score.

So, take a few extra moments to read the full question. Understanding exactly what is being asked increases your chances of getting it right the first time and saves you from second-guessing yourself later.

Narrow down your options

When you are not sure of an answer on the exam, using the process of elimination can help you make smarter choices. Start by crossing out any answers that clearly do not fit—maybe they are outdated, irrelevant, or just wrong. Getting rid of the obvious outliers helps you zero in on the more likely answers, instead of trying to juggle all the options in your head.

Take a question like, *Which of the following is a platform as a service (PaaS) offering in Azure?* If one of the choices is Azure Virtual Machines, you can cross that off immediately. The reason is that it is an IaaS option. By removing what does not fit, you make it easier to identify the correct response or at least make an educated guess.

This technique also improves your odds. If you can cut two out of four choices, your guess is suddenly a 50/50 probability. On top of that, it helps reduce mental fatigue.

Topics in the exam

In the next few sections, we will break down the major topics you will see in the exam. We will cover the core concepts, key services, pricing models, security fundamentals, and the essential management tools that Azure offers.

The foundations of cloud computing

You should know the definition of cloud computing, such as the one by Microsoft:

Cloud computing is the delivery of computing services—including servers, storage, databases, networking, software, analytics, and intelligence—over the internet ("the cloud") to offer faster innovation, flexible resources, and economies of scale. You typically pay only for cloud services you use, helping you lower your operating costs, run your infrastructure more efficiently, and scale as your business needs change.

You need to understand the three main cloud models:

- **Public cloud (for example, Azure, AWS, and Google Cloud)**: Shared resources, low cost, and low customization.

- **Private cloud**: Dedicated resources, high customization, suitable for regulatory or performance needs.

- **Hybrid cloud**: A mix of both, and supports complex and flexible workloads. Know how it differs from multi-cloud, which involves using multiple public cloud providers.

The following are the three service types:

- **IaaS**: You manage the OS and apps. Azure provides the infrastructure.

- **PaaS**: Azure manages infrastructure and the platform. You focus on apps.

- **SaaS**: You use the software (for example, Office 365). Everything else is managed.

Know what serverless computing is. This means that the cloud provider handles all server provisioning. Examples include Azure Functions and Azure Logic Apps, which are for lightweight, event-driven tasks.

Financial considerations are another key area. You should understand the following:

- **Capital expenditures (CapEx)**: Upfront, long-term investments.
- **Operating expenditures (OpEx)**: Pay-as-you-go, day-to-day costs.

You should also be familiar with the Azure Pricing Calculator, which helps estimate costs based on service configuration.

The shared responsibility model is important. Know who is responsible for what, depending on the service model (IaaS, PaaS, SaaS). For example, the customer always manages data, identity, and access.

Lastly, focus on the core benefits of cloud computing, as shown in the following section:

- **High availability**: Minimize downtime, often measured in *nines* (like 99.999%).
- **Scalability**: Vertical (more power per VM) vs. horizontal (more VMs).
- **Reliability**: Consistent performance and fault tolerance.
- **Predictability**: Steady performance and cost forecasting.
- **Security**: Multi-layered with physical, network, and data safeguards.
- **Governance and manageability**: Tools like Azure Policy and Azure Blueprints help maintain control and compliance.

Architectural components and services of Azure

Azure is powered by thousands of data centers worldwide. These are sophisticated facilities housing servers, networking gear, cooling systems, and backup power. They are highly secure and expensive to build and operate.

Understand Azure's geographic structure, described as follows:

- Geographies represent regions grouped by legal or compliance boundaries (for example, U.S. and Europe).

- Regions are specific locations within geographies, each containing multiple data centers (for example, East US and West Europe).

- Region pairs link two regions in the same geography to provide automatic replication and disaster recovery.

- Availability zones are distinct physical locations within a region. They provide high availability through redundancy and fault isolation.

One should also be familiar with sovereign regions. These are specialized Azure clouds designed for government or regulated industries with strict data residency and compliance requirements. Examples include Azure Government and Azure China. For the exam, remember that sovereign regions are isolated and offer high transparency and security.

Next, you should learn how Azure organizes and manages cloud resources:

- Resources are the individual services you deploy, like virtual machines or databases.

- Resource groups are logical containers for related resources. It is recommended that resources in a group share the same lifecycle.

- Subscriptions tie usage to billing and access policies. Different departments or projects may use separate subscriptions for better governance.

- Management groups sit at the top of the hierarchy and allow you to apply policies and access controls across multiple subscriptions.

You should also understand that hierarchy models function as *management groups | subscriptions | resource groups | resources*. Policies and permissions cascade from top to bottom, making access control and governance more manageable and consistent.

Also, know these important terms:

- **License**: The right to use Azure services, typically billed monthly.
- **Tenant**: The dedicated, regional environment that hosts services and user directories.

For resource deployment, you should know that:

- Azure resources can be created through the Azure portal, CLI, PowerShell, or resource manager templates.

- Availability zone configurations must be selected during deployment. They cannot be added later.

- CLI and templates allow for advanced automation and customization of deployments, which can be helpful in scaling applications efficiently.

Compute services

Azure VMs are at the core of IaaS. They allow you to run virtualized computing resources in the cloud. You must understand how to:

- Create and configure a VM (region, size, image, username, and key pair).
- Connect to a VM via RDP, SSH, PowerShell, or Azure Bastion.
- Understand pricing models, which depend on CPU/RAM use, storage, IP address type, and licensing.
- You should also be familiar with the **total cost of ownership** (**TCO**) and why VMs are often more economical and flexible than on-premises setups.

VMs have enhancements and supporting tools, such as the following:

- **Virtual Machine Scale Sets (VMSS)**: Automatically scale VMs up or down based on demand.

- **Availability sets**: Improve reliability by distributing VMs across fault and update domains.

- **Proximity placement groups (PPG)**: Reduce latency by placing VMs physically closer together.

Next, AVD provides a virtual desktop environment that users can access from any device. It is useful for remote work and comes with benefits like the following:

- Support for Windows multi-session.

- Cost savings.

- Easy scaling and centralized management.

You should also know about PaaS applications, and the following:

- **Azure app services**: A PaaS offering to build and deploy web apps, mobile backends, and REST APIs without managing infrastructure.

- **Azure Functions**: A serverless compute service ideal for small, event-driven tasks. Know that it offers automatic scaling and cost efficiency (one million free executions per month).

You should also understand the basics of containerization and Azure's offerings:

- **Azure Container Instances (ACI)**: A simple way to run containers without managing VMs.

- **Azure Kubernetes service (AKS)**: Fully managed Kubernetes with orchestration and scaling features.

- **Azure Container Apps**: A serverless container solution for microservices and background tasks.

- **Azure Container Registry (ACR)**: Used to store and manage container images. It integrates with AKS, App Services, and ACI, and supports geo-replication.

Networking

Understanding the fundamentals of networking is quite important. The following are the fundamentals of networking:

- **Packet switching**: Data is broken into small packets and reassembled at the destination. This is core to internet communication.

- **Common protocols**: Know terms like Ethernet (wired data transmission), TCP/IP (connects devices to the internet), and Fiber Channel (high-speed server-storage communication).

- **LAN vs. WAN**: LANs cover small areas (like offices); WANs span larger distances and interconnect cities or countries.

- **Software-defined WAN (SD-WAN)**: A virtualized approach to managing WAN networks using software.

Azure Virtual Networks are at the core of Azure's IaaS offerings. VNets let you build isolated private networks in Azure, connecting VMs and other resources securely. Subnets divide VNets into smaller segments. Each VM connects to a subnet via a **network interface card** (**NIC**). You can assign private IPs to subnets or public IPs if you want internet access, but this requires extra care with security.

You should know the following networking services in Azure:

- **Network security group (NSG)**: Acts like a firewall for your VNet. It controls inbound and outbound traffic using access control rules. Prioritization is based on rule numbers—lower numbers mean higher priority.

- **Peering**: Connects different VNets securely, allowing communication between them. This requires an **autonomous system number** (**ASN**) and avoids IP conflicts.

- **Azure DNS**: Resolves domain names to IP addresses. It supports internal DNS zones and custom domain naming, but it is not publicly accessible unless configured that way.

- **Azure VPN Gateway**: Secures traffic between on-premises networks and Azure using **point-to-site** (**P2S**) for individual devices (like laptops) and **site-to-site** (**S2S**) for entire network-to-network connections. The Azure VPN Gateway also uses encryption like AES-256 and includes options like **Border Gateway Protocol** (**BGP**) for routing.

- **ExpressRoute**: A dedicated private connection between Azure and your on-premises environment. This bypasses the public internet, offering greater speed, lower latency, and higher security.

Storage

Azure storage accounts serve as containers for your data and support multiple storage types, such as the following:

- **Blobs (binary large objects)**: Ideal for unstructured data like videos, images, logs, and documents.

- **Files**: Azure's version of a cloud-based file server.

- **Queues and tables**: More advanced types, not as heavily tested on AZ-900.

General-Purpose v2 (**GPv2**) accounts are most common for exam purposes. They support both blob and file storage and can scale to petabytes. Premium storage accounts offer lower latency using SSDs and are more expensive.

You should know the four redundancy types, which include the following:

- **Locally Redundant Storage (LRS)**: Cheapest, copies data within one data center.
- **Zone-Redundant Storage (ZRS)**: Replicates across three availability zones within one region.
- **Geo-Redundant Storage (GRS)**: Replicates from a primary region to a secondary region.
- **Geo-Zone-Redundant Storage (GZRS)**: Includes ZRS with geo-replication for high availability and disaster recovery.

The following are the four access tiers for storage:

- **Hot**: For frequently accessed data. It has higher storage costs and lower access costs.
- **Cool**: For infrequently accessed data (minimum 30-day retention).
- **Cold**: Lower storage cost than Cool. There is a minimum 90-day retention.
- **Archive**: Rarely accessed, lowest cost, but slow retrieval and 180-day retention required.

You should also have a good understanding of blob storage. There are three types available:

- **Block blobs**: General-purpose storage for files up to 190.7 TB.
- **Append blobs**: For log files that grow over time.
- **Page blobs**: Used as virtual hard drives (up to 8 TB).

Blobs are stored in containers, which are housed within a storage account. Moreover, access control is done via private or public settings and **Shared Access Signature** (**SAS**) tokens.

You should understand the file data management tools:

- **AzCopy**: CLI tool for efficient file transfer between containers. This reduces time and cost vs. downloading or uploading through the portal.
- **Azure Files**: Cloud-based file shares using SMB or NFS. This supports the hybrid cloud with Azure File Sync, which caches active files locally and stores others in the cloud.
- **Azure Migrate**: Assists in assessing and transferring on-premises workloads to Azure. It handles apps, databases, and storage, and supports dependency mapping.

Also, you should know about Data Box devices (100 TB, 40 TB disk, or 1 PB heavy box) for bulk offline data transfer during large migrations.

Identity, access, and security

Know about the different types of security threats:

- **Ransomware**: Locks systems until ransom is paid.

- **Phishing**: Tricks users into giving up sensitive information via messages or spoofed websites.

- **Denial of service (DoS)**: Floods systems with traffic.

- **Zero-day exploits**: Attacks targeting unpatched vulnerabilities.

- **Password and injection attacks**: Attempt to gain unauthorized access or run malicious code.

Understand identity and authentication with Microsoft Entra ID (formerly Azure AD). This is Azure's cloud-based identity and access platform. The following are its key capabilities:

- **Authentication**: Proves who the user is (via password, biometrics, etc.)

- **Authorization**: Controls what the user can access.

- **Single sign-on (SSO)**: Use one login for multiple applications.

- **Self-service**: Users can reset passwords without IT.

- **Conditional access**: Sets access policies based on location, device, time, etc.

Use cases include login flows for apps, secure access management, and integration with Microsoft 365 and other services.

You should also understand **multifactor authentication (MFA)** and passwordless. You need to know the three types of authentication factors, as follows:

- **Something you know**: Password, passphrase, PIN.

- **Something you have**: Phone, smart card, security key.

- **Something you are**: Biometrics like face or fingerprint.

MFA greatly reduces compromise risk. Passwordless login (for example, using FIDO2 or Windows Hello) improves both security and the user experience.

You should know about **role-based access control (RBAC)**. This limits what users can do based on roles, described as follows:

- **Reader**: Can view resources only.

- **Contributor**: Can make changes but not assign roles.

- **Owner**: Full control, including assigning permissions.

RBAC uses scopes (management group | subscription | resource group | resource). Always apply least privilege to reduce security risk.

You also should know about security models, such as the following:

- **Zero Trust**: Never trust by default. Always verify.

- **Defense in depth**: Layered security at multiple levels (for example, firewalls, MFA, network segmentation, monitoring).

Microsoft Defender for Cloud is a cloud-native protection suite that spans Azure, AWS, and Google Cloud. It offers the following features:

- Posture management (CSPM)
- Workload protection (CWPP)
- Security insights and recommendations
- Integration with DevSecOps

Cost management for Azure

Even though cloud services can reduce infrastructure and operations costs, Azure can still become expensive if not monitored. Costs accumulate through the following ways:

- VM runtime
- Storage and bandwidth
- IP addresses
- Monitoring and security
- Software licenses and support plans

Using Azure's cost management tools helps track usage, control budgets, and reduce waste. There are also some best practices to consider:

- **Understand pricing pages**: Every service has detailed pricing components (for example, storage costs include capacity, access frequency, and outbound data transfer).

- **Deploy resources close to users**: This may improve performance and reduce costs, but consider regulatory restrictions on data locality.

- **Use reservations and spot pricing**: Azure Reservations offer discounts for one-year or three-year commitments. Spot VMs, on the other hand, provide access to unused capacity at discounted rates but can be deallocated without notice.

- **Leverage existing licenses**: Known as the Azure hybrid benefit, this lets you use licenses (like SQL Server) to reduce Azure costs.

- **Organize resources**: Use management groups, subscriptions, and resource groups to streamline budgeting and governance.

Another helpful tool is the Azure TCO Calculator. It estimates cost savings from migrating to Azure from an on-premises setup. You must enter the following:

- Current servers, databases, storage, and network configurations.
- Assumptions like software assurance, electricity rates, and IT labor costs.

The report shows five-year savings and allows for adjustments to region, licensing, and assumptions.

There are also cost management tools built into the Azure portal:

- **Cost analysis**: Visualize monthly or quarterly expenses and track spending spikes.

- **Budgets**: Set financial limits and receive alerts when thresholds are hit.

- **Forecasting**: Predict future costs based on past usage patterns.

- **Export reports**: Send data to Power BI or other tools for deeper analysis and reporting.

Resource tags can also be helpful. They are key-value pairs used to organize and filter Azure resources. They are important for:

- Cost allocation by department, project, or business unit.

- Search and reporting—tags make it easier to manage large-scale environments.

- Bulk operations, such as setting permissions or generating reports.

Governance and compliance in Azure

While intuitive, the Azure portal lacks automation capabilities, making it less ideal for repeatable deployments. However, there are tools to help. One is Azure Arc, which has the following features:

- Manages on-premises, multi-cloud, and edge resources from Azure.

- Offers Kubernetes integration, certificate management, and telemetry data collection.

Only Azure services used (for example, Azure Monitor) incur charges—not Arc itself.

Then, there is IaC. This allows for the following capabilities:

- Define resources (VMs, databases, networks) in code or scripts.

- Supports repeatable deployments, disaster recovery, and version control. It also prevents configuration drift when paired with **Desired State Configuration (DSC)** tools.

There are also **Azure Resource Manager (ARM)** templates:

- Written in JSON, ARM templates describe the desired Azure infrastructure.

- Support parameterization, allowing reusability across dev, staging, and production.

- Can be stored in Git for versioning and collaboration.

- Enable deployments via Azure CLI, PowerShell, or Template Specs.

To receive personalized recommendations about your cloud implementation, you can use the Azure Advisor. It provides the following details:

- **Costs**: Suggests resizing or deallocating underutilized resources.

- **Security**: Flags issues like public access to storage accounts.

- **Reliability**: Recommends geo-redundancy or cross-region deployment.
- **Performance**: Identifies opportunities to improve response time or reduce latency.
- **Operational excellence**: Flags outdated APIs or nonstandard configurations.

Next, there is Azure Service Health. This tracks global Azure service incidents and notifies you if your region or services are affected. The following are its key features:

- Real-time alerts for service issues and planned maintenance.
- Ability to customize alerts by service, region, and notification channel (for example, email).
- Useful for maintaining SLA awareness and preparing for outages.

Finally, there is Azure Monitor. This provides a comprehensive view of resource health and application performance:

- Collects metrics (numerical data like CPU usage) and logs (event records).
- Integrates with tools like Power BI, Grafana, and Event Hubs.
- Supports alerts, autoscaling, and AIOps (machine learning for anomaly detection).
- Uses insights modules for specific environments (for example, App Insights, Container Insights).

Conclusion

In this chapter, we covered strategies for succeeding on the AZ-900 exam. We began with tips for staying calm and focused during the test. Then we explored techniques like pacing yourself, reading questions carefully, and narrowing down answer choices. We finished with a high-level review of the key topics that you are likely to encounter on the exam.

We are now finished with the book, in terms of the topics covered on the AZ-900 exam. In the next chapter, there are 40 practice questions that test your knowledge.

Join our Discord space

Join our Discord workspace for latest updates, offers, tech happenings around the world, new releases, and sessions with the authors:

https://discord.bpbonline.com

Appendix

Multiple choice questions

1. **A system's capacity to stay operational during unforeseen component failures or major incidents at a physical data center is known as what?**

    a. Scalability

    b. Elasticity

    c. Fault tolerance

    d. High availability

2. **For managing containerized applications in Azure, which two services are primarily used?**

    a. Azure Functions and Azure Virtual Desktop

    b. Azure Container Instances and Azure Kubernetes Service

    c. Azure Blob Storage and Azure SQL Database

    d. Azure Logic Apps and Azure Event Grid

3. **What is the consequence for resources located within an Azure resource group if the resource group itself is deleted?**

    a. The resources are temporarily disabled.

    b. The resources are automatically moved to a default resource group.

    c. The resources are permanently deleted.

    d. The resources remain accessible via the Azure portal but are unmanaged.

4. **Which Azure Storage access tier is best for data that is accessed infrequently but must be stored for at least 30 days, offering a balance of cost and accessibility?**

    a. Hot

    b. Archive

    c. Premium

    d. Cool

5. **To receive notifications about Azure service disruptions, planned maintenance, and other health advisories that might affect your resources, which Azure service should be used?**

    a. Azure Monitor

    b. Azure Advisor

    c. Azure Service Health

    d. Azure Active Directory

6. **A company needs to securely connect its web application running on Azure to an Azure SQL Database, minimizing exposure to the public internet. What is the recommended approach?**

    a. Use a public endpoint for the database.

    b. Implement an Azure Application Gateway.

    c. Configure a private endpoint for the database.

    d. Use a combination of public and private endpoints.

7. **For an application (App1) where code modification is necessary and OS management effort should be minimal, and another application (App2) requiring interactive OS access for custom scripting, which Azure service models are appropriate?**

    a. App1: IaaS, App2: SaaS

    b. App1: PaaS, App2: IaaS

    c. App1: FaaS, App2: PaaS

    d. App1: SaaS, App2: FaaS

8. **Which statement accurately describes the Azure portal?**

    a. It provides a GUI for managing Azure resources.

    b. It is a physical device required to access Azure.

    c. It is a command-line interface for managing Azure resources.

    d. It is only accessible via the Azure mobile application.

9. **An organization needs a tool to analyze resource consumption, get cost optimization recommendations, track budgets, and generate detailed cost reports for its Azure usage. Which Azure tool fulfills these requirements?**

    a. Azure Monitor

    b. Azure Advisor

    c. Azure Log Analytics

    d. Azure cost management and billing

10. **The initial, significant upfront investment in building a new data center is categorized as which type of expenditure?**

    a. OpEx

    b. Variable cost

    c. CapEx

    d. Recurring cost

11. **To manage Azure virtual machines running Windows Server, which set of tools can be used?**

    a. Azure portal, Azure CLI, Azure PowerShell, Azure SDK, and Azure API

    b. Azure PowerShell, Azure SDK, and Azure API only

    c. Azure portal and Azure CLI only

    d. Azure Virtual Desktop and Azure Functions only

12. **What cloud computing model enables businesses to manage, monitor, and integrate resources across both public and private cloud environments using a unified approach?**

    a. Hybrid cloud

    b. Private cloud

    c. Public cloud

    d. Multi-cloud

13. **What is the correct hierarchical order for organizing and managing resources in Azure, from the broadest scope to the most granular?**

    a. Subscriptions, resource groups, management groups

    b. Resource groups, subscriptions, management groups

    c. Management groups, subscriptions, resource groups

    d. Management groups, resource groups, subscriptions

14. **Which Azure service is specifically designed to provide desktop and application virtualization capabilities?**

    a. Azure Functions

    b. Azure Active Directory

    c. Azure Cognitive Services

    d. Azure Virtual Desktop

15. **A company migrating its on-premises file server to Azure needs to ensure users can continue accessing data via mapped Server Message Block (SMB) network drives on their Windows computers. Which Azure storage service should they use?**

    a. Azure Blob Storage

    b. Azure Cosmos DB

    c. Azure Files

    d. Azure Disk Storage

16. **To deploy and manage Azure resources as a collective unit, track dependencies between them, and apply RBAC, which Azure management service is essential?**

    a. Azure DevOps

    b. Azure Active Directory

    c. Azure API Management

    d. Azure Resource Manager

17. **What is the most accurate description of cloud computing?**

    a. Storing data exclusively on local servers.

    b. Transferring data between personal devices.

    c. Accessing software and hardware resources over the internet on demand.

    d. A type of computer powered by renewable energy.

18. **An administrator needs to automate Azure resource deployment and management using a standalone, cross-platform command-line tool. Which Azure tool is most suitable?**

    a.   Azure CLI

    b.   Azure Cloud Shell

    c.   Azure Functions

    d.   Azure PowerShell

19. **Which scenario represents an appropriate use case for a private cloud deployment model?**

    a.   A startup needing to rapidly scale infrastructure with minimal upfront investment.

    b.   A research consortium requiring collaboration across multiple external institutions.

    c.   A government agency needing to store highly sensitive data with stringent control requirements.

    d.   A retail company experiencing unpredictable seasonal traffic spikes.

20. **To deploy a complete Azure application environment, including the configuration of resources, role assignments, and policies, as a repeatable package, which Azure service should be used?**

    a.   Azure Resource Locks

    b.   Azure Policy

    c.   Azure Tags

    d.   Azure Blueprints

21. **In a SaaS cloud model, who is primarily responsible for managing and applying software updates and patches?**

    a.   The end-user

    b.   The customer's IT department

    c.   A third-party consultant hired by the customer

    d.   The vendor or provider of the SaaS application

22. **What term describes the capability of a cloud application to increase its processing capacity to manage a larger volume of work, often by adding more resources?**

    a.   Reliability

    b.   Agility

    c.   Scalability

    d.   Elasticity

23. **An organization wants to simplify user access to multiple applications by allowing them to log in once with a single set of credentials. Which Azure service enables this SSO capability?**

    a.   Azure App Service

    b.   Azure Information Protection

    c.   Microsoft Entra ID

    d.   Azure Key Vault

24. **Which of the following best characterizes Azure Blob Storage?**

    a.   A managed service for hosting and running virtual machines.

    b.   A file share service optimized for hosting web application content.

    c.   A NoSQL database service for structured and semi-structured data.

    d.   A scalable and cost-effective cloud storage solution for unstructured data like images, videos, and backups.

25. **What is a suitable use case for deploying resources in a public cloud model?**

    a.   A startup company needing to quickly scale its infrastructure up or down with minimal initial costs.

    b.   A healthcare provider needing to adhere to very strict, localized data privacy laws.

    c.   A financial institution requiring highly customized infrastructure with maximum control.

    d.   A government intelligence agency requiring complete isolation for its IT environment.

26. **A company is using Azure DNS to manage its domain name and wants to direct traffic to its website hosted on Azure. What is the primary role of Azure DNS in this context?**

    a.   Securing the website against cyberattacks.

    b.   Hosting the website's content and application logic.

    c.   Managing the domain name and resolving DNS records to route traffic.

    d.   Configuring SSL/TLS certificates for the website.

27. **By default, how is data stored in an Azure storage account replicated for durability?**

    a.   It is not replicated by default; replication must be manually configured.

    b.   It is automatically replicated at least three times across different Azure regions.

    c. It is automatically encrypted but not replicated by default.

    d. It is automatically replicated at least three times within the same Azure region.

28. **Can an Azure resource group contain resources that are located in multiple Azure regions?**

    a. No, all resources in a resource group must be in the same region as the resource group.

    b. Yes, a resource group can contain resources from multiple Azure regions.

    c. Only if the resource group is specifically configured with a global scope.

    d. It depends on the type of Azure subscription being used.

29. **To restrict the specific types or sizes of virtual machines that users can create within an Azure subscription, which Azure feature should be used?**

    a. Azure Resource Locks

    b. Azure Tags

    c. Azure Policy

    d. Azure Blueprints

30. **If a user is assigned permissions to manage an Azure resource group, can they manage all the Azure resources contained within that specific resource group?**

    a. No, they can only manage the resource group settings, not the resources within it.

    b. Yes, permissions assigned at the resource group level grant the ability to manage all resources within that group.

    c. Only if they also have subscription-level owner permissions.

    d. They can manage VMs and storage accounts, but not networking resources within the group.

31. **Identify three key benefits of migrating IT workloads to the cloud.**

    a. Increased physical server maintenance, limited geographic availability, enhanced local network control.

    b. Reduced infrastructure costs, greater scalability and flexibility, reduced operational complexity.

    c. Guaranteed data sovereignty in all regions, fixed monthly costs, elimination of security concerns.

    d. Full control over hardware, increased capital expenditures, simpler DR processes.

32. **In an IaaS cloud model, what is the customer's responsibility regarding software installation on the virtual machines?**

    a. The cloud provider pre-installs all necessary software; users cannot install additional software.

    b. Users do not need to install any software as it is fully managed by the provider.

    c. Users need to install all software themselves as they have full OS control.

    d. Users can install some approved software, but core OS software is managed by the provider.

33. **To identify and categorize Azure resources associated with specific cost centers, departments, or projects for better cost analysis and organization, which Azure feature should be used?**

    a. Azure Policy

    b. Azure Resource Locks

    c. Azure Blueprints

    d. Azure Tags

34. **Data transfers between Azure services located in different Azure regions are always free of charge.**

    a. True

    b. False

35. **If you assign tags to an Azure resource group, do the resources contained within that resource group automatically inherit those tags?**

    a. Yes, all resources within the group automatically inherit the parent group's tags.

    b. No, resources within a resource group do not inherit tags from the resource group.

    c. Only newly created resources in the group inherit the tags; existing ones do not.

    d. Tags are inherited, but they can be overridden at the individual resource level.

36. **What primary guarantee does Azure provide in its Service Level Agreements (SLAs) for most services?**

    a. Bandwidth speed

    b. Specific feature availability

    c. Data recovery time

    d. Uptime

37. **Which cloud computing benefit ensures that users can access a cloud-based application continuously with minimal interruptions or downtime, even if some components fail?**

    a. Agility

    b. Scalability

    c. Elasticity

    d. High availability

38. **A company needs to deploy its application in an Azure region that complies with specific data sovereignty laws requiring data to be stored within a particular geographic boundary. Which statement about Azure datacenters is true and relevant to this?**

    a. All Azure datacenters are located exclusively in North America.

    b. Azure datacenters are managed by individual customers, not Microsoft.

    c. Azure datacenters are globally distributed across multiple regions, allowing for data residency choices.

    d. All Azure datacenters offer the exact same set of services and features.

39. **What is the primary purpose of Azure Virtual Machine Scale Sets?**

    a. To provide a service for running virtual machines on Microsoft Azure.

    b. To offer automatic load balancing and inherent fault tolerance for individual virtual machines.

    c. To allow scaling up (increasing resources of a single VM) and scaling down based on demand.

    d. To automate the deployment, scaling (adding or removing VM instances), and management of a group of identical virtual machines based on demand or a schedule.

40. **What are three recognized advantages of high availability in cloud computing?**

    a. Decreased overall service cost, simplified data encryption, automated software patching.

    b. Resource redundancy for failover, load balancing across resources, and improved scalability.

    c. Increased data security from all attack vectors, guaranteed lowest latency, reduced need for backups.

    d. Single point of failure elimination, faster internet connectivity, enhanced AI capabilities.

Answer key

1. c

   Explanation: Fault tolerance ensures a system remains available even with component failures or catastrophic events, such as a data center outage.

2. b

   Explanation: ACI allows for running Docker containers without VM management, and AKS is a managed service for deploying and scaling containerized applications.

3. c

   Explanation: Deleting a resource group results in the deletion of all resources it contains, and this action is irreversible.

4. d

   Explanation: The Cool storage tier is optimized for data that is not accessed often and stored for at least 30 days, providing a lower-cost option compared to the Hot tier.

5. c

   Explanation: Azure Service Health offers personalized alerts and guidance regarding Azure service issues impacting your resources.

6. c

   Explanation: A private endpoint provides secure access to Azure PaaS services (like Azure SQL Database) over a private link, keeping traffic within the Azure network.

7. b

   Explanation: PaaS (e.g., Azure App Service) is suitable for App1 as it allows code modification with reduced OS management. IaaS is ideal for App2 as it offers full OS control for interactive access and customization.

8. a

   Explanation: The Azure portal is a web-based console offering a graphical interface for creating, managing, and monitoring Azure services.

9. d

   Explanation: Azure cost management and billing is specifically designed for managing and optimizing Azure costs, providing insights, budget tracking, and reporting.

10. c

    Explanation: Building a data center involves substantial upfront costs for land, construction, and hardware, which are considered CapEx.

11. a

   Explanation: A comprehensive set of tools, including the Azure portal, Azure CLI, Azure PowerShell, Azure SDKs, and Azure APIs, can be used to manage Azure Virtual Machines.

12. a

   Explanation: A hybrid cloud combines on-premises infrastructure (private cloud) with public cloud services, allowing applications and data to move between them, managed often through a single pane of glass.

13. c

   Explanation: Azure uses a hierarchy where Management Groups organize Subscriptions, and Subscriptions contain Resource Groups, which in turn hold the Azure resources.

14. d

   Explanation: Azure Virtual Desktop is a cloud-based service for virtualizing Windows desktops and applications, providing remote access.

15. c

   Explanation: Azure Files provides fully managed file shares in the cloud accessible via the SMB protocol, allowing for mapped network drives just like traditional file servers.

16. d

   Explanation: ARM is the deployment and management service for Azure, allowing you to work with resources in a solution as a group (resource group) and manage dependencies.

17. c

   Explanation: Cloud computing delivers on-demand access to shared computing resources (software, servers, storage, etc.) over the internet.

18. a

   Explanation: Azure CLI is a cross-platform tool for managing Azure resources via commands, ideal for automation and standalone use.

19. c

   Explanation: Private clouds are often used by organizations, like government agencies, that require a high degree of control and security for sensitive data.

20. d

   Explanation: Azure Blueprints enables the definition and deployment of a repeatable set of Azure resources, including configurations, policies, and role assignments, to ensure adherence to organizational standards.

21. d

    Explanation: With SaaS, the vendor or provider hosts and maintains the software, including the responsibility for updates and patches.

22. c

    Explanation: Scalability is the ability to increase the capacity of cloud applications to handle higher workloads, either by adding more resources to existing instances (vertical) or adding more instances (horizontal).

23. c

    Explanation: Microsoft Entra ID provides comprehensive identity and access management, including SSO, allowing users to access multiple applications with one authentication.

24. d

    Explanation: Azure Blob Storage is designed for storing massive amounts of unstructured data in a scalable, secure, and cost-efficient manner.

25. a

    Explanation: Public clouds are ideal for scenarios requiring rapid scalability and pay-as-you-go pricing with low upfront costs, which is beneficial for startups or businesses with fluctuating demand.

26. c

    Explanation: Azure DNS is a hosting service for DNS domains, providing name resolution using Microsoft Azure infrastructure, allowing you to manage DNS records for your domain names.

27. d

    Explanation: Azure Storage, by default (using **Locally Redundant Storage (LRS)**), replicates your data three times within the primary region selected for the storage account to ensure high durability.

28. b

    Explanation: A resource group is a logical container and can hold resources that are located in various Azure regions. The resource group itself has a location for metadata, but the resources within it can be in different regions.

29. c

    Explanation: Azure Policy allows you to create, assign, and manage policies that enforce rules over your Azure resources, such as restricting allowed VM SKUs (types or sizes).

30. b

    Explanation: Assigning permissions to a user or group to manage a resource group in Azure grants them the ability to manage all resources contained within that resource group.

31. b

    Explanation: Migrating to the cloud typically leads to reduced infrastructure costs, enhanced scalability and flexibility to adapt to changing needs, and simplification of operational tasks.

32. c

    Explanation: In IaaS, users have full control over the operating system and are responsible for installing, configuring, and maintaining all software on their virtual machines.

33. d

    Explanation: Azure Tags allow you to apply metadata (key-value pairs) to your Azure resources, which can be used to organize them for cost management, billing, and automation purposes, such as associating them with cost centers.

34. b

    Explanation: Data transfers between Azure services in different Azure regions are generally not free; charges typically apply, though some specific services or scenarios might have exceptions.

35. b

    Explanation: Resources in Azure do not inherit tags applied to the resource group or subscription they reside in. Tags must be applied directly to individual resources.

36. d

    Explanation: Azure SLAs for various services primarily guarantee a certain level of uptime, which refers to the percentage of time a service will be operational and accessible.

37. d

    Explanation: High availability is the cloud benefit that focuses on ensuring continuous user access to applications with minimal downtime through redundancy and failover mechanisms.

38. c

    Explanation: Azure has a global network of datacenters organized into regions, allowing customers to deploy resources and store data in specific geographic locations to meet compliance and data residency requirements.

39. d

   Explanation: Azure Virtual Machine Scale Sets enable you to deploy and manage a set of identical, auto-scaling virtual machines, automatically increasing or decreasing the number of VM instances in response to demand or a defined schedule.

40. b

   Explanation: High availability provides benefits such as resource redundancy, ensuring service continuity if one resource fails, load balancing to prevent overloading of any single resource, and enabling easier scaling of resources.

Join our Discord space

Join our Discord workspace for latest updates, offers, tech happenings around the world, new releases, and sessions with the authors:

https://discord.bpbonline.com

Glossary

- **Availability zones**: Physically separate groups of datacenters within an Azure region, designed to provide high availability and protect applications and data from datacenter failures. Each zone has independent power, cooling, and networking to ensure isolation.

- **AzCopy**: A command-line utility for copying data to and from Azure Blob Storage, Azure Files, and Azure Table storage with high performance.

- **Azure Advisor**: A free, personalized cloud consultant within Azure that provides recommendations to optimize your resources for high availability, security, performance, operational excellence, and cost.

- **Azure App Service**: A fully managed **PaaS** offering for building, deploying, and scaling web apps and APIs using various languages and frameworks, where Azure handles the underlying infrastructure.

- **Azure Arc**: A service that extends Azure management and services to infrastructure located on-premises, in multi-cloud environments, or at the edge.

- **Azure Bastion**: A fully managed PaaS service that provides secure and seamless RDP and SSH access to your virtual machines directly through the Azure portal, eliminating the need for a public IP address on the VM.

- **Azure Blueprints**: A service that allows cloud architects to define a repeatable set of Azure resources. It implements and adheres to an organization's standards, patterns, and requirements.

- **Azure CLI**: A cross-platform command-line tool used to manage Azure resources, enabling automation and scripting of Azure management tasks.

- **Azure cloud shell**: An interactive, authenticated, browser-accessible shell for managing Azure resources, offering a choice between Bash or PowerShell environments.

- **Azure Container Apps**: A serverless application-centric hosting service that enables users to run containerized applications without managing the underlying infrastructure or Kubernetes orchestrator.

- **Azure Container Instances**: A service providing the quickest and simplest way to run a container in Azure, without the need to manage virtual machines or adopt more complex orchestration services.

- **Azure Container Registry**: A managed, private Docker registry service based on the open-source Docker Registry 2.0, used for building, storing, and managing container images and related artifacts.

- **Azure Cosmos DB**: A globally distributed, multi-model database service supporting various data models like document, key-value, graph, and column-family databases.

- **Azure Cost Management**: A suite of tools within Azure that help you monitor, analyze, control, and optimize your Azure spending.

- **Azure Data Box**: A service providing physical devices for transferring large amounts of data to Azure, especially when online transfer is impractical due to time or bandwidth constraints.

- **Azure DNS**: A hosting service for DNS domains that provides name resolution using Microsoft Azure's global infrastructure, allowing management of DNS records for Azure services.

- **Azure ExpressRoute**: A service that enables the creation of private connections between Azure datacenters and on-premises infrastructure or colocation environments, offering higher reliability, faster speeds, and lower latencies than typical internet connections.

- **Azure File Sync**: A service that centralizes an organization's file shares in Azure Files while maintaining the performance, compatibility, and flexibility of an on-premises file server through local caching.

- **Azure Files**: A service offering fully managed file shares in the cloud, accessible via the industry-standard **Server Message Block (SMB)** and **Network File System (NFS)** protocols.

- **Azure Firewall**: A managed, cloud-based network security service that protects Azure Virtual Network resources from inbound and outbound threats.

- **Azure Functions**: A serverless compute service that allows you to run event-triggered code without having to explicitly provision or manage infrastructure, supporting various programming languages.

- **Azure Government**: A sovereign cloud platform specifically built to meet the unique compliance and security needs of U.S. government agencies and their partners.

- **Azure Kubernetes Service (AKS)**: A managed container orchestration service based on the open-source Kubernetes system, simplifying the deployment, scaling, and management of containerized applications.

- **Azure Load Balancer**: A service that distributes incoming network traffic across multiple virtual machines or services to ensure high availability and reliability for applications.

- **Azure Logic Apps**: A cloud-based platform for creating and running automated workflows that integrate apps, data, services, and systems using a visual designer and pre-built connectors.

- **Azure Migrate**: A service designed to help organizations discover, assess, and migrate on-premises workloads, applications, and data to the Azure cloud.

- **Azure Monitor**: A comprehensive solution for collecting, analyzing, and acting on telemetry from cloud and on-premises environments to maximize the availability and performance of applications and services.

- **Azure Policy**: A service in Azure used to create, assign, and manage policies that enforce rules and effects over resources, ensuring compliance with corporate standards and service-level agreements.

- **Azure portal**: A web-based, unified console that allows users to build, manage, and monitor Azure resources, offering a graphical interface as an alternative to command-line tools.

- **Azure PowerShell**: A set of cmdlets that use .NET Standard for managing Azure resources directly from the PowerShell command line, enabling scripting and automation.

- **Azure pricing calculator**: An online tool provided by Azure to help estimate the hourly or monthly costs of using Azure services based on specific configurations and usage requirements.

- **Azure Private Link**: A service that provides private connectivity from a virtual network to Azure PaaS, customer-owned, or Microsoft partner services.

- **Azure Resource Manager (ARM)**: The deployment and management service for Azure that provides a consistent management layer, enabling users to create, update, and delete resources in their Azure account.

- **ARM templates**: JSON files that define the infrastructure and configuration for a project, enabling automated and repeatable deployments of Azure resources.

- **Azure Service Health**: A service that provides personalized alerts and guidance when Azure service issues, planned maintenance, or health advisories could impact your resources.

- **Azure Site Recovery**: A service that facilitates business continuity by orchestrating replication, failover, and recovery of virtual machines and physical servers to Azure, or to a secondary on-premises datacenter.

- **Azure SQL Database**: A fully managed PaaS database engine that handles most database management functions like upgrading, patching, backups, and monitoring without user involvement.

- **Azure Stack**: A portfolio of products that extend Azure services and capabilities to your datacenter, edge locations, and remote offices, enabling a consistent hybrid cloud experience.

- **Azure Storage Explorer**: A standalone application that provides a graphical interface for managing Azure Storage data on Windows, macOS, and Linux.

- **Azure subscriptions**: Agreements with Microsoft that provide access to Azure services, acting as a unit for billing and access control for the resources consumed.

- **Azure Virtual Desktop (AVD)**: A cloud-based desktop and application virtualization service that allows users to access their Windows desktops and applications from virtually any device.

- **Azure Virtual Machine Scale Sets (VMSS)**: A service for creating and managing a group of identical, load-balanced VMs, where the number of instances can automatically scale based on demand or a schedule.

- **Azure Virtual Machines (VMs)**: On-demand, scalable computing resources that provide the flexibility of virtualization without needing to purchase and maintain the physical hardware.

- **Azure Virtual Network (VNet)**: The fundamental building block for private networks in Azure, enabling Azure resources like VMs to securely communicate with each other, the internet, and on-premises networks.

- **Azure VPN Gateway**: A specific type of virtual network gateway used to send encrypted traffic between an Azure virtual network and an on-premises location over the public internet, or between Azure Virtual Networks.

- **Binary Large Objects (Blobs):** Objects within Azure Storage designed to hold large amounts of unstructured data, such as text, images, videos, and backup files.

- **Capital expenditures (CapEx):** Funds used by a company to acquire, upgrade, and maintain long-term physical assets like property, buildings, technology, or equipment, typically involving upfront investment.

- **Cloud computing:** The delivery of various computing services, including servers, storage, databases, networking, software, analytics, and intelligence, over the Internet to offer faster innovation, flexible resources, and economies of scale.

- **Conditional access:** A feature within Microsoft Entra ID that enables organizations to enforce policies that control access to applications and data based on specific conditions related to the user, location, device, or application.

- **Containers:** Standardized, executable software units that package application code along with its dependencies, allowing applications to run consistently and reliably across different computing environments.

- **Data center:** A physical facility that organizations use to house their critical applications and data, encompassing servers, storage systems, networking equipment, and power and cooling infrastructure.

- **Defense in Depth:** A security strategy that employs multiple layers of security controls to protect an organization's assets, ensuring that if one layer is compromised, other layers are still in place to thwart an attack.

- **DP-900 (Microsoft Azure Data Fundamentals):** An entry-level Microsoft certification that validates foundational knowledge of core data concepts and how they are implemented using Microsoft Azure data services.

- **Fault domains:** A set of hardware components (servers, power, network) within an Azure datacenter rack that share a single point of failure; distributing VMs across fault domains protects applications from localized hardware failures.

- **Geo-Redundant Storage (GRS):** An Azure Storage redundancy option that first replicates data three times within a primary region (LRS) and then asynchronously copies that data to a single physical location in a secondary region.

- **Geo-Zone-Redundant Storage (GZRS):** An Azure Storage redundancy option that replicates data synchronously across three Azure availability zones in the primary region (ZRS) and also asynchronously replicates data to a secondary geographic region for protection from regional outages.

- **High availability (HA):** The ability of a system to operate without interruption for a defined period, ensuring continuous access to applications and data.

- **Horizontal scaling (scaling out or in)**: The process of adding or removing resources, like virtual machines, to a system to adjust capacity or performance in response to demand.

- **Hybrid cloud**: A computing environment that combines public cloud services with private cloud infrastructure or on-premises resources, allowing data and applications to be shared and managed across these environments.

- **Hypervisor**: Software that creates and runs VMs by abstracting the underlying physical hardware and managing the allocation of resources to each VM.

- **Infrastructure as a service (IaaS)**: A cloud computing model where a provider offers virtualized computing resources such as servers, storage, and networking over the internet, allowing users to manage the operating systems, applications, and data.

- **Infrastructure as code (IaC)**: The practice of managing and provisioning IT infrastructure through machine-readable definition files, rather than manual configuration, enabling automation and consistency.

- **Internet of Things (IoT)**: A network of interconnected physical devices (*things*) embedded with sensors, software, and connectivity, enabling them to collect and exchange data over the internet.

- **Load balancing**: The process of distributing network traffic or computational workloads across multiple resources, such as servers, to improve application availability, performance, and scalability.

- **Locally Redundant Storage (LRS)**: An Azure Storage redundancy option that replicates data three times within a single data center in the primary region, providing protection against server rack and drive failures at the lowest cost.

- **Management groups**: Containers in Azure that help organize subscriptions and apply governance controls, such as policies and role-based access control, across those subscriptions.

- **Microsoft Defender for Cloud**: A **cloud-native application protection platform (CNAPP)** that provides security posture management and threat protection for resources in Azure, hybrid, and multi-cloud environments.

- **Microsoft Entra ID (formerly Azure Active Directory or Azure AD)**: Microsoft's cloud-based identity and access management service that helps users sign in and access internal and external resources like Microsoft 365, the Azure portal, and other SaaS applications.

- **Microsoft Purview**: A unified data governance service that helps manage and govern data across on-premises, multicloud, and **software-as-a-service (SaaS)** environments.

- **Multifactor authentication (MFA)**: A security measure that requires users to provide two or more forms of verification (e.g., password and a code from a mobile app) to gain access to an account or application.

- **Multicloud**: The use of multiple public cloud computing services from different cloud providers within a single, heterogeneous architecture.

- **Network security group (NSG)**: A fundamental component of Azure networking that acts as a stateful firewall, filtering inbound and outbound network traffic to and from Azure resources within a virtual network.

- **Operating expenditures (OpEx)**: The ongoing, day-to-day costs a company incurs to run its business operations, such as cloud service consumption, utilities, and salaries.

- **Passwordless authentication**: Authentication methods that allow users to sign in securely without entering a password, typically using biometrics (like facial recognition), security keys, or authenticator applications.

- **Platform as a service (PaaS)**: A cloud computing model where a provider delivers a platform for customers to develop, run, and manage applications without the complexity of building and maintaining the underlying infrastructure.

- **Private cloud**: A cloud computing environment where IT services and infrastructure are dedicated to a single organization, offering greater control, security, and customization.

- **Proximity placement groups (PPGs)**: An Azure logical grouping capability used to physically co-locate Azure Virtual Machine resources within an Azure datacenter to minimize inter-VM latency for applications.

- **Public cloud**: A cloud computing model where IT services are delivered over the internet by third-party providers and are shared among multiple organizations (multi-tenant model), offering scalability and cost-effectiveness.

- **Region pairs**: Two Azure regions within the same geography that are paired for disaster recovery purposes, ensuring that one region is prioritized for recovery if an outage affects the other, with dedicated high-speed connectivity between them.

- **Regions**: Geographic areas around the world that contain one or more Azure datacenters, connected by a dedicated low-latency network, allowing customers to deploy resources close to their users.

- **Reliability**: The ability of a system or component to consistently perform its intended functions under predefined conditions for a specified period.

- **Remote Desktop Protocol (RDP)**: A proprietary Microsoft protocol that provides a user with a graphical interface to connect to and control another computer over a network.

- **Resource groups**: Containers within an Azure subscription that hold related resources for an Azure solution, allowing for collective management, deployment, and monitoring of those resources.

- **Resource locks**: A feature in Azure that prevents accidental deletion or modification of critical Azure resources by applying restrictions at the subscription, resource group, or individual resource level.

- **Resource tags**: Metadata in the form of key-value pairs that are applied to Azure resources to help organize them for purposes like cost management, billing, automation, and governance.

- **RBAC**: A method of restricting system access to authorized users based on their roles within an organization, ensuring users only have the permissions necessary to perform their job functions.

- **Scalability**: The capability of a system, network, or process to handle a growing amount of work, or its potential to be enlarged to accommodate that growth, either by adding more resources (scaling out) or increasing the capacity of existing resources (scaling up).

- **Serverless computing**: A cloud execution model where the cloud provider dynamically manages the allocation and provisioning of servers, allowing developers to build and run applications without managing infrastructure.

- **Service level agreement (SLA)**: A formal commitment between a service provider and a customer that defines the expected level of service, including aspects like uptime, performance, and responsibilities.

- **Shared responsibility model**: A cloud security framework that outlines the security obligations of the cloud provider (like Azure) and the cloud customer, clarifying who is responsible for securing different aspects of the cloud environment.

- **Single sign-on (SSO)**: An authentication scheme that allows a user to log in with a single set of credentials to access multiple independent software systems or applications.

- **Software as a service (SaaS)**: A software distribution model in which a third-party provider hosts applications and makes them available to customers over the Internet, where users typically only focus on using the application.

- **Sovereign regions (Sovereign Cloud)**: Azure cloud platforms specifically built to meet the unique data residency, security, and compliance requirements of governments and highly regulated organizations, operating as independent regions.

- **Secure Shell (SSH)**: A cryptographic network protocol for secure remote login and other secure network services over an unsecured network.

- **Storage tiers**: Different access tiers (Hot, Cool, Cold, Archive) for Azure Blob Storage that optimize costs by balancing storage expenses with access expenses based on data access frequency and retention duration.

- **Total cost of ownership (TCO)**: A financial estimate that includes all direct and indirect costs associated with purchasing, deploying, operating, and maintaining an IT asset over its entire lifecycle.

- **TCO calculator**: An Azure tool designed to help organizations estimate the potential cost savings of migrating their on-premises workloads to Azure by comparing their current infrastructure costs with equivalent Azure services.

- **Update domains**: Logical groupings of underlying hardware in an Azure datacenter that can be updated and rebooted at the same time during planned maintenance; distributing VMs across update domains ensures that not all VMs are rebooted simultaneously.

- **Vertical scaling (scaling up or down)**: The process of increasing or decreasing the capacity of an existing resource, such as a virtual machine, by adding or removing capabilities like CPU, RAM, or storage.

- **Virtual network encryption**: An Azure feature that encrypts traffic within an Azure Virtual Network between virtual machines, enhancing data security.

- **Zero Trust model**: A security framework centered on the principle of *never trust, always verify*, requiring strict identity verification for every person and device trying to access resources on a private network, regardless of whether they are sitting within or outside the network perimeter.

- **Zone-Redundant Storage (ZRS)**: An Azure Storage redundancy option that replicates data synchronously across three Azure availability zones in the primary region, providing high availability for data even if one zone fails.

Join our Discord space

Join our Discord workspace for latest updates, offers, tech happenings around the world, new releases, and sessions with the authors:

https://discord.bpbonline.com

Index

www.ingramcontent.com/pod-product-compliance
Lightning Source LLC
Chambersburg PA
CBHW061810210326
41599CB00034B/6953